T0214809

Performance Testing

An ISTQB Certified Tester Foundation Level Specialist Certification Review

Keith Yorkston

Foreword by Dr. David Rigler

Apress®

Performance Testing: An ISTQB Certified Tester Foundation Level Specialist Certification Review

Keith Yorkston
Ware, UK

ISBN-13 (pbk): 978-1-4842-7254-1   ISBN-13 (electronic): 978-1-4842-7255-8
https://doi.org/10.1007/978-1-4842-7255-8

Managing Director, Apress Media LLC: Welmoed Spahr
Acquisitions Editor: Susan McDermott
Development Editor: Laura Berendson
Coordinating Editor: Shrikant Vishwakarma

Cover designed by eStudioCalamar
Cover image designed by Freepik (www.freepik.com)

Distributed to the book trade worldwide by Springer Science+Business Media New York, 1 New York Plaza, New York, NY 10004. Phone 1-800-SPRINGER, fax (201) 348-4505, e-mail orders-ny@springer-sbm.com, or visit www.springeronline.com. Apress Media, LLC is a California LLC and the sole member (owner) is Springer Science + Business Media Finance Inc (SSBM Finance Inc). SSBM Finance Inc is a **Delaware** corporation.

For information on translations, please e-mail booktranslations@springernature.com; for reprint, paperback, or audio rights, please e-mail bookpermissions@springernature.com.

Apress titles may be purchased in bulk for academic, corporate, or promotional use. eBook versions and licenses are also available for most titles. For more information, reference our Print and eBook Bulk Sales web page at http://www.apress.com/bulk-sales.

Any source code or other supplementary material referenced by the author in this book is available to readers on GitHub via the book's product page, located at www.apress.com/978-1-4842-7254-1. For more detailed information, please visit http://www.apress.com/source-code.

Printed on acid-free paper

To Jacqui, Jared, and Kaitlin, love always.
And to my brother Dean, In Memoriam D. J. Y.

Table of Contents

About the Author

After a circuitous route into IT, **Keith Yorkston** has spent the last 20 years involved with software quality and risk. Cutting his teeth early in performance testing before good books were written on the subject, Keith went on to work as a consultant and trainer across the world. He currently works as an independent consultant specializing in performance and security.

About the Technical Reviewer

 **Steve Dennis** has more than 25 years of experience in delivering mission-critical IT change. His interest in software testing began as a junior developer with British Airways, learning testing before ever being allowed near code! This focus on early testing has continued throughout his career at Cresta and their subsequent acquisition by SQS (now Expleo) where he fulfilled several client-facing roles leading critical performance projects, end-to-end test engagements, and implementing the company's first graduate academy.

Skills development and bringing new people into our industry has always been a driving force, and Steve is proud to have led SQS's global training division, ensuring they maintained excellence in their delivery of ISTQB, technical tools, and skills training for both SQS staff and their customers. He both developed and delivered SQS's performance test training and Micro Focus's LoadRunner training; he still even has his Mercury Certified Instructor polo shirt!

Steve currently heads up Spike95, the UK's leading consultancy for major global retailers implementing transformative technology programs to enhance their business and their end customer's experience.

Acknowledgments

I would like to thank Steve Dennis and Dave Rigler for their input, reviews, and help with this book and for being great leaders and good mates. Gentlemen, the beers are on me.

I'd also like to thank all those from whom I learned this trade – my old instructor Mark Tomlinson (a legend in performance testing), Alan Gordon (the quiet man who has forgotten more than most will learn), Michael Blatt (in between rugby conversations and that one run where we did a few extra miles), and to my past and my current colleagues and students who put up with my bad jokes, cricket talk, and stories.

Importantly, I'd like to thank the first and best performance tester I worked with – Darryl Cording. Thanks for helping a once young guy become a nerd.

Foreword

Modern information technology is amazing, and the rate of change in the digital world is phenomenal. The benefits from humankind's technology-based ingenuity have the ability to improve life for all the residents of Earth and drive further exploration of our solar system. However, the lack of quality still blights the use of our digital inventions and often results in technology not behaving the way we want it to.

The quality challenges associated with making technology better require improved approaches to moving quality earlier and throughout the development and operations lifecycle. Some elements of early quality feedback, such as functional testing, are well understood and readily addressable by in-house and vendor-supplied teams. However, other aspects of quality are harder to address, and one of the biggest quality challenges that remains is ensuring the performance of technology is sufficient to meet our needs.

This book focuses on the thorny challenge of performance testing. It is based on a review of the standards that underpin best practice performance testing and combines it with Keith's extensive experience in practicing and teaching performance testing. This combination of theory, practice, and making performance testing understandable makes this book an important addition to the corpus of IT quality and testing literature. Keith has provided some great real-world examples, just the right number of jokes, and uses the recurring theme of Sherlock Holmes to emphasize the investigative nature of performance testing.

I met Keith for the first time in February 2006 as part of a two-week induction training course for a specialist testing consultancy called Cresta. The course was based in Durban, South Africa, and on day one, I found myself in a cramped, hot, and slightly fusty room with about a dozen nervous but expectant strangers waiting to see what we had signed up for. Any concerns about the challenges to be faced were soon dispelled, when Keith was introduced as one of the main trainers. It was obvious from the outset that Keith excels at three things: in-depth technical expertise, exceptional training capabilities, and livening up a room. By the end of the course, everyone had learned a lot, gelled as a team, and found a new friend called Keith.

Keith has trained thousands of people in a wide variety of subjects, but his real passion is for performance testing. He understands both the art and the science of performance testing and has enabled me, and many others, to build a performance testing career on the solid foundations he has provided. This book represents a lasting legacy that will enable others to benefit from Keith's ability to inform and entertain.

I was part of the review team for this book and I found, as always, that Keith has managed to bring performance testing to life and yet still hold true to the real detail that is required to understand this nuanced subject. I recommend that you read the whole book and then keep it nearby as a source of inspiration to help you solve your next performance testing challenge.

—Dr. David Rigler, UK, March 2021
Managing Director, Shift Left Group

Introduction

"This is indeed a mystery", I remarked. "What do you imagine that it means?"
"I have no data yet. It is a capital mistake to theorize before one has data. Insensibly one begins to twist facts to suit theories instead of theories to suit facts..."

—Conan Doyle, 1892

Performance testing has often been considered a black art. In many organizations, perhaps an individual or a small group of technical staff or contractors are given the task of "load testing" an extended system, network, or application. They may be given a set of goals to achieve in terms of a system, application, or transaction response time or a given number of users successfully using the system. It is expected that these single-minded experts in the technical field of information technology (a.k.a. nerds) will eventually create a stack of graphs and tables of figures. From this morass of numbers, an eventual answer will appear, accompanied by a description relating to "reducing the hard drive IOPS to increase throughput," "reducing the execution overhead of SQL SPs," or "replacing the rubbish G4 machines with a 3GHz quad core CPU, 32GB of RAM, and mirrored 500GB SSD drives."

Performance testing is like any other form of testing. It requires a defined test process very similar to other test types. It requires a disciplined approach to the definition of requirements and user stories, the creation of test conditions, test cases, and test procedures. It requires measurable goals against which the success or failure of the testing can be judged. It also requires (and this cannot be stressed highly enough) a definition and recognition of performance test failures.

But performance testing is also not like other test types. Performance testing is based in great part around psychology, forensic science, and scientific method. Performance testing requires much more input from the individuals conducting performing testing in not only the creation and execution of tests but also the interpretation of results and investigation of failures and associated defects.

Ultimately, as any tester would recognize, the goal of performance testing is to provide stakeholders with information on which they can base the success (or lack thereof) of the achievement of project goals. Key questions relate back to that simple point:

How much information is needed by the stakeholders?

Is the information they receive what is needed to make an informed decision?

The book has been designed to accompany the ISTQB Certified Tester Foundation Level – Performance Tester syllabus (2018), covering all its learning objectives, with additional references material to extend beyond the syllabus. It covers an overall methodology for managing and conducting performance testing, looking at:

- The importance of defining performance test goals/objectives/requirements/user stories

- The vital task of performance test planning

- The various test types that make up performance testing

- The definition of "load"

- The declaration and identification of performance defects

- The management of performance test assets – the performance test requirements and/or user stories (test conditions), the volume and quality of performance test data (test cases), and the performance test scripts (test procedures)

- The collection and analysis of performance test results

- The recognition of "what we think" vs. "what we know"

We also look at the characteristics of a performance engineer (a person with business, technical, and performance testing knowledge). Performance engineers are required to be good communicators, problem solvers, and have the ability, to paraphrase Holmes, "to *observe* rather than see." Performance engineers need to not only discover performance failures but, unlike many other test types, have the ability to investigate the associated defects to identify the root cause – and possibly advise how these can be repaired. They will need to possess knowledge of the technology and the business processes, even knowledge of the users of the system under test. They will need to have the ability to recognize patterns and discern the cause-effect relationships between the components that make up the system, be they hardware, software, data, infrastructure, and network, or even the behavior of the users themselves.

Importantly, they need curiosity:

My mind rebels at stagnation. Give me problems, give me work, give me the most abstruse cryptogram, or the most intricate analysis, and I am in my own proper atmosphere. I can dispense with artificial stimulants. But I abhor the dull routine of existence. I crave for mental exaltation.

—Conan Doyle, 1890

Performance testing isn't about writing and running the same manual steps against an application, recording little green ticks against steps. It isn't about identifying "a defect," sending it to someone, and waiting for a fix to be implemented to rerun the same steps. Irrelevant of experience, performance testing continues to challenge those involved.

This will be a "warts and all" look at performance testing.

Sherlock Holmes would make a great performance engineer. And, like Mr. Holmes, he also needs a Dr. Watson to keep a record of the tests – an area where previous performance engineers have been somewhat poor.

In the manner of Sir Arthur Conan Doyle (of which I confess a partiality), the book proposes many questions and, as any Holmes adventure should, answers all (it is hoped) by the conclusion.

The game is afoot…

—Shakespeare's King Henry IV, Part I, 1597

and

Conan Doyle, 1905

A Note on the Structure

This book refers to the ISTQB® Certified Tester Foundation Level – Performance Tester syllabus version 2018 and the relevant ISTQB® Glossary relating to this syllabus. Both the syllabus and the glossary can be found at www.istqb.org/. Note: Small spelling and grammatical corrections were made to the syllabus entries. Reference material such as the International Software Testing Qualifications Board (hereinafter called ISTQB®) syllabi or other reference material are copyright of the original author or organization.

The book chapters follow the structure of the syllabus – section headings and numbering follow the syllabus, with the learning objectives and syllabus sections included in the book highlighted as follows:

PTFL-1.1.1 (K2) Understand the principles of performance

The learning objectives correspond to the syllabus sections and outline the learning level needed for the exam. Each chapter has key learning objectives you should be familiar with to complete the exam successfully. The syllabus sections are shown as follows:

> *Accurate measurements and the metrics which are derived from those measurements are essential for defining the goals of performance testing and for evaluating the results of performance testing. Performance testing should not be undertaken without first understanding which measurements and metrics are needed.*
>
> —ISTQB_CTFL_PT

Key terms from the syllabus are listed at the beginning of each chapter, and relevant definitions appear throughout the book as follows:

Performance Testing

> *Testing to determine the performance efficiency of a component or system.*
>
> —ISTQB Glossary

The key points from the syllabus are summarized at the end of each section in the following way:

Summary   Performance is a component of a user's good experience and is part of an acceptable quality level.

If you're cramming for the exam, look for these!

The Basic Concepts of Performance Testing

ISTQB Keywords

capacity testing

Degree to which the maximum limits of a product or system parameter meet requirements [from ISO-25010].

concurrency testing

Testing to evaluate if a component or system involving concurrency behaves as specified.

efficiency

Resources expended in relation to the extent with which users achieve specific goals.

endurance testing

The type of performance testing conducted to evaluate the stability of the system over a timeframe specific to the system's operational context.

load generation

The process of simulating a defined set of activities at a specific load to be submitted to a component or system.

load testing

A type of performance testing conducted to evaluate the behavior of a component or system under varying loads, usually between anticipated conditions of low, typical, and peak usage.

performance testing

Testing to determine the performance of a software product.

scalability testing

Testing to determine the scalability of a software product.

1

© Keith Yorkston 2021
K. Yorkston, *Performance Testing*, https://doi.org/10.1007/978-1-4842-7255-8_1

spike testing

A type of performance testing conducted to evaluate the ability of a system to recover from sudden bursts of peak loads and return afterward to a steady state.

stress testing

A type of performance testing conducted to evaluate a system or component at or beyond the limits of its anticipated or specified workloads or with reduced availability of resources such as access to memory or servers.

Other Keywords

driver

A temporary component or tool that replaces another component and controls or calls a test item in isolation.

harness

A test environment comprised of stubs and drivers needed to execute a test suite.

service virtualization

A technique to enable virtual delivery of services which are deployed, accessed, and managed remotely.

stub

A skeletal or special-purpose implementation of a software component used to develop or test a component that calls or is otherwise dependent on it. It replaces a called component.

test case

A set of preconditions, inputs, actions (where applicable), expected results, and postconditions, developed based on test conditions.

test condition

A testable aspect of a component or system identified as a basis for testing.

test procedure

A sequence of test cases in execution order and any associated actions that may be required to set up the initial preconditions and any wrap-up activities post execution.

validation

Confirmation by examination and through provision of objective evidence that the requirements for a specific intended use or application have been fulfilled.

verification

Confirmation by examination and through provision of objective evidence that specified requirements have been fulfilled.

1.1 Principles of Performance Testing

PTFL-1.1.1 (K2) Understand the principles of performance

> *Performance efficiency (or simply "performance") is an essential part of providing a "good experience" for users when they use their applications on a variety of fixed and mobile platforms. Performance testing plays a critical role in establishing acceptable quality levels for the end user and is often closely integrated with other disciplines such as usability engineering and performance engineering.*

> —ISTQB_CTFL_PT

At this point, we already strike a problem. The issue in the preceding statement is derived from the use of the term "performance." When the syllabus speaks of a "good experience," it does so in terms of said performance. We could surmise a good experience would in part be dictated by good performance. Of course, a good experience will also relate to other functional ("what the system does") and non-functional characteristics of the product ("how the system does it" – in this case, usability and reliability – more on this shortly).

Putting those aside, let's focus on the key part in the syllabus section – performance testing plays a critical role in establishing acceptable quality levels for the end user. As a user, it can be sure you expect "good performance" as an important component of an acceptable level of quality. Hence, if you ask for good performance, there should be some definition of what you and other users would consider "bad performance." Unfortunately, performance isn't black and white. Performance is more closely related to a spectrum of gray rather than binary black or white outcomes.

The problem with performance is where the cut-off between "good" and "bad" performance exists. The often (mis)quoted US Supreme Court Justice Potter Stewart's statement is certainly applicable:

> *We will know it when we see it...*[1]

---

[1] Jacobellis v. Ohio, 378 U.S. 184 (1964), a US Supreme Court decision whether the state of Ohio could ban a film which the state had deemed to be obscene. This quote relates to Mr. Justice Stewart declining to define "hard-core pornography" when excluding it from the protection of the 1st and 14th Amendment. He wrote in his opinion, "I shall not today attempt further to define the kinds of material I understand to be embraced within that shorthand description; and perhaps I could never succeed in intelligibly doing so. But I know it when I see it, and the motion picture involved in this case is not that."

3

Unless performance engineers can define how performance quality will be quantified, it is difficult to provide a system with good performance. Consider the example – a user is standing at a busy train station attempting to use social media after being connected to the free station Wi-Fi. Yet they cannot initially connect immediately to the site, and when they eventually do, it is "very slow." It's usually accompanied by the statement, "You would think that [insert social media platform here] would have better performance than this...."

It might be the social media platform that is the problem. It could be that they are affected by some external event (be it an important global event such as the death of a celebrity or a national event such as a reserve bank interest rate change). It could be a technical issue within the social media platform infrastructure. It could be the telecommunications provider with an issue getting the user's request and response from the device to the social media platform. It could be the user's device, automatically downloading an update now they are connected to Wi-Fi. Or, it could be the 3000 other smart phone users connected to the same free Wi-Fi, complaining about the train delay due to "leaves on the track." Rest assured, if you've never traveled on the train in the UK, trains are occasionally delayed by fallen leaves![2]

It becomes the job of a performance engineer to not only discern what the actual "performance issues" might be but also to help the project with:

- Educating the stakeholders and users on the nature of performance testing

- Defining (in conjunction with the stakeholders) how performance is to be quantified and measured

- Creating (and/or reviewing) measurable non-functional requirements, user stories, and/or completion criteria

---

Summary   Performance is a component of a user's "good experience" and forms part of an acceptable quality level.

---

[2]When a train passes over fallen leaves, the heat and weight of the train bakes a thin lubricating film onto the track, becoming the railway's "black ice." This reduces acceleration and increases braking distance, hence slower running of trains (www.networkrail.co.uk/running-the-railway/looking-after-the-railway/delays-explained/leaves/).

*Additionally, evaluation of functional suitability, usability and other qual-
ity characteristics under conditions of load, such as during execution of a
performance test, may reveal load-specific issues which impact those
characteristics.*

—ISTQB_CTFL_PT

As mentioned, quality isn't focused on a single test type. In an ideal world,
performance is a single criterion in a criteria list both users and stakeholders focus upon
when considering the overall objective of the system/application under test to be "good
enough." Performance engineers need to not only understand what they can and cannot
measure with performance testing but also consider the impact performance may have
on other test types. Of note is usability – if the performance is "bad," usability could be
"bad." But it can also extend to reliability, security, and even functionality.

Summary   Poor performance can affect other quality characteristics/test types.

---

*Performance testing is not limited to the web-based domain where the end
user is the focus. It is also relevant to different application domains with a
variety of system architectures, such as classic client-server, distributed and
embedded. Technically, performance efficiency is categorized in the ISO
25010 [ISO25000] Product Quality Model as a non-functional quality characteristic with the three sub characteristics described below. Proper focus
and prioritization depends on the risks assessed and the needs of the various stakeholders. Test results analysis may identify other areas of risk that
need to be addressed.*

—ISTQB_CTFL_PT

The syllabus briefly dips into the definition of quality risk, a vast subject that gets
to the very heart of software testing. To explain the genesis of ISO 25010, we need to
consider the earlier ISO 9126, upon which the original test types and classifications were
derived (see Figure 1-1).

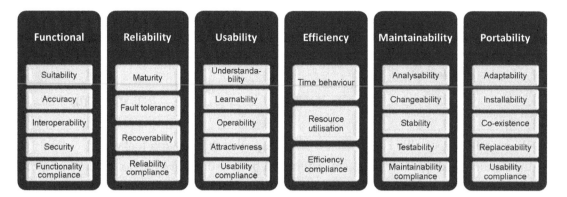

Figure 1-1. *The external and internal quality model from ISO 9126*

ISO 9126 was originally released in 1991. When we consider today how the information technology industry has changed, problems with this standard become evident. In 1991, for example, security was a functional characteristic as it dealt with a predominantly client/server infrastructure with almost no reference to what we would refer to today as "the Internet." Although ISO 9126 was subsequently updated, the decision was made to replace this standard. SQuaRE (Software product Quality Requirements and Evaluation) was developed, and in 2011, ISO 25010 was released (Figure 1-2).

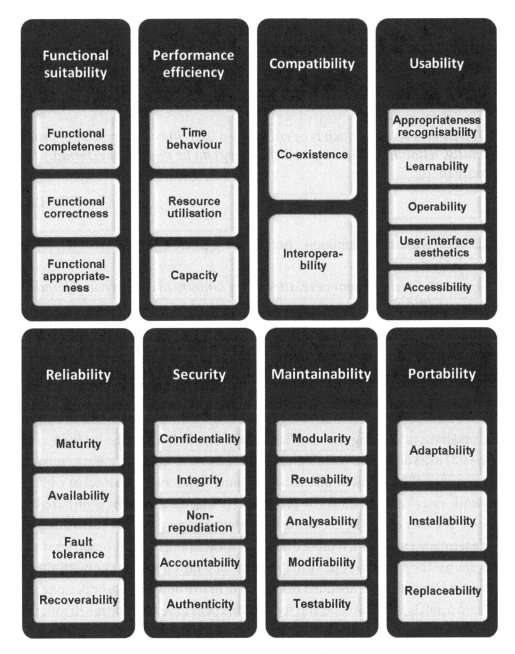

Figure 1-2. *The product quality model based on ISO 25010*

It is recommended that **anyone** involved with testing know this model. It allows a common approach to the categorization of quality attributes against the applications and systems measured. Of note to performance engineers is the reference to efficiency in both models. In ISO 9126, efficiency was defined as:

The capability of the software product to provide appropriate performance, relative to the amount of resources used, under stated conditions.

NOTE 1 Resources may include other software products, the software and hardware configuration of the system, and materials (e.g. print paper, diskettes).

NOTE 2 For a system which is operated by a user, the combination of functionality, reliability, usability and efficiency can be measured externally by quality in use.

—ISO 9126

ISO 25010 has a similar definition – performance efficiency:

...represents the performance relative to the amount of resources used under stated conditions.

—ISO 25010

These definitions are fascinating, in that the very nature of efficiency itself is dependent on the constituent parts that make up the system/application under test. In effect, we are looking at code executing in a defined environment that is creating, reading, updating, or deleting data as a basic definition. This forms the basis on which the ISO 9126 definition was created. Moving forward from the 1990s to modern times, those operations could be on a local machine, on a server on a local or wide area network, or a cloud instance. The processing of that data could be centralized or distributed. The users could be accessing the system using a variety of client interfaces, including terminal emulation, remote desktops, or via a range of web-based services or applications. The server may be virtualized. It could be a single-tier or multi-tiered system which may include embedded devices and/or IoT devices and/or peripherals.

The end result is both the code and the environment have become much more complex. The efficiency of any system is the combination of the efficiency of the code and the environments that make up that system. And yes, today we have faster processors, more bandwidth, and SSD storage. But notice where the focus is – people today are tempted to point at an increase in the environment capability. The environment can always be bigger/faster/more capable. But what about the code? What about the structure of the data, or how that data is used by the code?

Within the ISO 25010 performance efficiency category are the three subcomponents, on which we will speak shortly:

1. Time behavior

2. Resource utilization

3. Capacity

Yet, there hasn't been a mention of performance risk. This subject is covered in much more detail later. The basic risk definition defined by ISTQB relates to "any factor that could result in future negative consequences." Simply put – bad things can happen. What makes a bad thing we would hope can be defined based on the stakeholder requirements.

Summary   Performance relates to code running on an environment.

Time Behavior

Generally, the evaluation of time behavior is the most common perfor-mance testing objective. This aspect of performance testing examines the ability of a component or system to respond to user or system inputs within a specified time and under specified conditions. Measurements of time behavior may vary from the "end-to-end" time taken by the system to responding to user input, to the number of CPU cycles required by a soft-ware component to execute a particular task.

—ISTQB_CTFL_PT

Unfortunately, the metric most stakeholders identify with is time behavior. Although it can be a useful characteristic, in almost every case the stakeholders do not understand the implication of time behavior in terms of the environment and code.

time behavior

Degree to which the response and processing times and throughput rates of a product or system, when performing its functions, meet requirements.

—ISO 25010

Because time behavior is an easily quantified metric that anyone can relate to, it becomes the metric of choice for performance testing. For example, a common requirement any performance engineer would recognize is

The system should respond in two seconds.

On face value, the requirement looks defined, with a success criterion to be met. One thing that must be remembered about requirements and user stories is they are often written to communicate information to other people who write user stories and requirements, not to the people who use them. Irrelevant of any previous role you have had in IT or business – if you have worked in any IT project, it can be almost guaranteed that your project "had bad requirements." This is magnified when performance is added to the mix.

A huge number of questions can be raised from the preceding requirement. The first relates to the response time itself as a defined goal. If the response time after testing is exactly 2 seconds, does this constitute a failure? What about 2.01 seconds?

To which time measurement is the two seconds referring? Time can be measured differently – an average of two seconds is very different from a maximum of two seconds. It should become the standard practice of a performance engineer when stakeholders refer to ANY TIME MEASUREMENT, ask the following questions:

1. Is this time the maximum response time?

2. Is this time the average response time?

3. Is this time a percentile (and if so, which percentile)?

Increasingly, the percentile measure is being used. It can be more useful to know that 95% of the users responded within two seconds than defining an arbitrary maximum response time.

Another consideration would be, "Why two seconds?" What would be the impact if the system under test took longer to respond? Would the organization lose customers, or would the users wait longer? Could that longer wait time affect the user's productivity?

What does "respond" mean? Does this mean the timed transaction has completed the entire operation? Or that a connection to the target server has been completed?

What is "the system"? Is this transaction time measuring from the end user's machine through the application stack and back to the end user? Or is it measured from the point the web request passes the organization firewall through the application stack and back to the firewall?

And, most importantly, under what user behavior is the two-second response time required? Is a single user logging in, then logging out of the system? Five users? A thousand? Or are users logging in and completing a complex set of business transactions simultaneously? The total number of transactions needing to be completed (the throughput) can affect the time behavior. A single transaction being processed might complete quite quickly, whereas a thousand transactions being processed together (a much higher throughput rate) could take significantly longer.

Perhaps that requirement needs a little work.

Summary   Time behavior measures processing times and throughput rates.

Resource Utilization

If the availability of system resources is identified as a risk, the utilization of those resources (e.g., the allocation of limited RAM) may be investigated by conducting specific performance tests.

—ISTQB_CTFL_PT

resource utilization

Degree to which the amounts and types of resources used by a product or system, when performing its functions meets requirements.

—ISO 25010

Resource utilization is linked closely to the amount of load applied to the system under test. It relates very closely to the efficiency characteristic – the amount of resources used under stated conditions. As we saw earlier, the problem quite often lies in that specific statement of conditions. How we define the requirements associated with the environment and the code under test can dramatically affect the performance test itself.

A simple checklist against which resource utilization can be considered in almost any performance test consists of the following:

CPU Utilization

What is the CPU being asked to do? Note there may be multiple CPU cores across multiple machines within the system under test. Also, consider that the CPU utilization average might be capped at a measure (75% or 80%) as set by administrators – is this enough or too high?

Memory Utilization

How much available memory is consumed? What TYPE of memory – is it cached L1 or L2 memory on the motherboard, RAM, or HD/SSD memory?

Disk Input/Output

Reading and writing to a traditional disk platter in terms of performance is incredibly slow (this aspect will be considered later). Is the disk local to the machine, part of a RAID array, or was the storage cloud-based (AWS, Azure, OneDrive, or Dropbox)? Is the disk a traditional magnetic platter or a much faster (and more expensive) solid-state disk?

Bandwidth Consumption

When considering bandwidth, do not just think of the ethernet cable connected to the back of the machine. Bandwidth issues can exist internally in a machine as well as any networks used.

Queueing

Let's face it, no one likes a queue, especially a long one. Queueing is a sign that something has reached a point of saturation and could be the beginning of a performance issue.

More will be covered on these points later.

Summary   Resource utilization measures the effect of load on a system.

Capacity

If issues of system behavior at the required capacity limits of the system (e.g., numbers of users or volumes of data) are identified as a risk, performance tests may be conducted to evaluate the suitability of the system architecture.

—ISTQB_CTFL_PT

capacity

Degree to which the maximum limits of a product or system parameter meets requirements.

—ISO 25010

Before looking at capacity, it's important to clarify the terms operational profile and load profile. Within the performance engineering community, the terms are used interchangeably. The ISTQB syllabus clarifies the separation between them in the following way:

operational profile

An actual or predicted pattern of use of the component or system.

load profile

Documentation defining a designated number of virtual users who process a defined set of transactions in a specified time period that a component or system being tested may experience in production.

—ISTQB Glossary

Simply put, an operational profile describes what a user does in the system. A load profile defines how a performance engineer tests a system with a number of virtual users performing operational profiles.

Capacity relates to the basic definition of "how much" the system can support. This can be done in two general ways:

1. Establish a capacity goal and test to determine an operational profile on the system under test to meet the capacity goal – in effect answering the question of how much load will the system under test support

2. Establish an operational profile (an expected amount of load the system should support) to then build a load profile (and from this derive a performance test) and measure the system under test supporting the load

This raises a fundamental question. When considering performance, we are looking at how the system responds when subjected to "load." The fundamental question is

What is load?

It's worth noticing that the ISTQB syllabus speaks of load in relation to users performing actions in the system or volumes of data being processed. Unfortunately, this is not load. That is how we **DEFINE** load. Users performing tasks within the system have a cause-effect relationship with the system itself. The user performing the task is a cause, leading to an effect. What could the effect be?

At this point, we need to think about the systems and applications undergoing performance testing. Some would say that users performing tasks consume bandwidth or CPU cycles or memory. And that is true, in a manner of speaking. But it is not the true effect. CPU or memory consumption is a by-product of the effect of that user's actions. The true effect of a user performing an action in a system is **the execution of code**. From that, we derive CPU/bandwidth/memory consumption and so on.

Unfortunately, we cannot define load based on the hundreds, thousands, or even millions of lines of code executing per second in an environment.

We DEFINE LOAD by numbers of users performing tasks in a system.

ACTUAL LOAD is code executing in an environment linked to those previous actions.

Even a single user using a system generates load as code executes to support the user's actions.

Summary   Capacity measures the limits of a system.

On this basis, capacity brings these two elements together. Capacity considers the system's ability to support a defined load by a performance test subjecting the system to actual load based on the defined operational/load profile and measuring the time behavior and resource utilization.

> *Performance testing often takes the form of experimentation, which enables measurement and analysis of specific system parameters to take place. These may be conducted iteratively in support of system analysis, design and implementation to enable architectural decisions to be made and to help shape stakeholder expectations.*
>
> —ISTQB_CTFL_PT

This performance testing experimentation can be likened to a trip to the optometrist for new glasses. The performance engineer plays the role of the optometrist, flipping the little lens back and forth, asking

"Is it better or worse?"

Performance engineers spend a lot of time tuning a system in conjunction with various technical stakeholders and rerunning the tests, asking that question.

Summary   Performance testing is an iterative experiment gathering information for stakeholders.

The following performance testing principles are particularly relevant:

1. *Tests must be aligned to the defined expectations of different stakeholder groups, in particular users, system designers and operations staff.*

2. *The tests must be reproducible. Statistically identical results (within a specified tolerance) must be obtained by repeating the tests on an unchanged system.*

3. *The tests must yield results that are both understandable and can be readily compared to stakeholder expectations.*

4. *The tests can be conducted, where resources allow, either on complete or partial systems or test environments that are representative of the production system.*

5. *The tests must be practically affordable and executable within the timeframe set by the project.*

—ISTQB_CTFL_PT

These principles are true for all types of testing, whether functional or nonfunctional. Specifically, in terms of performance testing:

1. In any project, a diverse set of stakeholder groups will exist. A good (albeit coarse) example is the technical stakeholders (consisting of various administrators and/or developers) vs. nontechnical stakeholders (business users or management). In each case, the stakeholder groups may have different objectives, goals, and key metrics they require. Performance engineers should be mindful of common project requirements and goals, specific requirements/user stories and goals for each stakeholder group, and the relevant performance tests to prove these have been achieved.

2. One of the difficulties with performance testing is the variability of the system under test, the environment and infrastructure on which it runs, the tests performance engineers create, and even the data the system and performance tests use. This highlights a key point to performance testing vs. performance reality. Performance tests must be reproducible in that we would hope each test execution would yield the same results. But this creates an unrealistic real-world condition. The question of performance test randomness is always an important issue. In the real world, no load is consistent. There will always be slight variations in the way the load is applied to a system. The danger with performance testing is that unrealistic business scenarios are created, relying on fixed load profiles and user behavior with minimum randomness or variation. Although it is the ideal for repeatable performance tests, it does not match reality. Performance engineers must

consider this point when planning both the creation and execution of individual tests and the test scenarios in which they run. Often, it can be beneficial to create two sets of tests – a set that removes any randomness to create reproducible results and a second set that closer mimics the real-world random behavior of users.

3. In accordance with (1), the results must correspond with the performance requirements/user stories and key metrics. These results should be meaningful to all stakeholders, which may require some interpretation and translation by performance engineers to be meaningful.

4. Traditionally (and some would say ideally), performance testing should be conducted in a production environment with production-like volumes and types of data. Unfortunately, it is rare to meet that ideal. Much will be spoken of this in later sections, but suffice to say that the tests, the environment, and the data should be as lifelike as can be possible. It can be difficult to model the behavior of a production system when the system under test does not match the production expectations. This of course does not mean that performance testing cannot be conducted on a less than production-like environment – it means a skilled performance engineer will identify and assess the associated performance risks and be sure to present these to stakeholders. A change that has been underway in recent years is the "shift-left" effect of moving performance testing earlier in the development lifecycle. Running component-level performance tests as part of a DevOps sprint, for example, is today becoming normal practice. It could not be said this environment is "production-like," but it might be possible to test the component with a production-like load.

5. Performance testing must always remember that return on investment (ROI) exists. The very nature of performance testing could mean that we continue to execute tests for small improvements in performance that cannot be justified against

the cost of performance testing. In the same token, performance testing can sometimes be rejected by an organization as "too costly." This returns to performance risk, in that the time and cost required to conduct performance testing should be balanced by the performance risk the testing is attempting to mitigate.

Summary   Tests must align to stakeholder expectations; tests must be reproducible; test results must be meaningful; tests should be run in environments that are representative of the production system; tests must return good value for money and time.

Books by [Molyneaux09] and [Microsoft07] provide a solid background to the principles and practical aspects of performance testing.

—ISTQB_CTFL_PT

Both books mentioned earlier are excellent examples of an end-to-end view of performance testing. They are also two of a very small number in this genre. Unfortunately, like many IT books, they have become somewhat dated.

Another useful addition to a performance test library is George W. Anderson's *mySAP Tool Bag for Performance Tuning and Stress Testing.* Although technology specific (and a little old), it gives a good set of practices and principles for performance testing.

All three of the above quality sub-characteristics will impact the ability of the system under test (SUT) to scale.

—ISTQB_CTFL_PT

1.2 Types of Performance Testing

PTFL-1.2.1 (K2) Understand the different types of performance testing

Different types of performance testing can be defined. Each of these may be applicable to a given project depending on the objectives of the test.

—ISTQB_CTFL_PT

The types are influenced by the overall performance goals, objectives, user stories, and/or requirements. These create the framework for the business processes to be tested and their corresponding operational profiles. These are then combined into a load profile.

Performance Testing

Performance testing is an umbrella term including any kind of testing focused on performance (responsiveness) of the system or component under different volumes of load.

—ISTQB_CTFL_PT

performance testing

Testing to determine the performance of a software product.

—ISTQB Glossary

Performance testing is the overall type into which the performance test subtypes fit. The following diagram contains the types recognized by the ISTQB syllabus (Figure 1-3). You may recognize some of these or know these types by other names. There are also other types not included in this list that will be covered later.

Figure 1-3. *Performance test types*

Summary   Performance testing is the top classification.

Load Testing

Load testing focuses on the ability of a system to handle increasing levels of anticipated realistic loads resulting from transaction requests generated by controlled numbers of concurrent users or processes.

—ISTQB_CTFL_PT

load testing

A type of performance testing conducted to evaluate the behavior of a component or system under varying loads, usually between anticipated conditions of low, typical and peak usage.

—ISTQB Glossary

Load testing is almost always based on some real-world organization conditions. Load testing becomes an integral part of all performance tests as it is the basis from which the other performance test types are derived. The bases for load tests (the operational and eventual load profiles) are commonly known as *volumetrics* and are determined with the following questions:

Who

Who are the users? Do different user groups access the component or system for this load test? These could be different user groups performing different tasks or with different access privileges.

What

What business processes are being performed by the users? It is useful at this point to consider the way a business process (Figure 1-4) can be represented as part of a performance test.

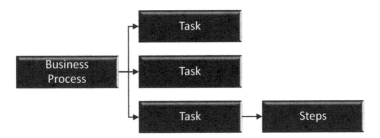

Figure 1-4. *Business process breakdown*

Consider the example of an online retail website. The business process represents some end-to-end action a user wants to perform (e.g., buying a book on performance testing). This end-to-end process can then be broken down into a series of reusable tasks (log in, search for a book, add to basket, purchase, and log out) which could represent a service or component within the system. Each reusable task can then be decomposed into a series of steps the user will perform (open the browser, navigate to the retailer's website, enter username and password, and click the login button).

Each of these business processes represents the definition of the load, or part of the load, that will execute the code within the environment to create the actual load. Part of the artistry of performance testing is to look at the "what" and understand how that business process operates across the system under test. For example, there was a performance test plan that looked at creating 80 separate reports to test the business intelligence reporting of an ERP system. But when it was looked at from the back-end servers, databases, and services, it was found that the 80 scripts could be cut down to seven, with each report variation managed with input data (and thus saving the performance engineer a mountain of work).

Where

Where are the users located? Are the users accessing the system from a concentrated location (such as an organization's office) or distributed (such as users working from home)? Another consideration is the use of geolocation[3] – load being redirected to different servers, services, components, or business processes based on the location from which the load originates.

---

[3] The process or technique of identifying the geographical location of a person or device by means of digital information processed via the Internet.

When

At what time of day does the load test represent? This could have a major impact on the amount of load the system could be subject to. Consider the example of entering weekly timesheets – it would be safe to bet that last thing on Friday afternoon might be busier in terms of organization staff entering time rather than Wednesday morning (and hence generating more load at that time)!

How

How are the users performing the business process steps? The example of a new user compared with an experienced user could mean the business process is completed differently by each. A new user may take more time or use a different path to the experienced user.

Consider a load test against a global online retailer. The user might be purchasing, checking order status, or browsing (different business processes). The users are generating a distributed load and hence are a non-concentrated load source. Geolocation may redirect users from the .com site to a more relevant regional site (.co.uk or .com.au). The load test might represent the load after 18:00 EST in the United States to represent the Christmas load on a weekday in December. This could also mean users are buying multiple items in one transaction to avoid the Christmas crowds, tinsel, and slightly tinny speakers playing Christmas carols in the local mall.

This scenario would go on to form an operational profile (and eventual load profile with the addition of virtual user numbers and so on) for the proposed load test.

Summary   Load testing tests how the system responds to real-world load conditions.

Stress Testing

Stress testing focuses on the ability of a system or component to handle peak loads that are at or beyond the limits of its anticipated or specified work-loads. Stress testing is also used to evaluate a system's ability to handle reduced availability of resources such as accessible computing capacity, available bandwidth, and memory.

—ISTQB_CTFL_PT

stress testing

A type of performance testing conducted to evaluate a system or component at or beyond the limits of its anticipated or specified workloads, or with reduced availability of resources such as access to memory or servers.

—ISTQB Glossary

Many people think of performance testing in terms of stress testing. In their eyes, performance engineers are trying to "break the system" with excessive load. Stress testing is a useful type in that it helps identify:

- The maximum capacity of the system under test

- Which part of the component or system fails first

Stress tests are usually a derivative of a load test that extends the load beyond the limits imposed by the operational profile (Figure 1-5).

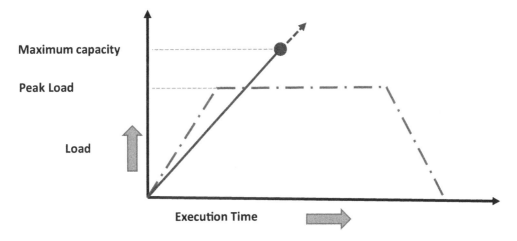

Figure 1-5. *The load profile comparison between a load test and stress test*

For example, a load test may run a system or service at peak load for a time to represent a defined business condition (the dot-dash line). A stress test (the solid line) would extend the load beyond this defined peak to identify the "breaking point" and the thing that breaks.

A point to note on stress testing is that it could continue indefinitely. Once the maximum capacity has been established and reported, alternatives exist:

- Stress testing can be used simply to inform stakeholders on the maximum capacity from a load definition point of view (users performing business processes linked to time behavior). No further action might be needed – we know that at a load of X, the system will become unstable.

- Stress testing informs developers and/or administrators as to the component that will fail if the load hits the maximum capacity (resource utilization). So, if the load hits X, the thing that breaks is Y.

- Further steps could then be undertaken to repair the component that initially failed to possibly increase the maximum capacity. And if the time and money are available, testing could then continue to the new failure point, as there will always be another component that will fail under load.

Summary   Stress testing tests the system beyond peak loads to identify the system's maximum capacity.

Scalability Testing

Scalability testing focuses on the ability of a system to meet future efficiency requirements which may be beyond those currently required. The objective of these tests is to determine the system's ability to grow (e.g., with more users, larger amounts of data stored) without violating the currently specified performance requirements or failing. Once the limits of scalability are known, threshold values can be set and monitored in production to provide a warning of problems which may be about to arise. In addition, the production environment may be adjusted with appropriate amounts of hardware.

—ISTQB_CTFL_PT

scalability

The degree to which a component or system can be adjusted for changing capacity.

scalability testing

Testing to determine the scalability of the software product.

—ISTQB Glossary

A commonly asked question is, "Is the system scalable?"

Remember, the answer is always yes! We can always increase the load on the system, service, or component and improve the ability to handle load.

Earlier we asked, "By how much does load affect the scalability of the system/service/code in terms of time behavior, resource utilization, and capacity?"

With scalability testing, we now answer a different question. Rather than ask "Is the system/service scalable?", a more accurate question would be

"**How** is the system/service scalable?"

There are two general types of scalability testing – horizontal and vertical (Figure 1-6).

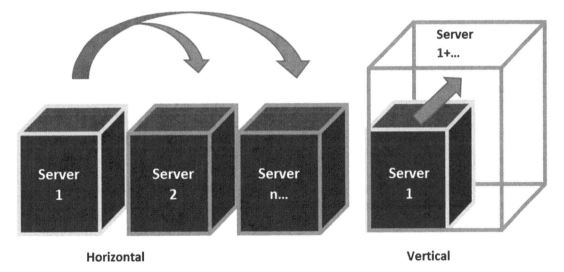

Figure 1-6. Horizontal and vertical scalability

Horizontal scalability adds more machines/pods/virtual machines of the same specification to the system, while vertical scalability replaces an existing machine/pod/virtual machine with a larger, more capable machine or more CPU and/or memory allocated to the VM/pod. Both methods have advantages and disadvantages.

In both cases, at first it's typical to gather time behavior, resource utilization, and capacity on a single server. A decision can then be made as to whether horizontal scalability (adding additional servers/pods/virtual machines) or vertical scalability (increasing the resources of a single server) will be measured to improve the overall ability of the system/service to handle a higher capacity load.

It should always be clear that there will always be an upper limit to scalability. A system or service might be scalable, but it could be too expensive to expand the necessary hardware/software licenses/infrastructure to the required level. It could be that the system or service becomes unstable or that adding more capacity may not have any benefit to the overall performance.

Summary   Scalability testing tests the system's efficiency to grow to handle larger loads.

Spike Testing

Spike testing focuses on the ability of a system to respond correctly to sudden bursts of peak loads and return afterwards to a steady state.

—ISTQB_CTFL_PT

spike testing

Testing to determine the ability of a system to recover from sudden bursts of peak loads and return to a steady state.

—ISTQB Glossary

Spike testing has become popular for looking at the system's performance if the load bounces above a defined peak for a short time (Figure 1-7). These peaks might be:

- A single event

- A series of regular spikes

- A series of random, unequal events

Examples might be online in-play betting – betting might increase:

- During halftime in a football match (a single event)

- At the end of an over in cricket or the end of a tennis game (a regular series)

- The first/next goal scorer in a football match (a series of unequal random events)

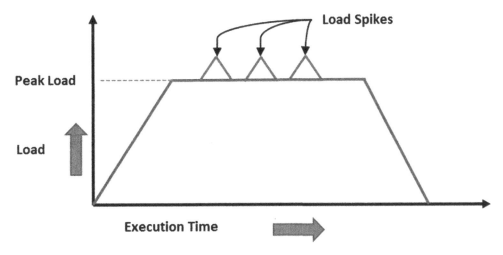

Figure 1-7. *Spike testing*

Spike testing's popularity has grown in cases of "what would happen if...." It allows performance engineers to measure the system's ability to recover after the load spike and any subsequent impact the spike may have on the system's continuing operations.

Summary   Spike testing tests the system's ability to recover from a load spike.

Endurance Testing

Endurance testing focuses on the stability of the system over a time frame specific to the system's operational context. This type of testing verifies that there are no resource capacity problems (e.g., memory leaks, database connections, thread pools) that may eventually degrade performance and/or cause failures at breaking points.

—ISTQB_CTFL_PT

endurance testing

Testing to determine the stability of a system under a significant load over a significant period of time within the system's operational context.

—ISTQB Glossary

Endurance testing is also referred to as soak testing. The difference between a load test and an endurance test is predominantly the length of time the test executes. Both are designed with a similar load profile. The difference lies where a load test may only execute for one hour; it's not unusual for endurance tests to run many hours, days, or even in extreme cases weeks in length. The challenge with endurance testing is obtaining enough test data to execute for an extended time and having enough storage space to capture the results. Endurance testing has become more critical, as the online 24 hours-a-day, seven-days-a-week nature of many organizations means there is little time for downtime or "rebooting the servers."

Summary   Endurance testing tests the system's stability over an extended time.

Concurrency Testing

Concurrency testing focuses on the impact of situations where specific actions occur simultaneously (e.g., when large numbers of users log in at the same time). Concurrency issues are notoriously difficult to find and reproduce, particularly when the problem occurs in an environment where testing has little or no control, such as production.

—ISTQB_CTFL_PT

concurrency

> *The simultaneous execution of multiple independent threads by a compo-nent or system.*
>
> —ISTQB Glossary

The concept of concurrency is a fundamental cornerstone of performance testing. Even though a single user or transaction generates load, that load may not be enough to truly exercise the system under test. By using concurrency, performance engineers can define how many business processes, tasks, or even steps are occurring simultaneously.

Three general types of concurrency can be considered. For example, if the system under test is an online retail site, many users might be performing a range of functions within the site at the same time. At a component level, it might be important to test the login component with a number of simultaneous login attempts. To break this down:

Application concurrency: There could be many users using the site to perform different business processes (searching, purchasing, checking order status, creating user accounts, etc.).

Business process concurrency: A smaller number of users may be performing a single business process simultaneously (searching the site).

Transaction concurrency: There may be a subset of the users performing a single business process (searching) that **all** click the search button simultaneously.

It could also be unexpected situations that could arise that fall more into the purvey of failover and disaster recovery, but still require performance testing. Concurrency testing might look at batch processing running concurrently with peak load, or a scheduled backup starts at a busy time.

Summary   Concurrency testing tests the ability to handle simultaneous business processes and transactions.

Capacity Testing

Capacity testing determines how many users and/or transactions a given system will support and still meet the stated performance objectives. These objectives may also be stated with regard to the data volumes resulting from the transactions.

—ISTQB_CTFL_PT

capacity

The degree to which the maximum limits of a component or system parameter meet requirements.

capacity testing

Testing to evaluate the capacity of a system.

—ISTQB Glossary

Capacity testing is like other already identified test types (stress and spike testing). The difference between capacity and stress testing is stress extends to a predetermined point of failure (e.g., a limit in throughput or resource utilization or a processing time being exceeded). Capacity testing may still extend beyond the peak load but is performed to achieve a performance test goal (e.g., how many users will the system support) rather than identify the cause of failure. Capacity testing focuses on achieving a defined level of performance rather than attempting to cause a failure (stress) or to "see what happens" (spike). Often, capacity testing has an underlying growth in load/performance relating to an organizational need. For example, the organization may have a global growth rate defined as 4% new customer growth per annum. Capacity testing could help answer the question regarding the system's ability to support this year-on-year growth.

Summary   Capacity testing tests the limit to which the system can grow while achieving its performance objectives.

1.3 Testing Activities in Performance Testing

PTFL-1.3.1 (K1) Recall testing types in performance testing

> *The principal testing types used in performance testing include static testing and dynamic testing.*
>
> —ISTQB_CTFL_PT

static testing

> *The process of evaluating a component or system without executing it, based on its form, structure, content, or documentation.*

dynamic testing

> *Testing that involves the execution of the test item.*
>
> —ISTQB Glossary

Static Testing

> *Static testing activities are often more important for performance testing than for functional suitability testing. This is because so many critical performance defects are introduced in the architecture and design of the system. These defects can be introduced by misunderstandings or a lack of knowledge by the designers and architects. These defects can also be introduced because the requirements did not adequately capture the response time, throughput, or resource utilization targets, the expected load and usage of the system, or the constraints. Static testing activities for performance can include:*
>
> - *Reviews of requirements with focus on performance aspects and risks*
>
> - *Reviews of database schemas, entity-relationship diagrams, metadata, stored procedures and queries*
>
> - *Reviews of the system and network architecture*
>
> - *Reviews of critical segments of the system code (e.g., complex algorithms)*
>
> —ISTQB_CTFL_PT

Static testing is an area that performance testing traditionally has not been directly linked. Because performance testing was always linked to the execution of the system (dynamic testing) and performed later in the test cycle, it was assumed that static testing was not relevant. This could not be further from the truth. We briefly mentioned earlier the trouble most experienced performance engineers uncover when they join a project. That is, either no performance test requirements/user stories have been written or those that do exist are not quantifiably and measurably adequate to conduct performance testing.

Actual static testing should not be dismissed. It could discover performance issues such as memory issues (the static analysis of the processor/main memory vs. processor/cached memory/main memory relationship, especially in embedded systems), thread locking (stopping a thread from executing for a myriad of reasons, but, when carelessly used, threads become deadlocked and cease processing), or even simple things such as the exponential multiplication of nested loops having an influence on performance. Static analysis, if a performance engineer is given the opportunity, can be valuable in reducing performance issues.

It's worth delving into each syllabus bullet point in more detail. In this, reference is made to another excellent book to add to a performance test library – André B. Bondi's *Foundations of Software and System Performance Engineering: Process, Performance Modeling, Requirements, Testing, Scalability, and Practice* (Bondi likes a long title). Bondi directly addresses the link between the quality of performance requirements and the impact they have on project success. From this point, when referring to the following requirements, both traditional requirements and user stories apply.

Reviews of Requirements with a Focus on Performance Aspects and Risks

The importance of the relationship between good performance requirements and good performance testing cannot be highlighted enough. Performance requirements are often derived from performance-related questions that organization stakeholders or users might ask. For example, from a business meeting the organization CEO has agreed with the board that the organization will adopt a new sales strategy to grow the organization's business at a rate of 5% per annum for the next four years. The CTO has subsequently asked the question:

"Will our business systems support a 5% revenue growth rate year on year for the next four years?"

And here lies the beginning of a performance test project. Of course, we cannot yet performance test against this requirement.

André Bondi lists the following points regarding performance requirements (point numbers have been added to the quote for reference):

Early and concise specifications of performance requirements are necessary because:

1. *Performance requirements are potential drivers of the system architecture and the choice of technologies to be used in the system's implementation. Moreover, many performance failures have their roots in poor architectural choices. Modification of the architecture before a system is implemented is cheaper than rebuilding a slow system from scratch.*

—Bondi, 2014

Traditionally, in many projects, performance testing is considered later in the software development lifecycle. And, if a performance defect is discovered, it can be extremely costly to rectify and bypass the advantage Bondi is suggesting. Similarly, it is becoming rarer today for an organization to write their own complete software systems. Much of the time development work consists of integrating various disparate products with various ages, technologies, and functionality together. It is important to note that in all the preceding instances performance engineers can have an impact on the overall performance of the end system. This might consist of performance testing existing systems to identify bottlenecks before an integration project starts, reviewing architecture diagrams to identify potential bottlenecks, and eventually reviewing (and possibly even writing from scratch) performance requirements to meet the organization's goals.

2. *Performance requirements are closely related to the contractual expectations of system performance negotiated between buyer and seller, as well as to any relevant regulatory requirements such as those for fire alarm systems.*

—Bondi, 2014

Performance engineers must always be conscious of service-level agreements (SLAs). These SLAs can be directly related to regulatory requirements (such as the EU PSD2[4] and related UK PSRs 2017[5]) or a customer contract. Indirectly, various business goals could also relate to performance around customer service, usability of systems for both staff and customers, and hence the perceived "quality" of the system.

> 3. *The performance requirements will be reflected in the performance test plan.*
>
> —Bondi, 2014

The performance test plan and performance requirements are inexorably linked. From the performance requirements, we will derive:

- The performance test types needed to meet the requirements

- The environment needs to achieve a production-like test environment with the necessary test data quality and volume

- The business processes to meet the performance requirements

- The quantifiable metrics identified to show the performance requirements have either been met or by how much the system needs to improve to meet them.

> 4. *Drafting and reviewing performance requirements force the consideration of trade-offs between execution speed and system cost, as well as between execution speed and simplicity of both the architecture and the implementation. For instance, it is more difficult to design and correctly code a system that uses multithreading to achieve parallelism in execution than to build a single-threaded implementation.*
>
> —Bondi, 2014

---

[4]The revised Payment Services Directive (PSD2), implemented in 2018, is the EU legislation which sets regulatory requirements for firms that provide payment services. The original Payment Services Directive (PSD) was introduced in 2007.

[5]PSRs 2017 – The Payment Services Regulations 2017 is the updated version for PSD2 which became a UK law through the Payment Services Regulations 2009 (`www.legislation.gov.uk/uksi/2017/752/contents/made`).

At this point, a brief explanation is required. Traditionally, people have always considered the "project triangle" as shown in Figure 1-8.

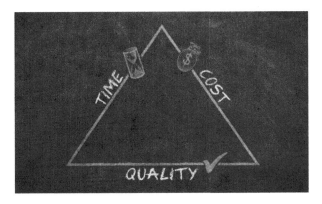

Figure 1-8.   *The quality triangle*

> There is always an appropriate catchphrase to go with this – "You can have any two you want...."
>
> Performance testing fits into this as to be expected. The preceding point considers system response time (or time behavior) as a function of quality. To achieve a reduction in system response time, more money could be spent to upgrade bandwidth or hardware (more on this in point 5). But the preceding diagram leaves out some important characteristics of any project. In using this diagram, we tend to focus more on one or two of these "sides" at the expense of the third. It does however show that all three are very closely linked.
>
> But if we expand the diagram to include "the missing bits," a different picture starts to appear. Ultimately, any project has the objective of achieving its goals – that of project success. Another thing missing from the preceding diagram is a simple reference to how much work is required to achieve the time/cost/quality the stakeholders desire.
>
> The final point considers quality itself. Quite often, the "quality" side is replaced with some expedient term to fit whomever creates the diagram. A common replacement is risk. Often, people consider quality and risk as opposites. But it could also be argued

that a system is "a high-quality system" that could also be risky (a point considered later – think of a system that is beautifully built and looks great that doesn't do the job as quickly as users expect). Because both could be considered separately, both deserve separate recognition in the preceding diagram.

We now have a more complete view of an IT project (Figure 1-9).

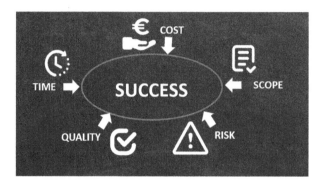

Figure 1-9. *The project success definition diagram*

The overall project goal as mentioned before is the success of the project. Each of the five project characteristics could have an influence on that success. If we imagine the success goal as a balloon, each of the five project characteristics can push either separately or together on that balloon to squeeze it out of shape (or even pop the balloon!). Importantly, if one characteristic has an adverse effect pushing on the balloon, the other four must change to keep the balloon intact. The time, cost, and quality are still there. Additionally, there is scope (how much we need to do to achieve the success) and risk (as an adjunct rather than opposite of quality).

5. *Development and/or hardware costs can be reduced if performance requirements that are found to be too stringent are relaxed early in the software lifecycle. For example, while a 1-second average response time requirement may be desirable, a 2-second requirement may be sufficient for business or engineering needs.*

Poorly specified performance requirements can lead to confusion among stakeholders and the delivery of a poor-quality product with slow response times and inadequate capacity.

—Bondi, 2014

Sometimes, these individual project attributes can be influenced by decisions made without reflecting on the impact these decisions will have on the other attributes. For example, the one-second vs. two-second average response time mentioned by Bondi is a classic performance engineer's quandary. Quite often, people will insist on a particular response time. Remember the three questions:

- Is the stated time the average response time?

- Is the stated time the maximum response time?

- Is the stated time a percentile (and if it is, what percentile)?

Once established as to which of the preceding three the stakeholder is referring to, the next very important question to ask is, "Why?" Why does the system need to respond within that maximum/average/percentile time? What is the impact if it doesn't? Was this time derived from any statistical data (such as looking at response times from a competitor's website), or was it derived using the process of inductive reasoning?[6] Where is this time being measured – is this from your uncle's old Pentium computer via an ADSL connection? From when the request hits the organization's firewall? But most importantly, if the "required response time" is needed, do the stakeholders understand the implications regarding quality, cost, time, risk, and scope to achieve that response time? Finally, can this be quantified into a requirement that contains all that is required for this to be tested?

6. *If a performance issue that cannot be mapped to explicit performance requirements emerges during testing or production, stakeholders might not feel obliged to correct it.*

—Bondi, 2014

---

[6]Inductive reasoning is a principle where an individual's experience and observation (including the learned experience and observations from others) is used as the basis to develop a general truth. It is also commonly known as a **guess**!

The very nature of performance testing systems of systems today is performance engineers quite often uncover undiscovered performance issues that could affect the system under test's overall performance. Unfortunately, performance engineers can also discover performance issues that are out of scope. Herein lies an important point – all such discoveries MUST BE REPORTED! It then becomes an issue for the stakeholders to decide upon. Performance engineers must always understand that, often, the stakeholders will look for advice on performance issues. That does not mean the performance engineer assumes the risk of the decision the stakeholder makes. It cannot be stressed highly enough the performance engineers must report what they find. It may be the discovery is beyond the scope of the project. But that does not mean that another stakeholder outside the project won't care about that discovery or that it's now "in scope."

Ultimately, static testing can allow performance engineers to ask relevant questions against the non-executable components of the project. These questions are too numerous to list, but the important point is to ask them. They can generally be grouped into the following areas:

Capacity

- Can the system support the defined peak load?

- Can the system cope with a sudden spike in load?

- What is the maximum capacity of the system?

- Does the system need to support an ongoing increase in capacity?

- Can functionality be added to the system without adversely affecting the system's performance?

Time Behavior

- Will the system respond within the defined time constraints? (Of course, this would include the load profile under which the desired time is required, with the desired load executing upon a defined, production-like environment, and include the start and end points between which the time will be measured.)

- Have all time constraints been specified in terms of average/ maximum/percentile response times?

- Have these response times been validated against real-world examples?

- Have these response times been evaluated by a range of stakeholders?

- Has the impact of aggressive time behaviors (i.e., very low response times) been assessed against the other project characteristics (cost, scope, quality, and risk)?

Resource Utilization

- Can the system running in the planned environment support the defined peak load?

- If they exist, can the system bottlenecks be identified?

- At maximum capacity, which system attribute causes the failure?

- Can the system be configured and/or tuned to meet a stakeholder requirement?

- Can changes to the system be measured both directly and indirectly against the resource utilization of the system?

- Can unpredictable behavior be diagnosed against resource utilization characteristics?

Finally, this section predominantly deals with the design of the systems under test. Whatever the form of this design – be it well-defined requirements, architectural diagrams, cause-effect graphs, state transition diagrams, function maps, database schema diagrams, or even pseudocode – all can (and should) be considered for static testing by performance engineers.

It is my business to know what other people do not know.

—Conan Doyle, 1892bc

Summary   Static testing allows performance engineers to remove defects early in the software development lifecycle before code execution by reviewing requirements, designs, and code.

Dynamic Testing

As the system is built, dynamic performance testing should start as soon as possible. Opportunities for dynamic performance testing include:

- *During unit testing, including using profiling information to determine potential bottlenecks and dynamic analysis to evaluate resource utilization*

- *During component integration testing, across key use cases and workflows, especially when integrating different use case features or integrating with the "backbone" structure of a workflow*

- *During system testing of overall end-to-end behaviors under various load conditions*

- *During system integration testing, especially for data flows and workflows across key inter-system interfaces. In system integration testing is not uncommon for the "user" to be another system or machine (e.g. inputs from sensor inputs and other systems)*

- *During acceptance testing, to build user, customer, and operator confidence in the proper performance of the system and to fine tune the system under real world conditions (but generally not to find performance defects in the system)*

—ISTQB_CTFL_PT

These preceding points from the syllabus basically define the role of performance testing against the various test levels. As a quick refresher to put these in context

component testing (module testing, unit testing)

A test level that focuses on individual hardware or software components.

—ISTQB Glossary

Component testing begins testing "a piece" of the system in isolation. It's important that at the beginning of any project a component is defined. It could be an object or method, a function, or some other defined module of code. This can be tested to ensure performance requirements established for that component have been met. Importantly, this level of testing might require mock objects, service virtualization, harnesses, stubs, and drivers to allow component testing to occur. Typically, it's performed within the integrated development environment (IDE) by people who can understand the code.

Although ISTQB have replaced the term unit testing with component testing, it is useful to distinguish between software and hardware components. Many performance engineers today anecdotally refer to unit testing when referring to code, and component testing when referring to a tier in the infrastructure (e.g., a web server in a three-tier system).

component integration testing

Testing in which the test items are interfaces and interactions between integrated components.

—ISTQB Glossary

Component integration takes the individual components tested in the previous level to now test them working together. It focuses on the interactions and interfaces between the previously tested single components. Once again, mock objects, service virtualization, harnesses, stubs, and drivers are needed to allow testing to occur – but this time the additional parts relate more to the component integrating into a larger collection of components rather than an individual component in isolation.

system testing

A test level that focuses on verifying that a system as a whole meets specified requirements.

—ISTQB Glossary

System testing now considers the system from an end-to-end business process point of view within that system. Traditionally, in sequential development methodologies, testing at this point consists of executing end-to-end business processes rather than individual tasks, with no access to the underlying code. This has changed in recent history with the introduction of agile-based iterative and incremental methodologies. But the premise remains the same – executing the end-to-end processes. It's important to note that system testing, like component testing, considers the **system** in isolation.

system integration testing

A test level that focuses on interactions between systems.

—ISTQB Glossary

As with component integration testing, system integration testing looks at a collection of systems working together – the interactions and interfaces between the previously system-tested systems. But not only systems – the addition of cloud-based microservices as an example might also need to be added to the environment. This can become quite complex, as the environment into which a system might fit could be closely integrated with many other systems. Some of these might be managed or owned by a third party – further complicating the issue!

acceptance testing

A test level that focuses on determining whether to accept the system.

—ISTQB Glossary

Acceptance testing can be broken down into a group of sublevels as defined in the ISTQB Foundation syllabus and glossary:

User acceptance testing (UAT)

*A type of acceptance testing performed to determine if intended **users** accept the system.*

Operational acceptance testing (OAT)

*A type of acceptance testing performed to determine if **operations and/or systems administration staff** can accept a system.*

Contractual acceptance testing (not called CAT)

A type of acceptance testing performed to verify whether a system satisfies its contractual requirements.

Regulatory acceptance testing (definitely not called RAT!)

A type of acceptance testing performed to verify whether a system conforms to relevant laws, policies and regulations.

—ISTQB Glossary

Before you look at the list and say, "Wait a minute, there's something missing...", alpha and beta testing were excluded from the list as these relate to the environment in which the test is executed. Alpha testing is acceptance testing run within the development environment; beta testing is acceptance testing conducted within the end user's environment.

Performance engineers could focus on any of these acceptance subtypes, and there is a role for performance testing within each. Special focus however will be on OAT as it is **acceptance testing performed by the administrators** of the system. Much of the time, OAT becomes a final check to ensure the likes of performance, security, reliability, and maintainability testing have been considered in earlier levels of testing to an adequate level and that existing system performance has been considered (i.e., regression testing the new/changed system against the existing systems). Similar to UAT being for users, OAT is for administrators to check the operational readiness of the system.

Summary   Performance testing plays a role in component, integration, system, and acceptance testing.

In higher test levels such as system testing and system integration testing, the use of realistic environments, data, and loads are critical for accurate results (see Chapter 4). In Agile and other iterative-incremental lifecycles, teams should incorporate static and dynamic performance testing into early iterations rather than waiting for final iterations to address performance risks.

—ISTQB_CTFL_PT

For iterative and incremental methodologies, performance testing can be broken down into two general sets of performance tests. The first are short directed performance tests embedded within the sprints to execute performance tests within each build – likely to be component or component integration level (multithreaded tests, queries, and simple load tests used as success criteria for user stories/definitions of done).

The second set are larger separate performance tests run outside the sprints developed by a performance team which may not be part of the sprint teams. These performance tests are more what are recognized as "traditional" performance tests (endurance tests, multiple load test scenarios on large environments). These are normally performed on a change-controlled environment, with the results fed back into the sprint teams to make changes as required.

Summary   In system and acceptance testing, performance testing should (in effect) replicate production environments. In agile projects, performance testing can begin earlier than sequential projects.

If custom or new hardware is part of the system, early dynamic performance tests can be performed using simulators. However, it is good practice to start testing on the actual hardware as soon as possible, as simulators often do not adequately capture resource constraints and performance-related behaviors.

—ISTQB_CTFL_PT

simulator

A device, computer program or system used during testing, which behaves or operates like a given system when provided with a set of controlled inputs.

—ISTQB Glossary

Summary   When required, simulators can replace components or systems not yet available for testing.

1.4 The Concept of Load Generation

PTFL-1.4.1 (K2) Understand the concept of load generation

In order to carry out the various types of performance testing described in Section 1.2, representative system loads must be modelled, generated and submitted to the system under test. Loads are comparable to the data inputs used for functional test cases, but differ in the following principal ways:

- *A performance test load must represent many user inputs, not just one*

- *A performance test load may require dedicated hardware and tools for generation*

- *Generation of a performance test load is dependent on the absence of any functional defects in the system under test which may impact test execution*

The efficient and reliable generation of a specified load is a key success factor when conducting performance tests. There are different options for load generation.

—ISTQB_CTFL_PT

Before moving on – a point on the "absence of any functional defects" in the preceding syllabus. The ISTQB Foundation syllabus refers to the seven testing principles, namely, Principle 1 – testing shows the presence of defects, not the absence. The syllabus isn't claiming the system be free of functional defects, which cannot be achieved because of Principle 2 – exhaustive testing is impossible. The point being made would be better to be thought of as any defects identified in functional testing should be repaired before performance test scripting begins.

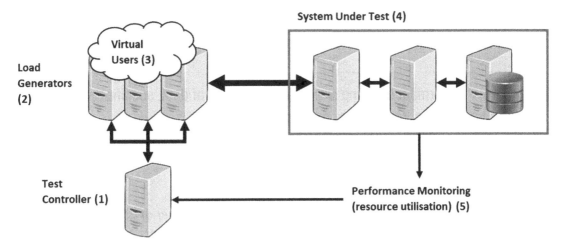

Figure 1-10. *View of the tool components of a performance test*

The load generator(s) (Figure 1-10 – 2) is/are the machine/machines on which the actual load applied to the system under test is generated. It enables performance tests to move beyond the scale of a single machine:

1. The performance test controller executes the performance test scenario and gathers the results from both the test execution and monitoring. The controller passes the performance test scripts to the load generator to execute.

2. The load generator runs the scripts – sending the requests to the system under test and capturing the responses.

3. The scripts act as "virtual users" – each script executing represents the actions of a single real user creating the individual business processes running against the system under test.

4. The system under test reacts to the load, generating metrics representing the system under test's response (response time and resource utilization). These metrics can be captured at different places within the performance test (e.g., transactional responses are sent back to the load generator/resource measurements are sent to the controller).

5. The response time and resource utilization are captured as a part of the performance test to enable root cause analysis to be performed on any defects or issues discovered.

This standard model has been adopted by many performance testing tools.

Summary   Performance testing needs large volumes of data, specific hardware, and tools to allow the load to be generated.

Load Generation via the User Interface

This may be an adequate approach if only a small number of users are to be represented and if the required numbers of software clients are available from which to enter required inputs. This approach may also be used in conjunction with functional test execution tools but may rapidly become impractical as the numbers of users to be simulated increases. The stability of the user interface (UI) also represents a critical dependency. Frequent changes can impact the repeatability of performance tests and may significantly affect the maintenance costs. Testing through the UI may be the most representative approach for end-to-end tests.

—ISTQB_CTFL_PT

UI performance testing is limited in scope, but it does address a major issue with many performance test tools. Most performance test tools work in the following way (Figure 1-11).

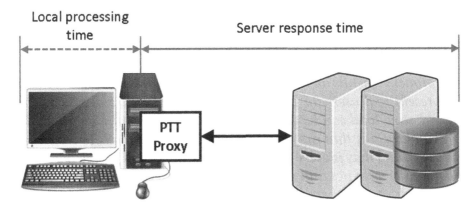

Figure 1-11. *A problem with some performance tests*

Many tools use protocol-based recording. When recording, the protocol request/response is captured via a performance test tool proxy (PTT proxy above). The tool does this by diverting the requests and responses from a defined communications port using a performance tool proxy and captures them. From this recording log through the performance tool recording proxy, the script is generated. On replay, the script replicates this request/response stream to simulate real user actions from the load generator to the system under test. But the performance test script does not capture any local client-side processing or rendering of the displayed information. Hence, these client-side actions are excluded from the transaction time. Accordingly, if the system under test uses client-side processes as part of the overall performance test, the performance engineer must specifically take actions to capture the client-side times.

UI performance tests are created similarly to functional automation scripts, in that they record by capturing the manipulation of the UI by the user and replay against the UI on replay.

Unfortunately, many fewer UI scripts can be run compared with a protocol-based script due to the limitation in running multiple end clients on a load generator.

UI performance testing can avoid the problem of proxy recording missing client-side processing by using "normal" proxy-based performance test scripts to generate a background load. A small number of UI virtual users can then be added to capture the client-side processing times from the end-user perspective.

Summary   Performance tests can be created by recording the UI but are dependent on the stability of the UI and can be limited to low user numbers.

Load Generation Using Crowds

This approach depends on the availability of a large number of testers who will represent real users. In crowd testing, the testers are organized such that the desired load can be generated. This may be a suitable method for testing applications that are reachable from anywhere in the world (e.g., web-based), and may involve the users generating a load from a wide range of different device types and configurations. Although this approach may enable very large numbers of users to be utilized, the load generated will not be as reproducible and precise as other options and is more complex to organize.

—ISTQB_CTFL_PT

A good performance test is repeatable. Three issues exist with crowd-based performance testing (also known as manual performance testing):

1. Controlling the "virtual users" – In this case, the virtual users are in fact real users who can all be streaming media/answering email/posting to social media/getting coffee while the performance test is running. Controlling these virtual users can be difficult as any performance engineer involved in manual performance testing will lack the fine degree of control they would have using performance scripts.

2. Capturing performance information – While the performance test is running, metric data can come from multiple sources. Keeping track of all the data sources without the use of tools can be almost impossible.

3. Correlating the performance metrics with the user actions – Because we cannot directly control the users, it becomes difficult to equate their actions with the performance metric data captured during the test.

Summary   Crowd performance tests use real people as crowd tester but can be difficult to control and reproduce.

Load Generation via the Application Programming Interface (API)

This approach is similar to using the UI for data entry but uses the application's API instead of the UI to simulate user interaction with the system under test. The approach is therefore less sensitive to changes (e.g., delays) in the UI and allows the transactions to be processed in the same way as they would if entered directly by a user via the UI. Dedicated scripts may be created which repeatedly call specific API routines and enable more users to be simulated compared to using UI inputs.

—ISTQB_CTFL_PT

Using API is a good method for the earlier levels of performance testing (component/component integration testing) and can continue to be used in later levels of testing. It has become popular in organizations using iterative and incremental methodologies for testing within the sprint. Performance engineers must be mindful of the limitations of conducting performance testing with API. In many cases, API will only represent single operations within a larger business process. For example, if we run API that performs a lookup in a database, it will return the result for that single API function being run. This can cause issues however (Figure 1-12).

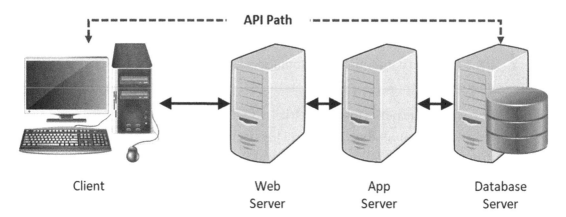

Figure 1-12. *An issue with API testing*

If the system is a three-tier system as shown earlier, and we run API to interrogate the database, we can exclude parts of the infrastructure and/or tiers in the load test. This can be a good thing for component and component integration testing, but as can be seen we are now avoiding the web and the app server by running the API. Hence, if we perform API testing in later levels of testing, we may be running the system in a nonproduction-like manner. But it shouldn't be dismissed – it can be a way of introducing stress as part of a stress test. For example, if the environment in Figure 1-13 is a test environment, and production will have two web servers and two databases, if we stress the web/app servers above 100%, the database will only be stressed above 50%. But, we could use API tests against the database server (i.e., running more queries against the database); it could increase the stress against the database to simulate another web/app server pair.

In many organizations using DevOps, teams develop and maintain one or a small number of related APIs building microservice architecture. API testing thus becomes a vital tool in component (directly testing the component itself) and component integration performance testing (testing the "neighbor" APIs) in these environments. This can even allow production-like loads to be applied, as the use of the microservice architecture allows containerized code to be applied in a "production-like" pod. A warning needs to be placed here – some of the components developed might be used by other systems without the knowledge of designers at creation. This "performance scope creep" can subsequently affect the performance of any system or service using that component, possibly causing it to fail under conditions never considered within the initial performance testing scope.

Summary   Performance tests via API avoid the UI and use the same API a user would use. They allow greater user numbers to be tested than UI load generation.

Load Generation Using Captured Communication Protocols

This approach involves capturing user interaction with the system under test at the communications protocol level and then replaying these scripts to simulate potentially very large numbers of users in a repeatable and reliable manner. This tool-based approach is described in Sections 4.2.6 and 4.2.7.

—ISTQB_CTFL_PT

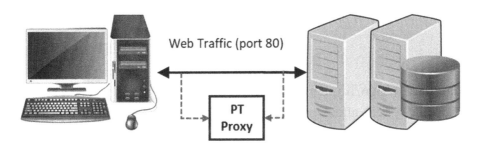

Figure 1-13.   The protocol recording mechanism

This recording method was mentioned earlier ("Load Generation via the User Interface"). The tool records the script based on the protocol calls through a nominated port or set of ports. The preceding example shows an HTTP web recording capturing the traffic via port 80. The tool captures the port once recording starts, and any request/response sent through port 80 is captured by the performance test proxy. These captured request/response calls are then used as the basis for the script. On playback, this script then regenerates the calls, and as far as the system under test is concerned, it's being contacted by real users. This method is used by almost all tools when creating performance tests.

Summary   Communication protocol capture allows many virtual users to be replayed.

1.5 Common Performance Efficiency Failure Modes and Their Causes

PTFL-1.5.1 (K2) Give examples of common failure modes of performance testing and their causes

> *While there certainly are many different performance failure modes that can be found during dynamic testing, the following are some examples of common failures (including system crashes), along with typical causes:*
>
> **Slow response under all load levels**
>
> *In some cases, response is unacceptable regardless of load. This may be caused by underlying performance issues, including, but not limited to, bad database design or implementation, network latency, and other background loads. Such issues can be identified during functional and usability testing, not just performance testing, so test analysts should keep an eye open for them and report them.*
>
> —ISTQB_CTFL_PT

Bad database design/implementation – A database can become a key performance bottleneck to any system, affecting the overall performance of the entire system. Factors to consider:

- Tables can contain too much data ("wide rows"), which can lead to data redundancy, or too little data, requiring more tables and more joins to retrieve data. As well as width, tables can be too tall – too many records without proper indexing and/or horizontal partitioning can slow the entire database.

- Normalization of data within tables can help eliminate redundant data and ensure relevant data dependencies. A set of rules exist for normalization – the first three are usually enough, but others exist beyond this set:

    - First normal form – Eliminate duplicate columns and repeating values in columns.

- Second normal form – Remove redundant data that apply to multiple columns.

- Third normal form – Each column of a table should be dependent on the primary identifier.

- Indexing compares with searching for a name in an old-fashioned phone book – it would be a lot harder to find the number you were looking for if all the people within this were listed by address rather than their last name. Poor indexing means the DB spends more time looking for the requested data.

- Queries and stored procedures are another (and some might subjectively say bigger) area of concern:

  - The first consideration is data volume. A simple query or stored procedure might return an unnecessary large volume of data. Is all the return data needed? SELECT * is a bad option.

  - A lot of concurrent queries can substantially degrade database performance. These queries will queue – and the shorter the queue waiting to be processed, the better the response time.

  - Even simple naming conventions can affect performance – for example, if stored procedures are prefixed with sp_, they are mixed with system-stored procedures, taking longer to find. Another tip is to add the schema name to the object name to reduce the possibility of searching multiple schemas.

- Database caching can also have a big effect on performance. Caching allows frequently used records to be stored in RAM, allowing faster access. Configuring DB caching can be an art – do we create a large cache at the expense of overall system memory, or do we reduce the cache, meaning users requesting information spend longer "spinning the disks…"?

- Database location – Remember latency? The further away the database is and the quality of the network between the database and the requestor can both affect the overall database performance.

- Database synchronization/harmonization can affect the overall performance based on such things as the update frequency and overall database size.

Network latency – Latency refers to the time it takes for data to complete a journey across the network. The best analogy for latency is pizza delivery (also having the advantage of including bandwidth). The first important characteristic is time. You can order pizza from two different pizza parlors – one that is 2 km from your house, the other 10 km away. If both the delivery drivers left at the same time, you would expect the closer to arrive first. It's the same with latency; the shorter the distance traveled, the faster the packets arrive at their destination.

But it's not as simple as that. Both bandwidth and congestion can also have an effect. Traveling 10 km on a multilane motorway (higher bandwidth) can be faster than 2 km in a narrow built-up city street (lower bandwidth). Traffic (congestion) can also have an effect – more traffic could mean a slower journey. Any of these can delay network packets, causing queueing (that line of traffic at the off-ramp) or the packets are dropped (the road to the pizza parlor is blocked – let's get a burger instead), leading to packets needing to be sent again or even active sessions being dropped and/or new sessions not starting.

To think of this in terms of a network, a TCP/IP connection between the client and server is about to commence. The TCP handshake is a means of commencing the transfer – initiated by the client. The client sends a SYN (synchronization) packet, the server then responds with a SYN-ACK (synchronization acknowledgment), and the client finally completes the handshake with the final ACK (acknowledgment) packet. The time taken to complete the handshake with a high latency (600 milliseconds) vs. a low latency (100 milliseconds) is stark:

High Latency		Low Latency	
SYN	600ms	SYN	100ms
SYN-ACK	600ms	SYN-ACK	100ms
ACK	600ms	ACK	100ms
TOTAL	**1800ms**	**TOTAL**	**300ms**

Background load – Background load could be linked to a resource becoming overloaded (similar to network congestion). A good example is a virtual machine server running several VMs. If one VM begins a resource-intensive process, and the server is set for dynamic resource allocation, other virtual machines could slow down as a result of a lack of resources now available to them. This issue is prevalent within some aspects of cloud computing (although less noticeable), as well as local VMs.

Background load may not be an issue during performance testing, as the system under test may be tested in isolation. As mentioned later, it's typical to run performance tests at night to reduce the effect of other traffic on the network affecting the performance test results. It must be stated however the system will run in that production environment, and some testing should be done to measure the effect of the system under test on the network during operational hours.

Summary   Slow response times at all load levels can be caused by bad database design or implementation, network latency, and other background loads.

Slow Response Under Moderate-to-Heavy Load Levels

In some cases, response degrades unacceptably with moderate-to-heavy load, even when such loads are entirely within normal, expected, allowed ranges. Underlying defects include saturation of one or more resources and varying background loads.

—ISTQB_CTFL_PT

An interesting conundrum that occurs is the link between resource saturation and load balancing. Of course, any resource saturation (CPU, memory, disk IO, bandwidth, and queueing) can degrade performance. But load balancing is a special case, in that quite often load balancing is included in the production system but is excluded in the test system due to cost.

Summary   Slow response times under moderate load can be caused by saturation of one or more resources and varying background loads.

Degraded Response over Time

In some cases, response degrades gradually or severely over time. Underlying causes include memory leaks, disk fragmentation, increasing network load over time, growth of the file repository, and unexpected database growth.

—ISTQB_CTFL_PT

Memory leak – Traditionally, memory leaks were a common problem for two reasons:

- Early computers didn't have a lot of memory.

- Developers wrote code in languages requiring them to manage memory.

memory leak

A memory access failure due to a defect in a program's dynamic store allocation logic that causes it to fail to release memory after it has finished using it.

—ISTQB Glossary

To demonstrate this in C:

```
void ml_function()
{
    int *pointer = malloc(10 * sizeof (int));

    /* Do stuff */

    return; /* Returns without freeing pointer memory*/
}
```

The preceding code creates a pointer variable (`pointer`) which will store the address allocated by the `malloc` function – malloc allocates a block of memory ten times the size of an integer (which can vary in size if the machine is 32-bit (4 bytes) or 64-bit (8 bytes)). But when the `return` statement returns control back to the code calling `ml_function`, the memory is still allocated. If this function is run again, another block of memory will be allocated. Herein lies the issue – a developer may forget the `free` statement. Adding in a `free(pointer);` just before the `return` statement would fix this problem.

Of course, this is a simple example. The trick is to find the offending process causing the memory leak.

If available memory begins to run low (for whatever reason), paging begins. A page is a block of memory managed by the operating system – when memory starts to run low, these pages, rather than be stored in RAM, are moved to the hard drive. If a program tries to access a page not stored in RAM, a page fault occurs (page faults are thus a useful thing to monitor – more on this later). The OS then must:

- Find the location of the page on the hard drive

- Find an empty page frame in RAM (which could mean moving another page out of RAM onto the hard drive) to use as a container for the required page

- Load the required page into the now available page frame

- Update the page table to refer to the new page frame

- Return control to the process and retry the instruction that caused the initial page fault

Compared to accessing the page in RAM, this process is incredibly slow and has a profound impact on performance. Accessing pages from disk is at least 100,000 times slower than RAM and over 2 million times slower than the CPU cache.

Disk fragmentation – Disk fragmentation occurs when a file is stored on disk. The storage process breaks up the file into blocks to store on the hard disk. These blocks may not always match the block size on the disk (e.g., a file block of 22 bytes will fit into a standard 32-byte disk block, but some memory will be wasted). As the disk fills up, less contiguous space is available, and the blocks are stored in any available space. Also, because files are constantly being created, deleted, and edited (getting bigger or smaller), fragmentation continues to occur. If a file is broken into many blocks over different locations, it takes substantially longer to read and write.

In terms of performance, the hard disk (both the traditional platter disk and to a lesser extent solid-state disk) is the primary bottleneck. File fragmentation adversely affects the read/write speeds of the disk. This can have a dramatic effect on database servers (which are always changing and rely on read/write speed for performance) or any server relying on disk access. Another effect is something called disk thrashing – constant writing and reading can add to the disk read/write queues and speed up eventual disk failure.

Increased network load – As mentioned previously, the more traffic on the road, the slower the pizza delivery…

File/database growth – File growth leads to disk fragmentation and the associated issues. Once again, looking at a database as an example, running a SELECT statement on a SQL Server table containing addresses with one million records and using the STATISTICS TIME counter:

```
SET STATISTICS TIME ON
SELECT [CustomerID], [AddressLine1], [AddressLine2], [City], [PostCode],
[MembershipStatus]
FROM [Customer].[Address]
SET STATISTICS TIME OFF
```

The results show:

```
SQL Server Execution Times:
CPU time = 1016 ms, elapsed time = 13645 ms.
```

And, if the table size is doubled to two million records:

```
SQL Server Execution Times:
CPU time = 2198 ms, elapsed time = 27015 ms.
```

The bigger the dataset, the longer any linear SELECT (or even worse a more complex INNER JOIN) or related search operation will take.

Summary   Degraded response over time can be caused by memory leaks, disk fragmentation, increasing network load over time, growth of the file repository, and unexpected database growth.

Inadequate or Graceless Error Handling Under Heavy or Overlimit Load

In some cases, response time is acceptable, but error handling degrades at high and beyond-limit load levels. Underlying defects include insufficient resource pools, undersized queues and stacks, and too rapid time-out settings.

—ISTQB_CTFL_PT

Insufficient resource pool – The term resource pool can be somewhat vague. Typically, resource pools referred to CPU, disk space, or memory resources for virtual machines. But it could also include the database and web application connection pools, thread pools, or queue pools as well.

Resource pools relate to the resources available to allocate to a cluster of VMs. It could be that a single VM doesn't have enough resource, or the entire cluster. In either case, it may be enough to allocate more resources to the VM/cluster.

The connection pool is slightly different. It's a cached collection of predefined connections users can draw from. This can speed up user transactions for both direct database users and dynamic database-driven websites and applications. Any user that can draw from the pool will connect and complete the transaction much faster than a user who must create a connection before completing the transaction. If the connection pool is too small, users without an available connection will slow down as they establish a fresh connection **for each transaction**. If the connection pool is too large, resources are used maintaining the connection pool. Tuning the connection pool can improve performance (setting minimum/maximum connections, maximum connection reuse, abandoned connection timeout).

Undersized queues/stacks – A queue is a buffer that allows a computer to handle varying load conditions. Queueing can occur in multiple places on a computer (processor, disk, and network (including messaging) are the main suspects). It works the same as the queue at the supermarket – the longer the queue and/or the more in the shopping trolley of people in front, the longer it will take. But on the other hand, if the supermarket analogy is continued, no queues could mean that the supermarket is paying for cashiers waiting with nothing to do. In the performance case, it shows the system may be overspecified (and hence more money was spent than needed).

The queueing theory is an interesting area (more on this later) – but basically in performance terms, a short queue is a good queue.

The stack is an area of memory that stores temporary function variables – when the function declares variables, it does so LIFO (last in, first out). Once the function returns, it frees the memory of the local function's variables. The stack size itself is limited by the operating system. Stack memory is faster than heap memory, but there are advantages and disadvantages to both.

If the stack is undersized, it can cause stack overflow, causing wild pointers (pointers aimed at addresses that don't store the required data) and overwritten variables.

Timeout settings – As a user logs in to a system/website, a session is created. It might be maintained by a session ID/token (stateless) or create a constant connection (stateful). These can be compared to making a phone call (stateful) – the call is connected and remains open until terminated by either user (or the train goes into a tunnel!). The stateless example would be a postcard – each one sent must be addressed to the recipient.

Timeout relates to idle sessions and unfulfilled requests. Session timeout determines the time a server maintains an idle session. Setting a high value for session timeout can impact performance by causing the server to maintain many sessions. Setting a low value can cause the server to terminate sessions too quickly, causing a usability issue. Waiting for requests is best seen with browser timeouts – the time the browser will wait for the next response. Once again, browser timeouts can be changed to wait longer (which just means a user waits longer without the browser timing out) or shorter (meaning if the response is delayed beyond the browser timeout, the user gets ERR_CONNECTION_TIMED_OUT[7]).

 It has long been an axiom of mine that the little things are infinitely the most important.

—Conan Doyle, 1894

Summary   Inadequate error handling under heavy or overlimit load can be caused by insufficient resource pools, undersized queues and stacks, and too rapid timeout settings.

---

[7]Other timeout messages are also available.

Specific examples of the general types of failures listed above include:

A web-based application that provides information about a company's services does not respond to user requests within seven seconds (a general industry rule of thumb). The performance efficiency of the system cannot be achieved under specific load conditions.

—ISTQB_CTFL_PT

Firstly, the "seven-second rule" relates to the time it takes to create a "good impression" and varies between:

- Meeting someone for the first time

- How long a piece of toast can sit on the floor before it becomes contaminated (although the "five-second rule" has been tested to show that bacterial transfer is dependent on time, the food type, and the surface onto which it falls[8])

- The amount of time a website has to capture a user's attention with the user's first visit to the site

Although no scholarly articles exist on the origins of the last statement, and little evidence on the validity of the rule exists, it continues to persist as a biased truth. If a situation arises where an individual insists on the truth of this statement (usually beginning with the statement, "Studies have shown…"), ask to see the studies!

The only clue here is that it's a web-based system that doesn't perform. This is a point to start thinking of what questions to ask the stakeholders about the system:

- At what user number is performance unacceptable? This could be an instance where the overall architecture could be an issue (poor DB performance).

- Is performance bad for certain user groups/transaction types (poor design/inefficient DB queries)?

- Is performance bad for users from a certain area (network latency)?

---

[8] Robyn C. Miranda, Donald W. Schaffner; *"Longer Contact Times Increase Cross-Contamination of Enterobacter aerogenes from Surfaces to Food"*; Applied and Environmental Microbiology; `https://aem.asm.org/content/82/21/6490?ijkey=FLERGaGuAWOEM&keytype=ref&siteid=asmj ournals`

This type needs a plain, old-fashioned load test to begin investigating these issues.

> *A system crashes or is unable to respond to user inputs when subjected to a sudden large number of user requests (e.g., ticket sales for a major sporting event). The capacity of the system to handle this number of users is inadequate.*
>
> —ISTQB_CTFL_PT

A sudden increase in load can put demands on the entire system infrastructure – the network with a sudden increase in traffic causing congestion, perhaps queueing at the network card, resource exhaustion with CPU/memory consumed (and perhaps paging starting). This type of condition can be anticipated as part of the operational profile and tested with a spike test.

> *System response is significantly degraded when users submit requests for large amounts of data (e.g., a large and important report is posted on a web site for download). The capacity of the system to handle the generated data volumes is insufficient.*
>
> —ISTQB_CTFL_PT

Once again, this could be one or a combination of several issues:

- Is the report generated with an inefficient query? (DB issue – running the query drains resources from other users.)

- Does the report contain unnecessary data from the query that needs to be modified by the web server? (Inefficient queries or an issue with the design – the user cannot preemptively filter the volume of data being returned.)

- Does the report change in size? Is there a point at which the report size links with both an acceptable and unacceptable response? (This could link to network bandwidth performance or DB performance.)

- Does the report need to be dynamically generated each run, or could it be cached within the DB cache or generated as a static page or .pdf and cached on the web server?

This is a prime candidate for a load test which increases the transaction. An example would be an online retail website being load tested with each order having 20 items ordered rather than a single item ordered. This would increase the system's processing to deal with the 20 items rather than one.

> *Batch processing is unable to complete before online processing is needed. The execution time of the batch processes is insufficient for the time period allowed.*
>
> —ISTQB_CTFL_PT

This example is a classic case of a part of the system becoming the bottleneck – the poor batch process performance slowing the entire system. Once again, questions to consider:

- Does this process vary with the size of the batch process? Does performance degrade upon a certain batch job size?

- Is the batch process itself inefficient?

- What response time is required – could the batch data be needed too quickly? This could come down to the cost to rectify vs. the organizational risk relating to slow response.

This could be a combination of load profiles built into load tests, based on the preceding answers.

> *A real-time system runs out of RAM when parallel processes generate large demands for dynamic memory which cannot be released in time. The RAM is not dimensioned adequately, or requests for RAM are not adequately prioritized.*
>
> —ISTQB_CTFL_PT

As mentioned earlier, low available RAM means the system will begin generating page faults as it starts to read/write to disk to free up memory. The syllabus answered the question itself in this case. For this example, scalability testing would be an option – determine the performance with the initial state system to determine the load required, then duplicate the load to test the new memory amount/memory prioritization.

A real-time system component A which supplies inputs to real-time system component B is unable to calculate updates at the required rate. The overall system fails to respond in time and may fail. Code modules in component A must be evaluated and modified ("performance profiling") to ensure that the required update rates can be achieved.

—ISTQB_CTFL_PT

This is interesting – it returns to the earlier question, "What is load?"

The efficiency of the code could be improved, and/or the environment could be changed to have more resources to execute. It will depend on the organizational risk associated with this issue. The event described here is a race condition – a sequence of events, threads, or processes that must occur in a defined order for the operation to be successful. A possible solution to this is semaphoring (discussed later), which could stop the system failure, but56 would not improve performance. Load testing component A could help diagnose and possibly help improve the performance inefficiency.

Chapter 1 Questions

1. Which of the following is NOT a performance efficiency attribute?

    A. Time behavior

    B. Scalability

    C. Capacity

    D. Resource utilization

2. During performance testing, which other quality characteristics apart from performance efficiency could be evaluated?

    A. Component and integration

    B. Capacity and resource utilization

    C. Usability and functional stability

    D. Usability and efficiency

3. Which of the following is a performance testing principle?

   A. The tests must build the defined expectations of different stakeholder groups, in particular users, system designers, and operations staff into the system.

   B. The tests must be executable within the timeframe set by the project but could be high in cost.

   C. The tests must yield results that are understandable and can be readily compared to stakeholder expectations when writing performance test user stories.

   D. The tests can be conducted, where resources allow, either on complete or partial systems or test environments that are representative of the production system.

4. Which of the following groups contains executable performance test types?

1. Availability Testing	5. Efficiency Testing
2. Spike Testing	6. Scalability Testing
3. Concurrency Testing	7. Capacity Testing
4. Endurance Testing	8. Stress Testing

   A.   2,3,4,6,7,8

   B.   1,3,4,5,7,8

   C.   1,2,4,5,6,8

   D.   1,2,3,5,6,7

5. Which of the following is the best description of endurance testing?

   A. Testing to determine the stability of a system under a significant load over a significant time period within the system's operational context

   B. Testing to determine the endurance of the software product

    C. Testing to determine the ability of a system to recover from extended bursts of peak loads and return to a steady state

    D. Testing conducted to evaluate a system or component at or beyond the limits of its anticipated or specified workloads

6. Which of the following performance testing activities should occur during integration testing?

    A. Testing to evaluate resource utilization and potential bottlenecks

    B. Testing end-to-end behavior under various load conditions

    C. Testing dataflows and workflows across interfaces

    D. Testing key use cases and workflows using a top-down approach

7. Which of the following is a disadvantage of load generation using crowds?

    A. Dedicated load generation scripts may be created which repeatedly call specific routines and enable more users to be simulated. (API)

    B. Load generated will not be as reproducible and precise as other options and is more complex to organize.

    C. Encryption of the generated communication protocol can impact the effectiveness of the performance scripts and slow down script creation.

    D. Frequent changes can impact the repeatability of load generation and may significantly affect the maintenance costs. (UI)

8. A colleague is analyzing performance test results and suspects the system under test has slow response under moderate-to-heavy loads. Which of the following causes would relate to this failure?

    A. Bad database design or implementation

    B. Disk fragmentation

    C. Too rapid timeout settings

    D. Saturation of one or more resources

9. A second colleague suspects the system under test's performance
    is degrading over time. Which of the following causes would relate
    to this failure?

    A. Bad database design or implementation

    B. Disk fragmentation

    C. Too rapid timeout settings

    D. Saturation of one or more resources

CHAPTER 2

Performance Measurement Fundamentals

ISTQB Keywords

measurement

The process of assigning a number or category to an entity to describe an attribute of that entity.

metrics

A measurement scale and the method used for measurement.

Other Keywords

driver

A temporary component or tool that replaces another component and controls or calls a test item in isolation.

test monitoring

The activity that checks the status of testing activities, identifies any variances from planned or expected, and reports status to stakeholders.

© Keith Yorkston 2021

K. Yorkston, *Performance Testing*, https://doi.org/10.1007/978-1-4842-7255-8_2

2.1 Typical Measurements Collected in Performance Testing

PTFL-2.1.1 (K2) Understand the typical measurements collected in performance testing

Before this chapter begins, a quick note to understand the nomenclature of monitoring:

- Performance engineers perform monitoring.

- Through monitoring, performance engineers gather metrics.

- Performance engineers define metrics with measurements.

To put that into context, a performance engineer is **monitoring** during a performance test, collecting CPU utilization (a **metric**). CPU utilization is the sum of work done (as opposed to not working) by a CPU, expressed as a percentage utilization (**measurement**) of the CPU. Hence, a 2GHz processor (capable of performing roughly two billion calculations per second) is doing a billion calculations per second; it's at 50% utilization. Of course, CPU utilization is more complex today – with GPUs and multicore processors – but the important point is to understand as a performance engineer:

- We do monitoring.

- We gather metrics.

- We report measurements.

Why Performance Metrics Are Needed

Accurate measurements and the metrics which are derived from those measurements are essential for defining the goals of performance testing and for evaluating the results of performance testing. Performance testing should not be undertaken without first understanding which measurements and metrics are needed. The following project risks apply if this advice is ignored:

- *It is unknown if the levels of performance are acceptable to meet operational objectives*

- *The performance requirements are not defined in measurable terms*

- *It may not be possible to identify trends that may predict lower levels of performance*

- *The actual results of a performance test cannot be evaluated by comparing them to a baseline set of performance measures that define acceptable and/or unacceptable performance*

- *Performance test results are evaluated based on the subjective opinion of one or more people*

- *The results provided by a performance test tool are not understood*

—ISTQB_CTFL_PT

As mentioned in the previous chapter, non-functional requirements/user stories are often not quantified. Stakeholders lacking in performance test experience unfortunately do not recognize these requirements/user stories cannot be successfully achieved from a quantitative perspective. By defining a set of standard metrics for performance testing, performance engineers can achieve two quick wins:

1. Performance engineers can automate the collection of the standard metrics to make the job easier.

2. Stakeholders can be educated as to the meaning of the standard metrics.

A temptation for many performance engineers is to gather as much metric information as possible and supply mountains of numbers to stakeholders. As mentioned previously, the stakeholders may not understand the implication of the metric information against the system under test. Performance engineers must develop an understanding of the Golden Rules of Monitoring:

1. Keep it simple!

2. When in doubt, refer to rule one!

Another consideration is the audience to which these metrics will be presented. Each stakeholder group will have different technical or business knowledge as well as performance test knowledge. A common language between these must be developed. Having a common set of metrics can help mitigate this.

Finally, there's the stakeholders who want "that extra bit of special data." Performance engineers should never dismiss these requests out of hand, as it's always worth validating why that data may be needed as well as the effort required to produce it. The gathered data may well be essential to prove a test objective or regulatory requirement. But it can also be demoralizing when effort is expended by performance engineers to report metrics to have stakeholders not turning past the executive summary on a performance test report.

Summary   Performance engineers perform monitoring, gather metrics, and report on the measurements of the metrics. Performance test goals are defined and achieved by the result metrics gathered during the test.

Collecting Performance Measurements and Metrics

As with any form of measurement, it is possible to obtain and express metrics in precise ways. Therefore, any of the metrics and measurements described in this section can and should be defined to be meaningful in a particular context. This is a matter of performing initial tests and learning which metrics need to be further refined and which need to be added.

For example, the metric of response time likely will be in any set of performance metrics. However, to be meaningful and actionable, the response time metric will need to be further defined in terms of time of day, number of concurrent users, the amount of data being processed and so forth.

—ISTQB_CTFL_PT

It should be noted a difference exists between accuracy and precision that causes confusion. Consider the following table:

- Accuracy – How close the measurement is to the real value

- Precision – How exact the measurement is

	Accuracy	Precision
$\pi = 3$	Yes (to one digit)	No
$\pi = 3.4268$	Yes (to one digit)	Yes
$\pi = 3.14159$	Yes	Yes

It is important to note that measurements can be precise without being accurate. Measurements can also be accurate without being precise.

Consider train timetables as an example of how monitoring can become a nightmare for stakeholders in terms of accuracy vs. precision. In the UK, the government publishes a Passenger Rail Performance Report[1] that reports on train punctuality. Train punctuality is important if:

- You live in the UK.

- You catch the train to and from work.

Consider the following taken from the report:

Great Britain - 2019-20 (April 2019 to March 2020)		Compared with 2018-19	
On Time	64.8%	⬆	1.4 pp
PPM	86.2%	⬇	-0.1 pp
Cancellations Score	3.4%	⬆	0.5 pp

So, 64.8% of trains were "on time" in the preceding time period. But what's the other figure? From further into the report:

*Using the **Public Performance Measure (PPM), 86.2%** of trains were punctual (early or less than 5/10 minutes after the scheduled arrival time) at their destination in 2019-20.*

But wait, there's more...

Train punctuality at recorded station stops: *On Time, Time to 3 and Time to 15 measure the punctuality of trains at each recorded station stop. These measures are different from the Public Performance Measure (PPM), which measures the punctuality of trains at their final destination only. The new punctuality measures also exclude station stops where the train fails to call. For PPM, all cancelled trains are included in the measure and counted as 'non-punctual' trains.*

---

[1] Passenger Rail Performance 2019-20 Q4 Statistical Release (Publication date: 21 May 2020)
https://dataportal.orr.gov.uk/media/1737/passenger-performance-2019-20-q4.pdf

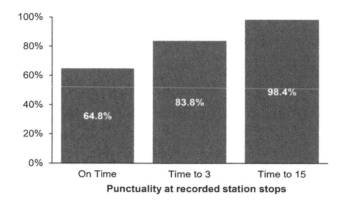

Punctuality at recorded station stops

Time to 3 and Time to 15 *measures the percentage of recorded stations stops arrived at early or less than three and 15 minutes respectively after the scheduled time.*

The percentages are cumulative, so for example, the Time to 15 measure will include the punctual (train) recorded station stops including the Time to 3 measure.

In the UK, train timetables are **precise** to the minute. But according to this, only 64.8% of the time are they **accurate**. Unless we adjust the requirement/definition of done – that is, the train is on time if it's within 15 minutes of the published time. And, hey presto, 98.4% of the trains are running on time! At least, so says the press release...

If we now think like a performance project stakeholder, the information required looks at the punctuality of the 07:41 train to London Liverpool Street. Will it be running on time for the stakeholder meeting at the office? Will the stakeholder care if 98.4% of the time, the trains are within 15 minutes of being on time of recorded stops? The key is not to provide a mass of information, but to answer the question that the stakeholder needs answered.

Performance engineers must ensure the definition within any requirements/user stories:

- The level of accuracy required – As shown earlier, is the train arriving within 15 minutes of the timetable "good enough"?

- The level of precision required – Do the stakeholders care that the precision is to a tenth of a percent?

In performance test terms, if a requirement is specified for a two-second response time, we should consider the level of precision required. Will a stakeholder care if a performance engineer gives a response time measured to the thousandth of a second? How accurately will this response time be measured – by a tool command within the performance test code or a user with a stopwatch?

Summary   Metrics and measurements should be defined to be meaningful in the context of the requirements/user stories. Measurements should be accurate and captured with a level of precision defined by the context.

The metrics collected in a specific performance test will vary based on the:

- *business context (business processes, customer and user behavior, and stakeholder expectations),*

- *operational context (technology and how it is used),*

- *test objectives.*

For example, the metrics chosen for the performance testing of an international ecommerce website will differ from those chosen for the performance testing of an embedded system used to control medical device functionality.

—ISTQB_CTFL_PT

Earlier, we covered five generic resource utilization metrics that can be monitored on any machine involved in a performance test. To consider these metrics in more detail:

CPU Utilization

CPU metrics include:

- % idle time – The percentage of elapsed time the processor spends idle

- % processor time – The percentage of elapsed time the processor spends executing non-idle threads (i.e., actually doing something!)

Memory Utilization

Memory metrics include:

- Available Mbytes – The amount of physical memory, immediately available for allocation to a process or for system use.

- Cache bytes – The size of the portion of the system file cache which is currently resident and active in physical memory.

- % committed bytes in use – The ratio of memory/committed bytes to the memory/commit limit.

- Committed bytes – The physical memory which has space reserved on the disk paging file(s).

- Page faults/second – The average number of pages faulted per second. It is measured in numbers of pages faulted per second because only one page is faulted in each fault operation; hence, this is also equal to the number of page fault operations.

- Page reads/second – The rate at which the disk was read to resolve hard page faults.

- Page writes/second – The rate at which pages are written to disk to free up space in physical memory.

Disk Input/Output (Physical Disk)

Disk IO metrics include:

- % disk read time – The percentage of elapsed time that the selected disk drive was busy servicing read requests

- % disk write time – The percentage of elapsed time that the selected disk drive was busy servicing write requests

- Disk read bytes/second – The number of bytes transferred from the disk during read operations per second

- Disk write bytes/second – The number of bytes transferred from the disk during write operations per second

Bandwidth Consumption

Bandwidth is interesting, as it exists externally on the physical/wireless network, along with each machine moving information internally between memory, the CPU, and storage (hard drive/SSD). Bandwidth metrics include:

- Bytes received/second – The rate at which bytes are received over each network adapter, including framing characters.

- Bytes sent/second – The rate at which bytes are sent over each network adapter, including framing characters.

- Split IO/second – The rate at which inputs/outputs to the disk were split into multiple IOs (a split IO may result from requesting data of a size that is too large to fit into a single IO you or that the disk is fragmented).

- IO data bytes/second – The rate at which the process is reading and writing bytes in IO operations. This counter counts all IO activity generated by the process to include file, network, and device IO.

- IO data operations/second – The rate at which the process is issuing read and write IO operations. This counter counts all IO activity generated by the process to include file, network, and device IO.

Queueing

Just like at the train station, queueing is a sign that the established system (in the train example, the station staff selling tickets) may be struggling to handle the subjected load (the Monday morning rush for tickets). Queues abound in systems, whether they be in disk storage, CPUs, printing and network devices. The queueing list could be quite long, but the following are typically used:

- Average disk queue length – The average number of read and write requests queued for the selected disk during the sample interval

- Average disk read queue length – The average number of read requests queued for the selected disk during the sample interval

- Average disk write queue length – The average number of write requests queued for the selected disk during the sample interval

- Output queue length – The length of the output packet queue (in packets) to the network adapter

Summary   Metrics vary based on the business context, operational context, and test objectives.

A common way to categorize performance measurements and metrics is to consider the technical environment, business environment, or operational environment in which the assessment of performance is needed.

—ISTQB_CTFL_PT

Categorizing performance metrics is extremely useful when analyzing potential performance issues. Determining the root cause of a possible performance issue relies on understanding the cause-effect relationship between various parts of the system. Categorizing the metrics allows the cause-effect relationships to be established much easier. The categories suggested by the syllabus are very high level and would need to be broken down further based on:

- The type of technical environment upon which performance testing is being conducted.

- The nature of the business processes in the performance test operational profile.

- The interaction between the business processes and the environment – For example, a business process that involves searches of a warehouse stock inventory will be affected by the performance of the search algorithm, the structure of the database, and the hardware on which the database resides.

Summary   Metrics can be categorized by technical, business, and operational environments.

The categories of measurements and metrics included below are the ones commonly obtained from performance testing.

—ISTQB_CTFL_PT

Technical Environment

Performance metrics will vary by the type of the technical environment, as shown in the following list:

- *Web-based*
- *Mobile*
- *Internet-of-Things (IoT)*
- *Desktop client devices*
- *Server-side processing*
- *Mainframe*
- *Databases*
- *Networks*
- *The nature of software running in the environment (e.g., embedded)*

—ISTQB_CTFL_PT

Each of the preceding environments has similarities (CPU, memory, and bandwidth). There are also vast differences between these (architecture, communication protocols, operating systems, and more).

The overall system performance is affected by its interaction with the environment and the efficiency of the code. Older hardware, operating systems, and limitations associated with each (such as memory limits on 32-bit machines) can severely impact the performance of the system overall.

Another important consideration is the complexity of the production environment. Organizations run projects dealing with "digital transformation" – an amorphous definition against which many senior executives apply their own meaning. From a performance point of view, digital transformation could mean integrating multiple disparate systems together. A system under test could consist of more than one of the technical environments listed earlier. An example could be a handheld stock control scanner (IoT), integrating with warehouse management software (desktop client/server-side processing), and sharing this data with the organization's ERP finance solution (which could be web or client/server with a database in the mix an absolute certainty).

All the "quirks" of each technical environment must be taken into consideration when considering overall system performance. A bottleneck in any part of the preceding environment has an impact on the overall performance of the end-to-end system.

In the following section, the syllabus draws a broad brush in selecting a set of generic metrics, much the same as was done earlier.

The metrics include the following:

- *Response time (e.g., per transaction, per concurrent user, page load times)*

—ISTQB_CTFL_PT

Consider the points from which these times are being taken – do the start and end points for this monitoring include the client/external network/firewall/internal network and infrastructure/system under test? Another consideration is the load under which these response times will be monitored. Response time was also mentioned earlier – are these times the maximum/average/percentile?

- *Resource utilization (e.g., CPU, memory, network bandwidth, network latency, available disk space, IO rate, idle and busy threads)*

—ISTQB_CTFL_PT

This list corresponds with the five generic metrics mentioned earlier – although we should never forget queueing as a measure of resource utilization.

- *Throughput rate of key transaction (i.e., the number of transactions that can be processed in a given period of time)*

—ISTQB_CTFL_PT

Throughput rate is an interesting area and key to any performance test. Throughput will vary depending on the rate at which transactions occur and the nature of the transactions conducted – for example, the transaction concurrency of users of the system logging on or off simultaneously. Another consideration is the type of transactions (database reads vs. writes) and how that transaction type may interact with the environment on which it executes.

- *Batch processing time (e.g., wait times, throughput times, data base response times, completion times)*

—ISTQB_CTFL_PT

Similar to response time, the start and end points of any batch process must be defined. Unlike response times monitoring business processes however, batch processes do not require continuous input from virtual users. In almost all cases, they are started, they run, and once the process completes, the processing time can be captured. Like response times, batch processes are dependent on a similar set of variables that can affect the batch processing time (capacity/resource utilization).

- *Numbers of errors impacting performance*

—ISTQB_CTFL_PT

The number and type of errors can be a good indicator of the location of a problem – a single issue may cause a cascade of error types or a linked chain of errors. Bear in mind the error is the effect – it's the job of a performance engineer to determine the cause of the error.

- *Completion time (e.g., for creating, reading, updating, and deleting data)*

—ISTQB_CTFL_PT

Although completion time seems obvious, predetermining completion points for transactions is an important step in planning a performance test. The measurement of time once again relates to the first point – determining the start and end points for the capture of response/batch processing/completion time. A subtle point is also made here – the categorization of operations can help not only with capturing time behavior of like processes but also with diagnosing errors later.

- *Background load on shared resources (especially in virtualized environments)*

—ISTQB_CTFL_PT

The strange duality of background load can be both a hindrance and a necessity in performance testing. For example, the environmental conditions for a load test to match the operational profile may require simulated traffic over a network segment. For virtualized environments, if the system under test is virtualized, characteristics such as the number of virtual machines on each server and the activity (and hence resource utilization) on these other virtual machines should be considered. It should be remembered that any virtual machine is sharing resources with the base operating system, as well as any other virtual machines on that server.

- *Software metrics (e.g., code complexity)*

—ISTQB_CTFL_PT

Software metrics have taken advantage of the push in software testing to "shift left." Traditionally, performance testing was generally conducted in the later levels of testing (system, system integration, and acceptance testing). These levels of testing typically don't have access to the code, as it's already been developed and compiled. Earlier testing during component and component integration testing allow access directly to the code. With the widespread use of Agile-based methodologies, interaction between developers and testers increased, and testing moves much closer to development.

Code complexity can be useful from a static testing point of view but has limited use for dynamic testing. Code complexity is normally used as a measure of the maintainability of the code. But high complexity can be an indicator of poor performance. In any performance testing, resource utilization and time behavior are key areas for monitoring.

Summary   Metrics vary depending on the type of the technical environment. Some common metrics exist across environments:

Response time   Resource utilization   Throughput rate   Batch processing time

Numbers of errors   Completion time   Background load   Software metrics

Business Environment

From the business or functional perspective, performance metrics may include the following:

- *Business process efficiency (e.g., the speed of performing an overall business process including normal, alternate and exceptional use case flows)*

—ISTQB_CTFL_PT

Performance engineers must always be considerate of the needs of users, continually asking the question "Is this what a real user would do?" Once again, performance engineers monitor using time behavior and resource utilization to capture information about the performance characteristics of the system under test. These results can then be used to inform stakeholders on the relative efficiency of business processes. From this, decisions can be made on the optimal processes to use and the processes that can be improved by configuration changes.

- *Throughput of data, transactions, and other units of work performed (e.g., orders processed per hour, data rows added per minute)*

—ISTQB_CTFL_PT

The very nature of performance testing means controlling the throughput as part of creating the operational profile. Occasionally, throughput forms the goal for the performance test – will the system support X users doing Y things (capacity testing) or how many transactions will the system support (stress testing)?

- *Service Level Agreement (SLA) compliance or violation rates (e.g., SLA violations per unit of time)*

—ISTQB_CTFL_PT

The key characteristic of an SLA is that it is quantifiable and realistic. Sometimes, it's up to performance engineers to test the system meets the SLA. It can also be the performance engineers' job to establish the SLA in the first place. For example, the business might require an overall average response time under load of a business process of three seconds. A performance engineer might then need to break this end-to-end three-second time down into a group of sub-second goals for components within the business process.

- *Scope of usage (e.g., percentage of global or national users conducting tasks at a given time)*

—ISTQB_CTFL_PT

The scope of usage definition is somewhat simplified. The preceding point speaks of a percentage of global or national users, which could be broken down further into user groups based on:

- Physical location – The point or points from which the load is generated

- User groups – The role/access rights of each of the users

- Business processes – The process path each user follows

- *Concurrency of usage (e.g., the number of users concurrently performing a task)*

—ISTQB_CTFL_PT

Earlier, concurrency was broken down into application/business process/transaction concurrency:

- Application – The total number of users concurrently using the system. Note that in a stateful environment, an idle user consuming a connection but not actively using the system might need to be included in the performance test. An example might be the number of users on a shopping website.

- Business process – The subset of the total users actively engaged in a defined business process. Note the users could be at any step within that business process. The example might be the number of users currently within the "create new account" business process.

- Transaction – The sub-subset of users that are at the same point in a business process at that point in time. For example, the number of users simultaneously clicking the "create account" button.

As mentioned previously, decomposing a whole into its constituent parts is an absolute necessity for performance testing, whether it's an environment or an end-to-end business process. As Holmes would say

Never trust to general impressions, … but concentrate yourself upon details.

—Conan Doyle, 1892ci

- *Timing of usage (e.g., the number of orders processed during peak load times)*

—ISTQB_CTFL_PT

Timing of usage in this case does not refer to time behavior. It relates to the rate at which the load is applied to the system. To define the load profile, the performance test will consist of a set of user groups (each of which has a defined number of users). Each of those users will be performing one or more tasks (as mentioned earlier, a task being a defined part of a business process). It needs to be emphasized that the task rate and the number of users are two distinctly different parts of the load profile. It's easy if, in the performance test, a single user performs one task. But it is never as simple as that.

Let's say we are testing an online shopping platform. The goal of the performance test is to measure the search task resource utilization with a total transaction rate of 400,000 searches per hour.

We need to consider the following:

- The number of users performing the task (300 users)

- The number of tasks to be completed during the performance test (400,000 searches)

- The time it takes the user to complete the task (each search task takes a user 30 seconds)

- The total time of the performance test to achieve the desired outcome (one hour)

This information will be required to calculate the load profile. But where did these figures come from? It is worth considering how these numbers will relate to real users accessing the system. For example, does this shopping site allow anonymous searches (in that the user is not a registered user and logged in), or does it allow only logged in users to search? Another consideration would be when will the users be performing these searches:

- Where the search task fits within the end-to-end business process

- The search count done by each user (e.g., an individual who knows the exact item they require will do one search, another might be looking for gift ideas for a child's 12th birthday and could perform multiple searches)

- The time of day the search is performed (in many time zones, the Internet becomes busy between 19:00 and 23:00 on weekdays[2])

All the preceding information falls under the timing of usage. The output of this will be the operational and load profiles which will be covered later in Chapter 4.

_____

[2]Known as the "Internet rush hour."

Summary   Business performance metrics include

Business process efficiency	Throughput of data, transactions	SLA compliance
Scope of usage	Concurrency of usage	Timing of usage

Operational Environment

The operational aspect of performance testing focuses on tasks that are generally not considered to be user-facing in nature. These include the following:

- *Operational processes (e.g., the time required for environment start-up, backups, shutdown and resumption times)*

—ISTQB_CTFL_PT

These operational processes could form part of the background load in a performance test and thus become part of the performance test itself. An interesting consideration here is user timeout periods. It could be a few user session IDs could still be active after a performance test. If another test is started directly after the end of the previous performance test, these sessions will still be running. Those redundant sessions could, in fact, affect the performance of the system under test in the next performance test. These operational processes could also form part of maintainability or reliability testing performed in conjunction with performance testing.

- *System restoration (e.g., the time required to restore data from a backup)*

—ISTQB_CTFL_PT

System restoration is an important consideration during the execution of performance tests, especially if the system data needs to be restored before each performance test execution.

A real-world example was a very large city council testing a system managing local council tax for each household. Performance testing was using the entire city council address database, which although was production-like became a problem. It took 27 hours to roll the test data back to an initial state once a performance test had been completed, and it needed to be done at the end of every performance test.

Once again, it could also be that the data restoration could be part of a reliability or maintainability test being conducted in conjunction with performance testing.

- *Alerts and warnings (e.g., the time needed for the system to issue an alert or warning)*

—ISTQB_CTFL_PT

Although alerts and warnings may not be a direct part of the performance test, these may fall within the scope, once again, of reliability and maintainability testing. The ability to capture these though may form an important part of the performance test being a reflection on the capacity of the system under test.

Summary   Operational performance metrics (non-user facing) include

Operational processes	System restoration	Alerts and warnings

Selecting Performance Metrics

It should be noted that collecting more metrics than required is not necessarily a good thing. Each metric chosen requires a means for consistent collection and reporting. It is important to define an obtainable set of metrics that support the performance test objectives.

—ISTQB_CTFL_PT

From earlier, remember the Golden Rules of Monitoring (keep it simple). Performance engineers should always use metrics to answer the questions posed by the performance goals/objectives/requirements. A generic set of metrics as mentioned previously can always be presented to allow stakeholders to understand this general dataset. Further metrics sets should also be specific for the stakeholders to which they will be presented – business stakeholders will require different metrics from technical stakeholders.

Summary   Only collect the metrics necessary to prove/disprove the objectives/ goals/requirements/user stories.

For example, the Goal-Question-Metric (GQM) approach is a helpful way to align metrics with performance goals. The idea is to first establish the goals, then ask questions to know when the goals have been achieved. Metrics are associated with each question to ensure the answer to the question is measurable. (See Section 4.3 of the Expert Level Syllabus – Improving the Testing Process [ISTQB_ELTM_ITP_SYL] for a more complete description of the GQM approach.) It should be noted that the GQM approach doesn't always fit the performance testing process. For example, some metrics represent a system's health and are not directly linked to goals.

—ISTQB_CTFL_PT

Summarized from the ISTQB Expert Level Improving the Test Process syllabus, GQM defines a method of categorizing the metrics sets required. It uses three levels:

1. Conceptual level relating to the GOALS for the organization regarding the quality of products, processes, and resources including the people, officers, hardware, and software

2. Operational level relating to the QUESTIONS characterizing the products, processes, and resources with respect to their quality

3. Quantitative level relating to the METRICS which may be objective (quantitative, factual) or subjective (qualitative, viewpoints)

A good general way to refer to these is to think of conceptual metrics relating to high-level organization stakeholders, operational-level metrics relating to key user stakeholders, and quantitative metrics relating to technical stakeholders. Of course, there will always be exceptions to these associations, but as a rough rule it's a good reference point.

Summary   Goal-question-metric aligns the goals, questions relating to the goals, and metrics answering the questions. GQM isn't always appropriate for every performance project.

It is important to realize that after the definition and capture of initial measurements further measurements and metrics may be needed to understand true performance levels and to determine where corrective actions may be needed.

—ISTQB_CTFL_PT

This point will be covered much further in Analyzing Results and Reporting, but suffice to say that the Golden Rule of Monitoring still applies. Each of the stakeholder groups will require specific information in addition to the generic metrics set. If testing discovers a performance issue, there are two general approaches that can be considered.

The deductive approach conducts multiple iterations of end-to-end performance testing business processes with changes to single items for each iteration. As part of the results analysis, the effect of those single changes is observed. For example, an online shopping system might have problems with the search task. The deductive approach would vary the test data used as an input and observe the results of this data variation. It might be found, for example, that searches for a certain item or groups of items might take much longer. The deductive approach would then drill down on this as a possible problem – does it relate to the search algorithm or the database indexing?

The diagnostic approach looks at the problem slightly differently. It involves gathering more information earlier with more intensive monitoring performed initially. If a problem is discovered, the results data is analyzed by tracking from the beginning/ end of a business process through the results dataset to discover the issue. To continue the preceding example, if a problem exists with the search task, these transactions would be tracked through the dataset to ascertain where the problem might lie. The diagnostic approach potentially skips the additional iterations of performance testing, as the wider results dataset might contain the causal factor of the issue.

Both approaches have their advantages and disadvantages. Every performance engineer will use both without question. And, every performance engineer will have a preference. No approach is right or wrong or best practice. But every performance engineer, irrelevant of preference, must get better at whichever approach is **not** their preference!

Summary   After initial metrics are captured, further metrics might be needed to diagnose issues.

2.2 Aggregating Results from Performance Testing

PTFL-2.2.1 (K2) Explain why results from performance testing are aggregated

> *The purpose of aggregating performance metrics is to be able to understand and express them in a way that accurately conveys the total picture of system performance. When performance metrics are viewed at only the detailed level, drawing the right conclusion may be difficult—especially for business stakeholders.*
>
> —ISTQB_CTFL_PT

A key to this area is having a comparison framework from which to work. For example, to include the time when errors occurred with CPU activity on a particular server in the performance test environment, a common reference point is important for results to be correlated. Much will depend on how information is gathered, but the most common reference frame is the absolute time against which the performance test is executed (the actual time events occurred according to a centralized time reference) or elapsed time (the time since the start of the performance test).

If monitoring is being performed within a single performance test tool capturing the results, elapsed time (starting at 00:00:00 when the performance test starts) may be enough.

Although elapsed time can be convenient for a single tool, as soon as other information from outside the tool is required, absolute time is a much better reference point. Absolute time allows other tools, logs, and result sets to be brought into the performance test results for direct comparison. It also facilitates a more natural conversation – "Hey Julie – did anything unusual happen on the network between 01:00 and 02:00?"

If any doubt exists, performance tests should use absolute time.

Summary   Aggregating performance metrics can help explain system performance to stakeholders.

For many stakeholders, the main concern is that the response time of a system, web site, or other test object is within acceptable limits.

—ISTQB_CTFL_PT

Once again, as mentioned earlier, many stakeholders relate to response time because of two reasons:

1. The stakeholder personally relates to the response time due to it relating to a business process they are either performing or a process their team is performing

2. The stakeholder automatically relates response time to performance testing for the simple reason being that's the first thing they think about when performance testing is mentioned

An interesting phenomenon that occurs when establishing performance test goals/objectives/requirements/user stories is the origin from which they stem. Although performance requirements are derived from other higher-level requirements or organization risks, quite often they start with a question. These questions could relate to capacity ("How many more users will the system support?"), resource utilization ("Can we fit another virtual machine on the server?"), or time behavior ("How long will the batch run take?"). This can be taken one step further in that questions being asked can help determine the types of performance testing needed:

- "How long does it take to enter a timesheet on Friday afternoon?" (load)

- "What happens to the website when the sale starts?" (spike/stress)

Performance engineers should never accept the first answer from the stakeholders. In fact, the role of a performance test teacher is often a secondary job for many performance engineers. An important job in any project involving performance testing is educating the stakeholders to move beyond measuring response time.

Summary   Response time is a key stakeholder metric.

Once deeper understanding of the performance metrics has been achieved, the metrics can be aggregated so that:

- *Business and project stakeholders can see the "big picture" status of system performance*

- *Performance trends can be identified*

- *Performance metrics can be reported in an understandable way*

—ISTQB_CTFL_PT

Performance engineers gain a deeper understanding of the behavior and performance of the system under test not only by collecting metrics but by analyzing these metrics and establishing the cause-effect relationship between them.

The deeper understanding for the stakeholders comes from:

1. The generic metrics set

2. The stakeholders learning more about performance testing and performance issues

3. The performance engineer analyzing the metrics to outline performance against the requirements/user stories and highlighting issues if they exist

4. The performance engineer creating specific targeted reports for stakeholder groups

5. The performance engineer remembering the Golden Rules of Monitoring[3]

Summary   Aggregated metrics let stakeholders see the big picture, identify performance trends, and allow clear reporting.

---

[3] Keep it simple!

2.3 Key Sources of Performance Metrics

PTFL-2.3.1 (K2) Understand the key sources of performance metrics

Launch the probe!

—Dr. Evil

System performance should be no more than minimally impacted by the metrics collection effort (known as the "probe effect"). In addition, the volume, accuracy and speed with which performance metrics must be collected makes tool usage a requirement. While the combined use of tools is not uncommon, it can introduce redundancy in the usage of test tools and other problems (see Section 4.4).

—ISTQB_CTFL_PT

probe effect[4]

An unintended change in behavior of a component or system caused by measuring it.

—ISTQB Glossary

The simplest way to understand the probe effect is to think of checking the pressure in a tire. To check the tire pressure, a small amount of air will be released into the pressure gauge, allowing the current pressure to be measured. Once the measurement is taken, the gauge is removed, and the air filling the gauge is released. Thus, the pressure is now slightly lower than when it was measured. Depending on the precision of the measurement taken by the tire pressure gauge, this may never be detected. On the other hand, a bicycle tire with a smaller volume might show the relative pressure loss greater than a huge mining truck tire with an immensely greater volume.

---

[4]This is the updated ISTQB Foundation Certificate V3.1 2018. The previous version of this term for reference:*The effect on the component or system by the measurement instrument when the component or system is being measured, e.g., by a performance testing tool or monitor. For example, performance may be slightly worse when performance testing tools are being used.*

The performance and/or monitoring tools being used to monitor the system under test can vary greatly, and all tools will add some measure of load to the system under test. How much of an effect will depend on two factors:

1. The level of measurement precision required (e.g., the timing measurements taken rounded to the nearest second or thousandth of a second)

2. The ratio of effect the tool measurement load will have on the overall system (e.g., an embedded PCB with limited CPU/memory – the bike tire – or a high-end server with multicore processors and hundreds of GB of memory, the mining truck)

Summary   Monitoring uses resources, which could affect the system performance.

There are three key sources of performance metrics:

1. Performance test tools

2. Performance monitoring tools

3. Log analysis tools

Performance Test Tools

All performance test tools provide measurements and metrics as the result of a test. Tools may vary in the number of metrics shown, the way in which the metrics are shown, and the ability for the user to customize the metrics to a particular situation (see also Section 5.1).

Some tools collect and display performance metrics in text format, while more robust tools collect and display performance metrics graphically in a dashboard format. Many tools offer the ability to export metrics to facilitate test evaluation and reporting.

—ISTQB_CTFL_PT

The amount of information available from a performance test tool can vary. Some tools present a huge number of monitoring options; others are much more rudimentary. Some tools have built-in monitoring; others rely on integration with external monitors (such as Windows perfmon) to gather metrics.

Certainly, in recent history there has been a drive within the performance tool market to consider the usability of tools. Commercial tools have always been ahead of open source tools in terms of usability, but today that gap is shrinking.

Two basic types of performance test monitoring information exist (and note that the same monitoring information may be displayed in both types):

Summary displays information at a "point in time," such as the CPU utilization at 19:07:30 during a performance test. Typically, summary information includes maximum/minimum/average results. Summary information is normally displayed as a table (Figure 2-1).

Transactions: Total Passed: 320 Total Failed: 0 Total Stopped: 0   Average Response Time

Transaction Name	SLA Status	Minimum	Average	Maximum	Std. Deviation	90 Percent	Pass	Fail	Stop
C_DataTansfer_MakeDir	⊘	0	0.005	0.144	0.021	0.001	64	0	0
C_DataTransfer_10GB	⊘	0.081	0.131	0.246	0.042	0.198	64	0	0
C_DataTransfer_1GB_bin	⊘	0.084	3.926	10.494	4.618	9.608	64	0	0
C_DataTransfer_1GB_zip	⊘	0.08	4.005	10.633	4.711	9.779	64	0	0
C_DataTransfer_lessthan1GB	⊘	0.079	0.853	9.598	2.058	1.734	64	0	0

Figure 2-1. *Performance test summary results*

Progress displays information representing changes over a defined time during the performance test. Many data points are sampled during the defined time and usually displayed as a graph displaying the line of best fit through the sampled data points (Figure 2-2).

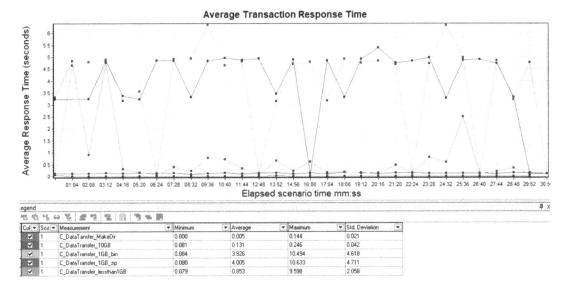

Figure 2-2. *Performance test progress results*

Summary   Performance tools vary in the quality and number of metrics they can display and export for analysis.

Performance Monitoring Tools

Performance monitoring tools are often employed to supplement the reporting capabilities of performance test tools (see also Section 5.1). In addition, monitoring tools may be used to monitor system performance on an ongoing basis and to alert system administrators to lowered levels of performance and higher levels of system errors and alerts. These tools may also be used to detect and notify in the event of suspicious behavior (such as denial of service attacks and distributed denial of service attacks).

—ISTQB_CTFL_PT

He sits motionless, like a spider in the center of its web, but that web has a thousand radiations, and he knows well every quiver of each of them.

—Conan Doyle, 1893

Performance monitoring could cover a range of tools, each gathering information on the performance of the system. These tools could be embedded into the operating system (Microsoft Performance Monitor, or "perfmon"), applications (VMware vSphere), or stand-alone tools (Cisco AppDynamics or Splunk). These tools have a wide range of counters and can monitor individual systems (perfmon – Figure 2-3) or the entire infrastructure (vSphere/AppDynamics/Splunk).

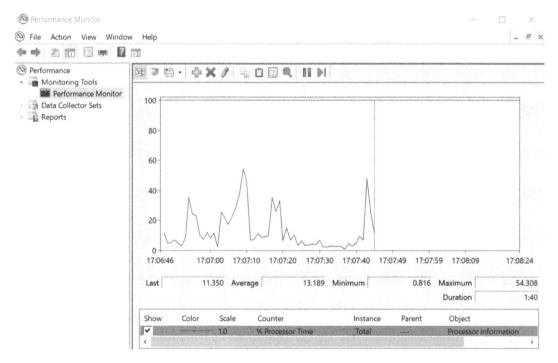

Figure 2-3. *Microsoft Performance Monitor (perfmon)*

To the advantage of performance engineers, some performance test tools integrate with performance monitoring tools to allow a connection between the executing performance test and the results data gathered by the monitoring tool. Without this, it can be problematic associating the results data with the executing performance test, especially if multiple monitoring tools are used in conjunction with the performance test tool. A big help in overcoming this problem is the common absolute time reference mentioned earlier – allowing both the execution of the performance test and the gathering of results data have a common frame of reference. This simple step won't make correlation easy, but it will certainly make it easier.

Summary   Monitoring tools supplement performance tools for monitoring, can alert suspicious behavior, and can monitor the system on an ongoing basis.

Log Analysis Tools

There are tools that scan server logs and compile metrics from them. Some of these tools can create charts to provide a graphical view of the data. Errors, alerts and warnings are normally recorded in server logs. These include:

- *High resource usage, such as high CPU utilization, high levels of disk storage consumed, and insufficient bandwidth*

- *Memory errors and warnings, such as memory exhaustion*

- *Deadlocks and multi-threading problems, especially when performing database operations*

- *Database errors, such as SQL exceptions and SQL timeouts*

—ISTQB_CTFL_PT

A good example of a log analysis tool is Splunk – a set of ever-expanding tools that can aggregate and analyze multiple datasets into a dashboard allowing instant access to information. With the addition of AI in recent years, these tools have become much more capable in helping performance engineers correlate the cause-effect relationship between components in the system under test.

Summary   Log analysis tools convert text logs to graphic data, alerting based on predefined performance criteria.

2.4 Typical Results of a Performance Test

PTFL-2.4.1 (K1) Recall the typical results of a performance test

> *In functional testing, particularly when verifying specified functional requirements or functional elements of user stories, the expected results usually can be defined clearly, and the test results interpreted to determine if the test passed or failed. For example, a monthly sales report shows either a correct or an incorrect total.*
>
> *Whereas tests that verify functional suitability often benefit from well-defined test oracles, performance testing often lacks this source of information. Not only are the stakeholders notoriously bad at articulating performance requirements, many business analysts and product owners are bad at eliciting such requirements. Testers often receive limited guidance to define the expected test results.*
>
> —ISTQB_CTFL_PT

Herein lies the fallacy of performance testing. This fallacy relates in much part to the difference between functional and performance testing. Functional testing considers what the system does, whereas performance testing is looking at how the system behaves. From a functional point of view, it can be easier most of the time for functional testers to know if a defect exists. But consider a performance engineer in the following scenario:

> *An on-site shopping website has a performance requirement stating that under a certain level of load, the search transaction will respond in less than two seconds. A performance engineer regarding the two second limit would immediately ask if the defined two second limit was a maximum time, average or percentile time. Once established (let's say in this case it's maximum time), a clear goal has now been established. Accordingly, a performance test was subsequently run measuring the search transaction response time. The test found in the 15,000 search transactions conducted, seven searches responded in a greater than two second response time. Based on this, the test would be a failure.*

A magistrate in Australia[5] was once quoted speaking of the law – "It's a set of black and white rules for a collection of grey circumstances..."

---

[5] Alan Yorkston – Magistrate and my father!

This is much the same as establishing quantitative performance requirements and/
or user stories. Many points related to this have already been covered, including:

- Measurable non-functional goals – Much of the time, without the
  input of a performance engineer, the usual people who create
  performance test goals/objectives/requirements/user stories do
  not have the necessary technical or performance test knowledge
  required. They default to response time to define quantifiable,
  measurable goals.

- Lack of performance test understanding – Project staff often do not
  appreciate the technical requirements for performance testing.
  Things like configuration management, version control, an adequate
  performance test environment, and necessary types and amounts of
  performance test data should be shared by the performance engineer
  with the stakeholders.

- Interpreting the results of performance testing – Performance
  engineers can create many reports with colorful graphs and tables
  of information, but if the stakeholders cannot understand how these
  relate to the performance test goals/objectives/requirements/user
  stories, these reports will be of little value.

If a maximum response time of two seconds is defined, the first question would be,
"Why two seconds?"

Experienced performance engineers often see the same response times occurring
when establishing time-related requirements. Typical answers include the system
responding in:

- Instantly/instantaneously

- Two seconds

- Five seconds

- Seven seconds

- Ten seconds

- Multiples of five seconds

There is an urban myth behind some of these (five and seven seconds), a desire of the stakeholders (instantly/instantaneously), or psychological reasons (two, five, ten, and multiples of five seconds). Another psychological factor is the impact of unconscious bias – specifically the anchoring effect.[6]

But we must return to the preceding question – why is that time significant? It could be because the stakeholders have a perception that real users of the system will not wait longer for the task to complete. It could be a regulatory requirement or a service-level agreement. Or, more often, it is based on a reasoning principle mentioned earlier called inductive reasoning, a fancy name for the process of guessing.

It cannot be stressed enough that whatever the goals/objectives/requirements/user stories are based upon, it should be realistic, quantified, and relevant.

It can also be useful to build in a tolerance to any defined goals/objectives/requirements/user stories. To return to the initial two-second response time example, where in 15,000 transactions the performance test failed due to seven measured response times exceeding the maximum of two seconds. It is at this point we should consider building in a gray area rather than thinking of the target time as black or white. It might be that the performance engineer suggested a tolerance of 10% to that goal. In effect, the following would apply:

Green	**Within the 100% goal**	**<=2 seconds**
Amber	**Within the 10% tolerance**	**2.0–2.2 seconds**
Red	**Exceeding 110%**	**2.2 seconds +**

Thus, if the seven response times were within the 10% tolerance, it gives the stakeholders more information. In effect, the maximum time was exceeded, but only by a little. In most performance testing today, this tolerance method is well used.

---

[6] Anchoring is a cognitive bias where an initial piece of information is heavily favored when making a decision. For example, is the Golden Gate Bridge shorter or longer than 600 m? Irrelevant of the answer to this question, if a person is then asked to estimate the length of the Golden Gate Bridge, the distance in the previous question (600 m) becomes the anchor upon which the person estimates the length.

Summary   Defining both adequately quantifiable requirements and gathering results data to definitively show pass or fail is difficult in performance testing, due to a lack of stakeholder performance knowledge.

When evaluating performance test results, it is important to look at the results closely. Initial raw results can be misleading with performance failures being hidden beneath apparently good overall results. For example, resource utilization may be well under 75% for all key potential bottleneck resources, but the throughput or response time of key transactions or use cases are an order-of-magnitude too slow.

The specific results to evaluate vary depending on the tests being run, and often include those discussed in Section 2.1.

—ISTQB_CTFL_PT

Performance engineers obtain the return on investment in two parts of the overall performance test – the performance test planning to make sure the right questions are being answered and the analysis of the results to show the system has positively or negatively answered the questions posed.

It is the ability of performance engineers to diagnose the cause-effect relationships between various metrics that help to answer the questions posed by the performance requirements/user stories. An apt analogy is identifying the forest through the trees. Knowing what to look for in a mass of lines on a graph or numbers in a table is a vital skill. In fact, too much monitoring during a performance test can hinder identifying where an issue may lie. A good performance engineer will also know when to use the diagnostic or deductive approaches mentioned earlier if an issue is identified. Quite often, the first sign the system under test has a performance issue is a transaction time slows down. Ultimately, this slow transaction is the effect, and it's the job of the performance engineer to determine the cause.

Summary   Initial results can be misleading and can hide potential performance problems.

Chapter 2 Questions

1. Which of the following is NOT a technical environment metric?

   A. Alerts and warnings (the time needed for the system to issue an alert or warning).

   B. Numbers of errors impacting performance

   C. Throughput rate of key transaction (the number of transactions that can be processed in a given period of time)

   D. Background load on shared resources (especially in virtualized environments)

2. Performance testing should not be undertaken without first understanding which measurements and metrics are needed. Performance planning went well, with sets of user stories developed by the business stakeholders. Unfortunately, the project you are joining has been running several performance test cycles without any metric planning. An argument over the captured response time results has been long running between stakeholders. Which of the following project risks would apply to this problem?

   A. The results provided by a performance test tool are not understood.

   B. Performance test execution will not be completed on time due to the continuing argument.

   C. It may not be possible to identify trends that may predict lower levels of performance.

   D. The performance requirements are not defined in measurable terms.

3. Which of the following is NOT a reason for aggregating results?

    A. Business and project stakeholders can see the "big picture" status of system performance.

    B. Performance metrics can be reported in an understandable way.

    C. Performance metrics can be viewed at the detailed level allowing business stakeholders to understand the system.

    D. Performance trends can be identified.

4. Which of the following is NOT a source of performance metrics?

    A. Metric tools

    B. Test tools

    C. Monitoring tools

    D. Log analysis tools

5. Which of the following describes the "probe effect"?

    A. The impact performance testing has on the system performance

    B. The effect of redundancy in using multiple monitoring tools

    C. The impact metric collection tools have on system performance results

    D. The volume, accuracy, and speed at which performance metrics are collected

6. In what way are performance monitoring tools helpful for collecting metrics?

    A. They create the system load and monitor the system performance.

    B. They monitor the systems while the performance tests are conducted and report on the behavior during the tests.

    C. They scan the various server logs and compile metrics for events that were recorded during the test execution.

    D. They write the performance results to the server logs for later manual analysis.

7. Which of the following is a failure that would typically be found by conducting an endurance test?

   A. The system performance gradually degrades.

   B. The system provides inconsistent responses to errors.

   C. The system handles a sudden burst of activity but can't resume a steady state.

   D. The system performs well for the expected load but can't scale to a larger load.

CHAPTER 3

Performance Testing in the Software Lifecycle

ISTQB Keywords

metric

A measurement scale and the method used for measurement.

risk

A factor that could result in future negative consequences.

software development lifecycle

The activities performed at each stage in software development, and how they relate to one another logically and chronologically.

test log

A chronological record of relevant details about the execution of tests.

3.1 Principal Performance Testing Activities

PTFL-3.1.1 (K2) Understand the principal performance testing activities

> *Performance testing is iterative in nature. Each test provides valuable insights into application and system performance. The information gathered from one test is used to correct or optimize application and system parameters. The next test iteration will then show the results of modifications, and so on until test objectives are reached.*
>
> *Performance testing activities align with the ISTQB test process [ISTQB_FL_SYL].*
>
> —ISTQB_CTFL_PT

© Keith Yorkston 2021
K. Yorkston, *Performance Testing*, https://doi.org/10.1007/978-1-4842-7255-8_3

From the 2018 ISTQB Certified Tester Foundation Level Syllabus, the test process is summarized in Figure 3-1.

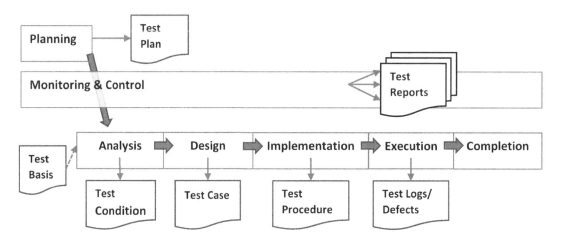

Figure 3-1. *The ISTQB fundamental test process*

It might seem these test process phases are better suited for functional testing. In fact, more functional testers recognize this than performance engineers. The model is also designed for non-functional (performance) testing. Where it differs from functional testing are the steps within each of the test process phases that are undertaken.

Before commencing, it can be useful to have a means through which to track the planning and creation of performance tests. As stages are completed and checked off, it is possible to show stakeholders the progression. Of course, there may be project tracking software used by the project, and performance testing can always be built into these applications. But if you work on a project without this software, Table 3-1 could be used as a starting point.

Table 3-1. *Performance Testing Task List*

Requirement	Showstopper	Status	Notes
Test requirements approved	Y		
Volumetric data approved	Y		
Performance test plan approved	Y		
Test tool is available and working after POC	N		
Business process list approved	Y		
Test environment designed	N		
Test scripts designed	N		
Test scenarios designed	N		
Test data design/volume approved	Y		
Test monitoring designed	N		
Initial recording environment accepted	Y		
Test scripts created and approved	Y		
Test scenarios created and approved	Y		
Test data created	Y		
Test monitoring completed	Y		
Test tool setup complete (with licenses)	N		
Test result collection set up	N		
Execution environment completed and checked	Y		
OVERALL STATUS	**Not Ready**	**0%**	

Summary   Performance testing is iterative (running cycles of testing) and complies with the ISTQB test process.

Test Planning

Test planning is particularly important for performance testing due to the need for the allocation of test environments, test data, tools and human resources. In addition, this is the activity in which the scope of performance testing is established.

During test planning, risk identification and risk analysis activities are completed, and relevant information is updated in any test planning documentation (e.g., test plan, level test plan). Just as test planning is revisited and modified as needed, so are risks, risk levels and risk status modified to reflect changes in risk conditions.

—ISTQB_CTFL_PT

As mentioned earlier, planning is an important part of any performance test. In earlier times, a performance engineer would make some notes and start scripting. Much of the time, this was adequate, as the project stakeholders for which the performance engineer was working didn't want to know the level of detail required. It was soon discovered however that an old military axiom came into play:

Failing to plan is planning to fail...

As performance testing matured, the need for test planning became evident. Experienced performance engineers then started to tweak the standard planning process to become better suited for performance testing. Today, thanks to standards like ISO 29119, both the test process and especially test planning are suited to non-functional testing.

As part of the planning process, it is useful to think of the final output of this phase. To complete a test plan, a lot of information needs to be gathered from the project. As well, a performance engineer will have a lot to add to any ideas the project has on performance testing. Working backward from the test plan, the following steps are needed within test planning:

Initial Workshop

The initial workshop is a meeting where both the stakeholders involved in both the project and performance testing are brought together with the performance engineer. This is an opportunity for the performance engineer to inform the project stakeholders on the basic rules, requirements, and procedures for performance testing. It is also an opportunity for the project stakeholders to elicit requirements and the background from the project.

Business and Technical Overview

This may be done in conjunction with the initial workshop or separately depending on the availability of key stakeholders in both the business and technical aspects of the project. This is an opportunity for the performance engineer to get a clear view of the nature of the application/infrastructure (software, hardware, protocols, business processes, and required data). This may be a point at which the performance engineer can highlight any early potential performance weaknesses in the system giving forward notice that more information on these weaknesses may be required.

Definition of Requirements/User Stories

Requirements definition is where the basis, the reasoning, and the outcome of the project are outlined. It's important that in conjunction with the requirements/user stories, an indication of the performance engineering effort is also linked to the requirements/user stories. From this, explicit success criteria can be derived (for both requirements and user stories, as both require a measurable way of knowing if the eventual test will pass).

Linked to the definition of requirements/user stories is the discovery of performance product risk. This includes potential technical-related performance risks and business-related performance risks. For example, a technical risk relates to an older database with a limited connection pool linked to a system that requires more connections than is available. A business-related performance risk could possibly be linked to this in that there is now a business process delay while users wait for a database connection to become free to access information.

More information regarding risk is covered later. At this point, it should be noted that risk isn't the opposite of a requirement.

Project risk should also be considered. These risks relate to the successful completion of performance testing unrelated to the performance of the system under test. Examples of performance project risk include problems with the test environment or test data.

A final point is to reinforce the emphasis around measurable quantitative requirements/user stories and associated completion criteria. If the requirement/user story cannot be measured, it makes it more difficult to achieve this requirement and pass the test.

Volumetric Analysis

Referring to points covered earlier in Chapter 1.2, this becomes the who/what/where/ when/how of the performance test. Ideally, a real-world usage model should be constructed. These should be based on both average, peak and worst-case scenarios (end of week, end of month, end of quarter, or end of financial or calendar year, or an expected peak next year or in five years' time). Volumetric analysis enables a performance engineer to determine which performance test scenario will be appropriate for the upcoming performance tests. These scenarios will relate back to the performance requirements/user stories and risks mentioned earlier.

The product of this step is the operational profile and subsequently the load profile (the ISTQB syllabus considers the operational and load profile as related, but not the same – more on this in Chapter 4).

Performance Test Environment Analysis

Based on the volumetric analysis, a determination on the required performance testing environment can now be done. If an existing test environment is available, it should be assessed as to whether it will be suitable for performance testing. It should also include a gap analysis of the key differences between the proposed/available test environment and the production environment. If gaps exist, the question as to how the gap impacts can be mitigated with the existing environment could be considered.

If an opportunity exists to specify a performance test environment, this should be "production like." Ideally, if the actual production environment is available, the performance test should use this.

Performance Test Tool Analysis/Proof of Concept

In almost every instance, performance testing needs tools. A vast range of both commercial and open source tools are available, and choosing the right tool will make performance testing easier. It's important to note that no tool is right for every situation, and no tool is perfect for any situation.

With any performance test, the timeframe, budget, technologies, performance product risk (if any), the current toolset used by the organization and/or project must be considered (performance tools are looked at in Chapter 5).

Performance Project Planning

The final step in the planning process is determining the performance project timeline. From the overall project timeline and completion date and working backward, the test plan phases for performance testing can be documented. Further detail will be required, but at this point it will give an overall picture of the estimated performance test timeline. It's useful at this point to generate a Gantt chart to add to the performance test plan. It should also be remembered that the planning process can always miss tasks or random events that might happen, but with the benefit of experience (or maybe a good previous performance test plan to "copy"), this can be reduced.

Performance Test Plan

At this point, the performance test plan won't be completed. It is appropriate however to involve project management and stakeholders to review the performance test plan. This document becomes the expected result for the performance test project, and it's useful to get feedback from the stakeholders to ensure that both the performance test goals/ objectives and the overall project goals/objectives are being achieved.

A useful performance test plan template can be found in Chapter 4. Another example is from the test plan template found in ISO 29119.

Summary   Test planning defines the performance test scope, test environments, test data, tools, and human resources needed and completes risk identification and analysis. The output is an updated project test plan and/or performance test plan.

Test Monitoring and Control

Note the monitoring mentioned here refers to monitoring the progress of the performance test project and not the monitoring performed during performance testing.

Control measures are defined to provide action plans should issues be encountered which might impact performance efficiency, such as:

- *increasing the load generation capacity if the infrastructure does not generate the desired loads as planned for particular performance tests*

- *changed, new or replaced hardware*

- *changes to network components*

- *changes to software implementation*

The performance test objectives are evaluated to check for exit criteria achievement.

—ISTQB_CTFL_PT

The performance test plan (expected result for the performance test project) will almost always change. It should be outlined at this point that monitoring and control extends throughout the performance test project. All phases of the performance test project can and should be monitored. Monitoring at this stage of the project concentrates on the performance test project risk rather than performance product risk. Performance test project risk reflects on the time, cost, and resourcing implications of the performance test project going "off course." It allows performance engineers and project staff to implement controls to mitigate these performance test project risks. The main aim of these controls is to mitigate performance project risk and get the performance test project back on track to finish on time, on budget with the required level of product quality and risk.

Based on this, flexibility becomes an important requirement for any performance test plan. As stated earlier, there will be a necessity to change the performance test plan, based on information discovered as part of the performance test project. Any changes made must be documented to capture the actual results of the performance test project. The importance of documenting these changes cannot be emphasized enough, as these changes will feed back into the performance project lessons learnt/retrospectives to improve the performance test planning process.

Summary   Monitoring checks if the performance test exit criteria have been met. Control provides potential mitigation actions to performance project risks.

Test Analysis

Effective performance tests are based on an analysis of performance requirements, test objectives, Service Level Agreements (SLA), IT architecture, process models and other items that comprise the test basis. This activity may be supported by modelling and analysis of system resource requirements and/or behavior using spreadsheets or capacity planning tools.

Specific test conditions are identified such as load levels, timing conditions, and transactions to be tested. The required type(s) of performance test (e.g., load, stress, scalability) are then decided.

—ISTQB_CTFL_PT

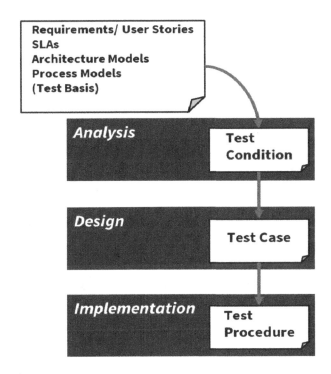

Figure 3-2. *Creating a test*

To put the next sections of the test process into context, it's best to consider the output from each of the next phases in the process (Figure 3-2).

Basically put, a test is formed of the three constituent parts of a test condition, one or more test cases, and one or more test procedures. To use a functional example, there might be a requirement within the project that specifies opening different document types using Microsoft Word. A test condition contains some testable aspect of the system. Thus, a high-level test condition might be

To test opening a document successfully using Microsoft Word.

This test condition is high level, as it contains little detail about the documents to be opened. The advantage of a high-level test condition is that it doesn't take a lot of effort to create these. The disadvantage is the test condition isn't specific and will require many test cases to obtain adequate coverage. This could also hurt in that there may be an obsolete document type as part of a test case (e.g., WordPerfect 5) that fails, and hence the high-level test condition would show a failure. If lower-level test conditions were written, it might show that only the "opening a WordPerfect 5 document" failed, which may be acceptable to stakeholders.

The test cases contain the precondition, postcondition, input data, and expected result. Thus, the test cases might contain:

- Microsoft Word is open, with no document open – the precondition.

- A list of the different types of document to be opened (e.g., .doc, .docx, .pdf, .rtf, .txt, etc.) – the input data.

- The screenshot showing how the document will display in Microsoft Word (the expected result).

- Microsoft Word now has a document open that could subsequently be edited, printed, and/or saved.

The test procedure contains the steps that the test could follow to execute the test cases against the system under test. In this case, there are ten different ways to open a Microsoft Word document – see if you can find them all! Don't forget the command line and right-click options...

Each of these different sets of steps might need to be tested against each of the different document types.

By combining all the constituent parts (test condition, test cases, and test procedures), tests are formed. This approach emphasizes the modularity required with testing, as the test cases and test procedures might be reused across a series of test conditions.

To consider the idea of modularization further, we can also look at the business process model specified earlier (Figure 3-3).

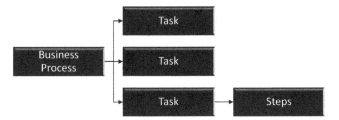

Figure 3-3. *Business process breakdown*

To extend this to an approach that we could use with performance testing, this breakdown extends to the test we write in the following way (Figure 3-4).

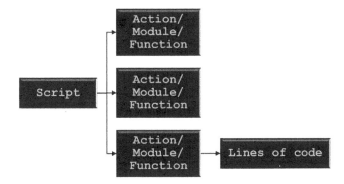

Figure 3-4. *Performance test breakdown*

In the preceding automated performance test example:

- The test condition relates to the script (which itself relates to the end-to-end business process).

- The test procedure is represented by the task level, with the steps represented by the lines of code.

- The test cases feed into the test procedures/test conditions to denote the start and end points and give the test data and expected results.

Test Script Design

Based on the performance test requirements/user stories and associated performance product risks identified earlier, the business processes associated with these can now be identified. As outlined earlier, the business process can be broken down into a series of reusable tasks, each of which will have associated sets of steps, input test data, and expected results.

It's important at this point to consider the actual users of the system. Quite often, the test conditions, test cases, and test procedures can be designed on a theoretical basis that somebody has decided the users will follow. And just as often, the users find different ways of using the system.

Performance engineers need to consider the steps a real user might follow, as not all users do "everything right":

> *A gambling company, at the beginning of online gambling in the late 1990s, created a set of performance test scripts following the assumed behavior of users. For each iteration of one of the tests, the script logged the user in, placed a bet on a horse or dog race, and logged out.*

> *When the site went live however, the actual users behaved differently.*

> *The system administrators noticed problems with the number of concurrent sessions being maintained affecting performance. When a user logs in, a session ID was created and stays persistent until either:*

> a) *the user logs out (a user-terminated session); or*

> b) *the session times out (a server-terminated session).*

> *The problem was identified relating to session maintenance - it was discovered the users behaved in a different way from that that was tested. In the performance test every user login, placed a bet, AND LOGGED OUT. When the real users placed bets they logged in, placed one or more bets, and then either close the browser or navigated to a different website, leaving the session ID to time out.*

> *When the administrators went back and looked at the ratio of user-terminated and server-terminated sessions, they found only 2% of the sessions were user terminated. Hence, 98% of the user sessions were sitting idle waiting to timeout, consuming resources on the Web server.*

Occasionally, actual users do things the stakeholders don't expect. It's essential that the test conditions, test cases, and test procedures replicate the behavior of real users.

Test Scenario Design

In conjunction with the requirements/user stories identified earlier and the test script design identifying the business processes to be executed, the overall performance test is the next thing on the list. Earlier, different performance test types were covered. These now need to be combined with the outputs from earlier in the test process:

- The requirements/user stories

- Business processes

- Performance risks

- The chosen performance tools

- Volumetric information

- Project scope and constraints

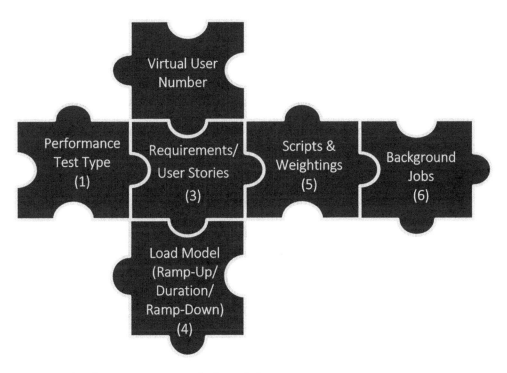

Figure 3-5. *Performance scenario breakdown*

To create the scenario (Figure 3-5), the following need to be included:

1. The performance test type mentioned earlier

2. The total number of virtual users and the distribution between the user groups

3. The business processes to be tested

4. The load model – the rate at which virtual users log in (ramp up), the duration of the test, and how the virtual users log out (ramp down)

5. The total number of transactions broken down over the business processes

6. Any required background jobs to be added to the load during the performance test

Monitoring Design

The monitoring approach is the next consideration. The software, hardware, and infrastructure will dictate how the monitoring will be done, and the requirements/user stories will determine the amount of monitoring required. Things to consider include:

- The chosen performance and monitoring tools – Will one tool cover all the required monitoring, or will multiple tools be required?

- Result storage – How much storage will be required to store the result set, and will the tools be able to access this storage area?

- Security access – Will the performance monitoring tools be able to access the required counters for monitoring?

- The metrics required – Consider both the default metric set and specific metrics associated with performance test requirements/user stories and stakeholder needs.

Performance Test Data Planning

Coupled with the script and scenario design, a part of the testing trifecta has been neglected. Both the test condition and test procedure have been considered, but now we need an important part of the test case – the performance test input data. It's important to note that whatever data is required, a lot of it will be needed. The volume of required data is something most project stakeholders underestimate dramatically. The performance test might require hundreds of users doing tens of iterations, requiring tens of thousands of input data records. The next problem will be sourcing the volume of data and populating the data into the performance test environment.

Scheduling

The final step is to create a more detailed low-level schedule for performance test creation and execution. This schedule should consider not only when performance tests will be created and run but also by whom. The Gantt chart that was created earlier can be filled out with lower-level detail to show the day-by-day plan to include the creation of specific performance tests planned in this phase and the subsequent execution.

Summary   Performance tests are based on an analysis of the test basis (performance requirements, test objectives, service-level agreements, IT architecture, process models, and other items), supported by modeling and analysis of system resource requirements and/or behavior. Specific test conditions such as load levels, timing conditions, and transactions to be tested determine the type(s) of performance test (e.g., load, stress, scalability).

Test Design

Performance test cases are designed. These are generally created in modular form so that they may be used as the building blocks of larger, more complex performance tests (see section 4.2).

—ISTQB_CTFL_PT

Remember from earlier, the performance test case includes:

- Test precondition
- Test postcondition
- Input data
- Expected results

Test Case Data Preparation

 "Data! Data! Data!" he cried impatiently. *"I can't make bricks without clay."*

—Conan Doyle, 1892cb

The required data specification from the earlier planning stage makes this task easier. The focus now is to develop the datasets to allow both the performance test scripts and scenarios to be created. This input data can be thought of in three loose categories. Consider the online shopping website example from earlier.

Master Data

Master data is contained within the system before the performance test is executed and isn't expected to change as part of the test. It includes existing user accounts, the product catalogue, and so on.

User-Defined Data

User-defined data is data to be input by the test during execution. Some of this will be existing master data (user accounts/product codes/etc.) with some being added to the test (order quantities, delivery addresses, etc.). It's this data that forms the input data during the performance test.

Transactional Data

Transactional data is created dynamically as part of execution by the system under test (order numbers/delivery docket numbers/etc.). To correlate the input data with the results, transactional data will be captured as part of the test execution results.

The performance data poem to remember is:

We need master data before we start,

We input user-defined data at runtime,

And we capture transactional data for the results.

I never claimed it was a good poem!

Due to recent improvements in data privatization and data security, this area has now become somewhat more regulated. Performance engineers need to source data that is both realistic and compliant with local data privacy regulations. Familiarity with data privacy regulations and what is covered by them is invaluable when sourcing or creating test data.

Negative data is also required. One of the primary mistakes made when sourcing test data performance testing is the dataset is made up of positive data only. Negative testing is an aspect that is rarely considered when performance testing is being built. It should be argued however that negative testing is not a functional only activity. If performance tests only exercise positive paths through the system, potential performance issues may be missed. It should never be assumed that all users will always do the right thing in the system under test. For example, users that try to log in with incorrect user credentials or attempt to submit partially completed forms could be added to the business processes.

Summary   Performance test cases are created in modular form to be used as the building blocks of larger performance tests.

Test Implementation

In the implementation phase, performance test cases are ordered into performance test procedures. These performance test procedures should reflect the steps normally taken by the user and other functional activities that are to be covered during performance testing.

A test implementation activity is establishing and/or resetting the test environment before each test execution. Since performance testing is typically data-driven, a process is needed to establish test data that is representative of actual production data in volume and type so that production use can be simulated.

—ISTQB_CTFL_PT

As stated by the syllabus, test implementation is the last building phase of the performance tests. It should be noted at this point that the following stages are not sequential. It may be that after the initial environment acceptance check, the subsequent stages are performed simultaneously by one or more performance engineers.

Initial Environment Acceptance Check

This initial stage allows the performance engineer to verify the functionality of the test environment used to prepare the performance test scripts and scenarios. This may not be the performance execution environment to be used later unless of course it is available. Typically, the environment used to build scripts and scenarios is a functional test environment. It is at this point where the paper-based planning exercises have concluded; this and the technical work commences.

Script Construction

Performance test scripts are created using the chosen performance test tools. The starting point for these is the requirements/user stories, the test script and scenario designs, and the test cases produced earlier. These scripts are designed to replicate the business processes selected performance test in the way the designated users would complete them. The overriding objective of creating scripts is to make them as realistic as possible given the constraints of the available tool and data.

As this is a scripting activity, the usual rules of writing good code should apply. Things to consider when building scripts are:

1. Naming conventions – Naming conventions should be developed, for everything from variables/parameters to actions/methods/functions to the scripts and scenarios themselves. Beyond that, results, analyses, and reports would also need naming. Try and be descriptive as possible with any name – don't call a variable that counts iterations a, b, or x, call it iteration_counter! It will be much easier to maintain the scripts later and keep the myriad of files in order if these principles are followed:

   a. With dates, use YYYYMMDD or YYMMDD to allow dated files/variables to be ordered chronologically.

   b. Special characters (~ ! @ # $ % ^ & * ( ) ` ; < > ? , [ ] { } ' " |) should be avoided.

   c. When using numbering, using leading zeros adds clarity ("001, 002, ...010, 011 ... 100, 101, etc." instead of "1, 2, ...10, 11 ... 100, 101, etc.").

   d. Use underscores (file_name.xxx) or camel case (FileName.xxx) with any multiword names.

   e. Use prefixes/suffixes to denote specific types (e.g., a load test scenario or result set might begin with LO_, a stress test with ST_).

2. Standard headers – Headers are the "back of the book" information every script and function needs. Basic information such as the author, script and business process information, and dependencies are extremely useful when maintenance is needed. A typical header should contain creation information and revision history to track the script or function development. An example is as follows:

```
\*******************************************************************
* Project: Merlin - Online Sales Performance
*
* Script name: SingleAnonymousSearch
*
* Author: jonesh
*
* Date created: 200612
*
* Purpose: Single item search by a guest user (no login)
*
* Revision History:
*
* Variables:
* Item - search item
* SearchCount - item count after search
* Filter - optional search filter
*
* Data File - Search.csv
*
* Dependencies: function Online_Search
*
```

```
* Date       Author    Ver    Revision
* 200709     jonesh    1      Added verification check
*
********************************************************************/
```

3. Comments – Commenting is a must in any programming. It allows for new people looking at the code to understand what the original author of the code was thinking when it was written (including the original author, who might not have seen the code in a while). Of course, there is an argument that states "good code is self-commenting" – if you can't read the code, you should learn more! The opposite end is to comment everything, wasting development time for little benefit. Of course, the middle ground between the two extremes is to think of comments as "deodorant for smelly code."[1] In terms of effective commenting, the rules to follow are

   a. Make comments brief.

   b. Keep comments relevant.

   c. Write comments for the least experienced person to view the code.

4. Verification – It helps to know if the business process completed successfully. Based on this, many performance engineers add some form of verification to the test. This is an interesting area though, as much of the time the checks done are somewhat rudimentary. Just capturing a single order number (transactional data) does not constitute verification. As well, the fact the script did not stop in error does not mean that it has passed. A type of performance testing not mentioned by the syllabus is functionality under load (FUL). Every performance test can have elements of checking functionality under load by treating any performance test as if it were an automated functional test. It's not unusual that functional errors occur under load, for example, a system that under load fails to generate transactional data in a timely manner

---

[1] Thanks to the Refactoring Guru – https://refactoring.guru/smells/comments

(or display it at all). Rather than create the message "standard order 12345 saved" and display it as it did during functional testing, the system would respond with "standard order saved." After execution when testers checked the database, the order number was written within the record. Upon investigation, the system while under load was found to delay creating the order number, and hence the end user wouldn't see the order number saved at completion of the business process. It's advisable to think of every performance script as a functional test as well as a performance test. Under load the system can behave differently and uncover errors such as these that although they appear to be a functional error, they only appear under load conditions.

5. Standardized error handling – Many tools already have standard error handling based on such things as the HTTP return codes, where return codes in the range of 400 or 500 are immediately captured as errors. Where this error capturing ability does fall short is recovery from an error condition. Some tools allow a predetermined response to an error condition (e.g., restarting the next test iteration on error). Many systems though will have a set of error conditions specific to that system. It is worth considering writing custom functions to capture and recover from these internal errors.

6. Common libraries/repositories – Every good developer would agree with the premise of modularization and the use of reusable code. The same stands true for performance scripts. To use common function libraries and data repositories to minimize the maintenance overhead needed to keep the scripts up to date.

A checklist can be useful to track the progression of script creation, allowing both the performance engineers and stakeholders visibility of this stage (Table 3-2).

Table 3-2. *Performance Scripting Development Checklist*

Performance Script Development			
	Purchase_Single	Purchase_Multi	Purchase_Special
Manual execute script business processes			
Initial recording			
Replay success with original recording			
Parameterize			
Correlate			
Add checkpoints			
Transaction timing			
Replay with original data			
Replay with multiple iterations			
Replay multiple users/iterations			
Replay in perf test scenario			
READY TO RUN			

Scenario Construction

Scenarios should be created as per the Test Scenario Design developed earlier. Once again, a scenario development checklist is a useful aid (Table 3-3).

Table 3-3. *Performance Scenario Checklist*

Performance Scenario Development			
	Load_Ave_Day	**Load_Peak_Day**	**Stress_Peak_Day**
Conform scenario design			
Initial scenario creation			
Add scripts			
Initial test run (single Vuser)			
Set scenario runtime settings			
Set and check monitoring			
Final test shakedown run (5 Vusers)			
READY TO RUN			

Test Data Preparation

Again, this is a simple matter of putting the test data plan into practice. A small amount of data will need creating for use in building the scripts. The next concern is to create the volume of data required to run a full performance test. This will consist mainly of master data, with some user-defined data thrown in. The focus now will be feeding data into the performance execution environment. Data can be copied from the production environment, especially if it doesn't relate to any data covered by privacy regulations. Private data SHOULD NOT BE USED in testing.

To recreate private data, tools like the example in Figure 3-6 can be used.

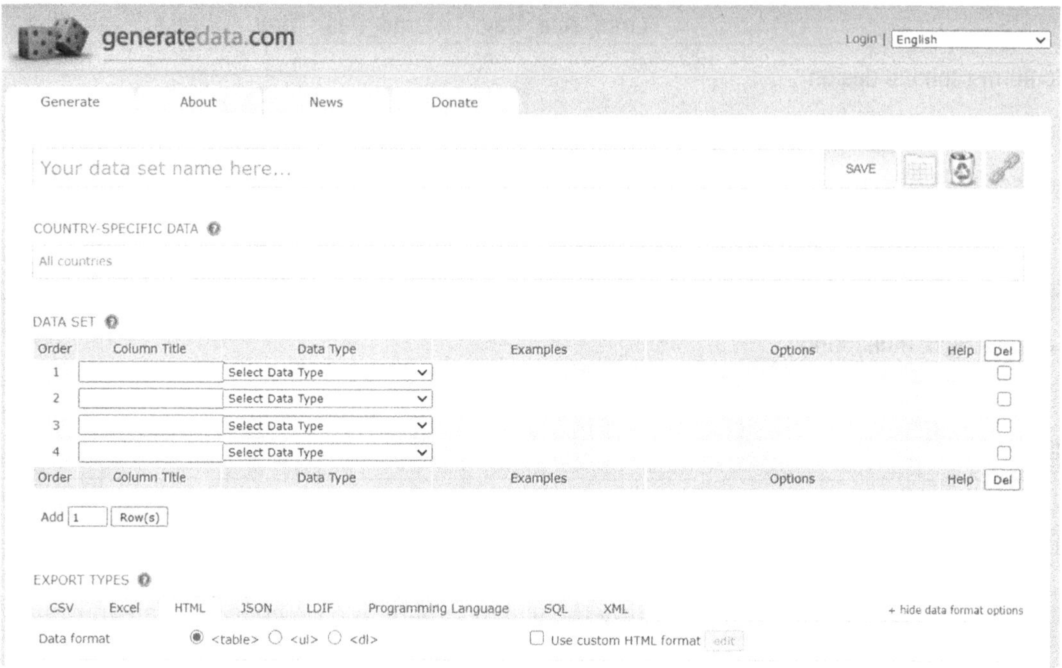

Figure 3-6. www.generatedata.com/

Generatedata.com allows random private information to be recreated to be added to records for use in performance tests (or any other type as well). It allows the development of a custom dataset via an easy-to-use interface and can generate up to 100 records using the free version or, for a small license price, generate thousands of records based on the configured dataset defined. It can then output these in different formats. Tools like this make data generation and data management much easier. A wide range of tools exist, including Excel macros up to full data management toolsets. This dataset should be quick to build, quick to refresh, and compliant with all data privacy and security regulations.

This data preparation process can be tested in the environment used to create the performance test scripts and scenarios with a cut-down dataset. The execution environment can then be populated with the full dataset.

Test Environment Preparation

The test environment needs to be configured to allow the full performance test to be run. This environment should be built as per the test environment design. Any shortfalls with the environment could lead to the performance test objectives not being achieved. Once again, an environment checklist can be useful to ensure whoever is building the environment covers all that is required. This also includes the dataset mentioned previously, and any tools and/or monitoring is also added.

As well, this environment from this point should be managed, subject to both change control and configuration management. As some performance engineers have found, if changes are made to the environment without the performance engineer's knowledge, time can be wasted diagnosing nonexistent problems as a result of changes to the environment.

Test Tool Preparation

Based on the work in the planning phase, a proof of concept may already have led to the tool being installed. This stage now prepares the tool to begin recording scripts, creating scenarios, and executing a full performance test. Some tools, such as LoadRunner by Micro Focus, have a set of tools, each of which performs a specific function within the performance test. Other tools, such as JMeter, have everything incorporated into a single tool. At this point, it's important to set up the tool to run the full suite of planned performance tests. As per other stages, a checklist is valuable to ensure everything is considered (Table 3-4).

***Table 3-4.** Performance Execution Checklist*

Performance Tool Preparation Checklist		
Hardware		
Checks	Pass/Fail	Action on Failure
Is the test controller available (via physical or remote access)?		Obtain access (physical is preferred) from the supplier/environment administrator
Are load generators available (physically or remotely)?		Obtain access/schedule load generator availability

(continued)

Table 3-4. (*continued*)

Performance Tool Preparation Checklist

Check permissions on controller and load generator machines	Obtain local admin on the relevant machines
Can the controller gain network access to the load generators?	Obtain access via environmental support/ vendor support
Can the load generators gain network access to the system under test?	Obtain access via environmental support

...

Software

Controller machine – are the prerequisites/ controller installed?	Obtain local admin and complete installation
Load generators – are the prerequisites/ load generators installed?	Obtain local admin and complete installation
Monitoring – are all monitors installed and working correctly?	Obtain local admin and complete installation
Are the necessary tool licenses available and installed?	Obtain access via environmental support/ vendor support
Can the controller connect and maintain connection to the load generators?	Obtain licenses via vendor support
Can the load generators execute the scripts against the system under test?	

...

This list will vary depending on the nature and design of the tool. Both open source and commercial tools will have similar characteristics, and many tools work in a similar manner.

Monitoring Preparation

Some performance test tools have the monitoring built within the tool; others integrate with external tools. Some performance tools have a vast array of monitoring options; others are limited.

Monitoring should be set up based on:

1. The requirements of the performance test specified earlier in the monitoring planning

2. The capabilities of the performance test/monitoring tool(s) to capture the required metrics

It will be important if multiple monitoring tools are being used to correlate the monitoring with the actions of the performance test. The usual method for this is to set all monitoring to use absolute time (i.e., the local clock time), allowing the various metrics to be matched.

Just like the performance tests themselves need to be checked, the monitoring too needs testing. It should become a standard practice that every time the "performance test" test is executed, the opportunity should be taken to test fully the monitoring as well.

In preparing monitoring for performance testing, four issues exist:

1. Permissions – As mentioned previously in the checklist, permissions involve environment and network administrators granting permissions to run monitoring services like perfmon or opening ports to allow the tool to communicate with the machines being monitored.

2. Knowledge of the metrics – It's the responsibility of performance engineers to educate themselves on the "art of the possible" in terms of the available monitoring counters.

3. Collection and consolidation – Having a common storage area for results is an important consideration. Having the ability to compare the metrics produced will aid in finding the root cause of issues. Some of this can be automated – never forget that Excel macros and other useful scripts can cut down on the performance engineers' legwork to consolidate results.

4. Storage – An aspect of performance monitoring that sometimes gets overlooked is the amount of data that is gathered due to monitoring. Sufficient disk space for the storage of results is an absolute necessity (considering some result sets on longer soak tests might run into gigabytes of data).

Results Capture and Analysis Preparation

At this point, the next consideration is displaying the analysis work after execution. As mentioned before in monitoring preparation, if some of this can be automated, it will save time. Standard summary information from the performance test along with average and maximum transaction times will always be of interest and are prime candidates for automatic capture.

The results return to the original objectives of the performance test. Ultimately, the results are the answers to these questions. An important consideration is the needs of the stakeholders, some of which will be technical and some less so. A simple pass/fail on these allows the overall outcome of the test to be quickly determined.

Table 3-5. *Performance Test Objective Results*

Performance Test Objectives	Outcome	Notes
To verify the system can support the current peak user load	☑	System supports 100% current peak load with • 92% transaction times met • 99% transaction success rate
To determine if the current system is scalable to the 5-year growth target	☑	System supports 150% current peak load with • 86% transaction times met • 97% transaction success rate
To verify the integration between the system and Optimus 3.2 with current peak load	☒	System supports 67% current peak load before errors with • 42% transaction times met • 87% transaction success rate

Deep analysis is unfortunately difficult to automate, but as tools be☑come more advanced it becomes easier for performance engineers to conduct analysis sessions with the tool's assistance. More details on analysis and reporting follow in Chapter 4.

Final Environment Acceptance Test and Readiness Report

The final environment acceptance test is like that done at the beginning of the test implementation test process phase. The difference now is that the execution environment is being tested. This test will include the hardware and infrastructure, software, test data, performance, and monitoring tools required to conduct the full performance test.

The performance test readiness report covers off the test process until this point. It's the final checklist to track progress until execution. The example in Table 3-6 might be recognized as the checklist from the planning phase – hopefully now completed.

Table 3-6. *Performance Readiness Check*

Requirement	Showstopper	Status	Notes
Test requirements approved	Y	**Pass**	
Volumetric data approved	Y	**Pass**	
Performance test plan approved	Y	**Pass**	
Test tool is available and working after POC	N	**Pass**	
Business process list approved	Y	**Pass**	
Test environment designed	N	**Pass**	
Test scripts designed	N	**Pass**	
Test scenarios designed	N	**Pass**	
Test data design/volume approved	Y	**Pass**	
Test monitoring designed	N	**Pass**	
Initial recording environment accepted	Y	**Pass**	
Test scripts created and approved	Y	**Pass**	
Test scenarios created and approved	Y	**Pass**	
Test data created	Y	**Pass**	
Test monitoring completed	Y	**Pass**	
Test tool setup complete (with licenses)	N	**Pass**	
Test result collection set up	N	**Pass**	
Execution environment completed and checked	Y	**Pass**	
OVERALL STATUS	**Ready**	**100%**	

This table becomes a key deliverable to the project to provide the status and (hopefully) the evidence of the completion of the preparation of the performance test.

Summary   Performance test procedures contain the steps implementing the performance test cases. Performance testing is reliant on production-like amounts and types of test data to simulate real users.

Test Execution

Test execution occurs when the performance test is conducted, often by using performance test tools. Test results are evaluated to determine if the system's performance meets the requirements and other stated objectives. Any defects are reported.

—ISTQB_CTFL_PT

Unusual as it may seem, performance test execution can be the boring part of performance testing. The automated performance test scenarios can take hours to complete, with the only excitement for the performance engineer being small graphs slowly creeping across a dashboard. Another point is in most instances, later levels of performance test execution is done outside of normal working hours. Methodologies such as DevOps have changed the traditional view of performance testing, as component performance testing may now be run similar to automated functional tests within each sprint (even to the point that they are automated as part of the build process).

Performance testing can add large amounts of load to the network, which can adversely affect the overall performance of the network for other users. As well, the load from other users can affect the results of the performance test. At this point, performance engineers can become a creature of the night, sitting in an empty office watching those small graphs creep across the screen...

The following stages cover test execution. Incorporated into this will be analysis and remediation.

Initial Test Setup

Initial test setup ensures the entry criteria for the performance test to be executed have been completed. Things to be added to this test setup checklist can include:

- Support – Administrator support for the system under test, network, database, and infrastructure can be helpful. Being able to immediately diagnose issues is a bonus, and the above administrators can certainly help with this.

- Monitoring – Before each execution, a quick monitoring check to ensure all the monitors are up and able to record the test results should always occur.

- System under test state – Things to investigate include checking the system state and any user sessions still running. Often after a previous test is completed, some leftover user sessions might still be running. These can either be left to time out or terminated before the next execution.

- Data setup – Any test data required should be checked, such as:

  - Master data, both that used by the test and the amount required for the database to behave in a production-like manner

  - User-defined data that is both lifelike and in enough quantity to allow the performance test to execute per the operational and load profiles successfully

  - Transactional data or business processes in a specific state to be used in the test and the means to capture transactional data during the test

- Tools – Any specific requirements for the tools and/or scripts, such as:

  - Specific runtime settings for that scenario execution.

  - Specific result names or settings for the execution.

  - Specific run logic for the tasks within the business process.

  - Specific environment or other variables are set for the execution.

Test Execution

Run the performance test, ensuring the proper controls are in place to allow meaningful results. It sounds obvious, but it's surprising how often things are forgotten before execution leading to invalid results and wasted time. Performance testing is usually run in cycles – there may be one or a number of performance tests that will be executed against a version/build of the code/application/system. One difference with other types of testing is a performance test cycle may be completed quite quickly. A functional cycle might take a week, whereas a performance test cycle consisting of a load test and a stress test might only take a few hours.

Results Analysis

Analyze the results of the execution. This can begin during the execution as data is incoming from the tools and continue after the execution is complete. Results analysis is a subject that is deserving of its own chapter, which in fact comes a little later. At this point, some simple questions require answering (Figure 3-7).

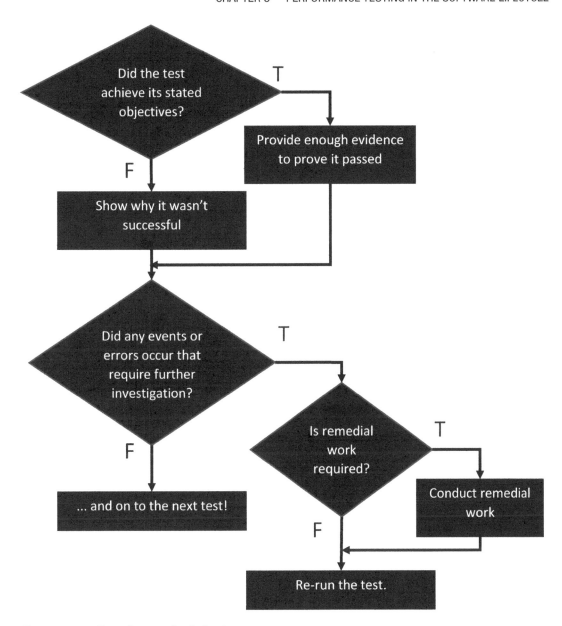

Figure 3-7. *Results analysis logic*

Interim Test Report

After each test, a results summary should be written. The interim report should be a brief summary (an email or a one-page report) of the success or failure of test objectives. This may not be possible if you are running hundreds of tests; obviously, a report for each of them is impractical, and a single report for a test cycle may be more appropriate.

Importantly, this summary will give the stakeholders a view of the objectives to make decisions as required. Deeper analysis can be included within this report, or it may require several execution cycles to determine the deeper issues.

Remedial Action (If Needed)

At the completion of each performance test execution, a decision point should exist deciding whether the test was completed satisfactorily.

In the preceding flowchart, the represented remedial work could focus on the script (change or update), the test data (change or refresh), the infrastructure, or the system under test. Any remedial work must be documented, as one of the traditional issues is the lack of changes being documented.

Test Cycle Report

At the completion of a performance test cycle, a test cycle report shall be completed. This is more comprehensive from the interim test report, containing additional information not included in the interim test report. It's at this point that comparisons in performance can be made between the tests within the cycle, along with earlier executed cycles.

Results Review Meeting

The purpose of this meeting is to analyze the results with stakeholders (both technical and business). It's at this point that information from the review meeting can be used by stakeholders to make informed decisions about the performance test project. The performance engineer:

- Proves the performance tests have been executed successfully.

- Identifies new potential performance risks.

- Identifies and shows documented any changes to the test plan.

- Shows documented any remedial work undertaken.

- Shows documented any further opportunities for system and process improvements.

System and Process Improvement

This covers both improvements to the system (tuning) and improvements to the performance process. This state will be entered only if outstanding performance project risks still require further mitigation. The goal should be to improve the performance testing process and/or procedures being followed. The process loops once this is completed back to the initial test setup.

If performance testing has been completed, the test completion activities are next.

Summary Test execution runs the performance tests; results are evaluated to see if the system's performance meets the stated objectives and any defects are reported.

Test Completion

Performance test results are provided to the stakeholders (e.g., architects, managers, product owners) in a test summary report. The results are expressed through metrics which are often aggregated to simplify the meaning of the test results. Visual means of reporting such as dashboards are often used to express performance test results in ways that are easier to understand than text-based metrics.

—ISTQB_CTFL_PT

First, a quick anecdote. As the success of the LEGO Group proves, many people of all ages love to build. Performance test execution can be compared to building with LEGO. By the end of building, there is usually LEGO spread all over the table or the floor. But once building is complete, there is still some work to be done. Test completion can be compared to this point – it's time to pick up the LEGO!

Test Completion Report

The test completion report is a consolidation of the test cycle reports in conjunction with the performance test plan. It not only provides information on the test cycles executed but details the performance test project and product risks, the defects found, and how both were mitigated.

Once again, it needs to be emphasized that there are multiple stakeholders viewing this report. All stakeholder requirements, both technical and business, must be considered in this final report.

Presentation and Recommendations

It can be easier to present the findings and recommendations to the project stakeholders in a meeting. This allows the stakeholders to clarify any points they don't understand. This stage is extremely important in terms of giving performance testing and performance engineers a positive impression to those stakeholders present in this meeting. Performance engineers must consider the differences in both business and technical knowledge – it could be that two meetings are required. It's a good practice to give business information with little technical detail in the first meeting and get "down and dirty" in the technical details with the relevant nerds in a subsequent meeting.

Performance Test Pack Creation

At this point, it's time to create a regression test pack which will contain all performance test assets and enough documentation for those assets to be reusable as is.

Most organizations have comprehensive regression sets. The failing of many of them is they almost exclusively contain functional tests only. If any change is made to a system, the potential for defects to be present has increased; by how much though is dependent on a variety of factors. The normal reaction is of course to test to hopefully discover these defects. The unfortunate issue is when defects are mentioned, people think of functional defects.

Summary   Performance test results are provided to the stakeholders in a test summary report, shown as metrics and dashboards aggregated to simplify the test results to be understood by stakeholders.

Performance testing is often considered to be an ongoing activity in that is performed at multiple times and at all test levels (component, integration, system, system integration and acceptance testing). At the close of a defined period of performance testing, a point of test closure may be reached where designed tests, test tool assets (test cases and test procedures), test data and other testware are archived or passed on to other testers for later use during system maintenance activities.

—ISTQB_CTFL_PT

The system maintenance activities mentioned earlier mean changes. Non-functional testing (including performance testing) within the regression set is vital in uncovering performance-related issues introduced by these changes.

Transition

The main transition action is to pass the performance test pack onto the next owners and to walk them through it. The next owner could be operations support, application support, or the testing department. This pack can be used for multiple jobs:

- Regression testing

- Go-live assurance monitoring

- Availability monitoring after go-live

Summary   Performance testing is an ongoing activity performed at multiple times and at all test levels. Once testing is completed, the tests, test tool assets (test cases and test procedures), test data, and other testware are archived or passed on to others for use during maintenance activities.

3.2 Categories of Performance Risks for Different Architectures

PTFL-3.2.1 (K2) Explain typical categories of performance risks for different architectures

As mentioned previously, application or system performance varies considerably based on the architecture, application and host environment. While it is not possible to provide a complete list of performance risks for all systems, the list below includes some typical types of risks associated with particular architectures.

—ISTQB_CTFL_PT

These risks should be thought of as a tiered set of product risks. And an example could be the failure of a single server in a multi-tiered system because of excessive resource consumption on that machine. That single machine failure could cause the entire system to fail.

Performance engineers should always be considering the cause-effect relationship. It's the goal to identify the root cause of a problem, when often the first sign is the system is "a bit slow." This could relate to a bottleneck caused by high CPU utilization, low memory, low bandwidth, and so on. Performance engineers should always refer to the fundamental question looked at earlier:

What is load?

If performance engineers always consider the code executing in a defined environment, they think beyond "the CPU is running at 100%." They will identify the code that's causing the CPU to run at 100%.

Hopefully…

Summary   Performance varies based on the architecture, application, and the host environment.

Single Computer Systems

These are systems and applications that run entirely on one non-virtualized computer. Performance can degrade due to:

- *excessive resource consumption including memory leaks, background activities such as security software, slow storage subsystems (e.g., low-speed external devices or disk fragmentation), and operating system mismanagement.*

- *inefficient implementation of algorithms which do not make use of available resources (e.g., main memory) and as a result execute slower than required.*

—ISTQB_CTFL_PT

Excessive resource consumption relates back to the generic monitoring elements mentioned in Chapter 1:

- CPU utilization:

  - Note should be taken on any system that continuously runs above 70% for an extended time. Running above 70% CPU utilization leaves little room for other operations that may run (such as operating system actions).

  - Consider how the CPU utilization is spread across the available processors. If the application being tested is single threaded, only one processor might be busy in a multicore processor or a multithreaded application where the load is being spread unequally across the available processors.

  - Examining which processes are consuming the processors can also be of value.

  - Look out for heat – a CPU running above 70% can heat up and could possibly reduce the life of the processor!

- Memory utilization:

  - Memory could refer to cached memory (L1 – part of each CPU core, small but fast; L2 and L3 between the CPU and RAM, slightly slower than L1 and has more storage) as well as RAM itself. Cached memory is used for instructions and data the CPU needs to access quickly or instructions/data to be reused. The more L2 and L3 memory the machine has, the faster it will run.

  - Memory utilization should be closely tracked, both in terms of the overall memory use and memory use by each process. Watching both will help uncover memory leaks and more importantly which process is causing this.

  - If available memory starts running low, paging starts (paging is a memory management function that stores and retrieves blocks of memory). If a process references a page that isn't in RAM, a page fault occurs. The CPU must then find the page on the HD/ SSD, find room in memory to place the retrieved page (meaning something might need to be written to disk), move the paged information into RAM, update the page table, and return the control back to the code needing the data. Monitoring page faults can indicate the amount of paging occurring during the test.

- Disk input/output:

  - Hard disks – Retrieving from or writing to the HD involves moving the disk arm to position the disk heads over the correct track (seek time), waiting for the data to be under the heads (rotational latency), and then transferring the data. Excessive HD activity can become a bottleneck in the system and can lead to HD read/write queueing.

  - Solid-state disks – SSD avoids the seek time and rotational latency and hence is much faster (five or more times faster to read/write than HDs, depending on the technology). If a HD is a bottleneck, SSD can improve this between 200% and 800%. However, the downside of SSD is the price (more expensive than HDs, although the price is dropping dramatically).

- Bandwidth consumption:

  - Bandwidth isn't just relevant to the ethernet cable out the back of the machine, as bandwidth also exists internally within machines.

  - Network bandwidth can directly affect transmission time (how much data fits down the network segment), coupled with latency (how long it takes to traverse the network segment) and packet loss (the quality of the network segment).

  - To the same extent, bandwidth can also affect moving data internally between the CPU, memory, disks, network card, etc.

- Queueing:

  - Queued processes, threads, and/or read/write transactions are indicators of congestion. All can become system bottlenecks.

- Queue lengths should be snapshot as an actual queue length, or queue length/sec, rather than looking at the average queue length over the length of the test. The average may hide a short-term high spike in queueing.

- Queueing can cause cascades, where multiple queues increase as a result of a single queue. For example, a HD read queue may lead to a processor queue as the processor waits for values to continue working.

Summary   Performance on single systems can degrade due to excessive resource consumption (memory leaks, background activities, slow storage subsystems, and operating system mismanagement) or inefficient implementation of algorithms.

Multi-tier Systems

These are systems of systems that run on multiple servers, each of which performs a specific set of tasks, such as database server, application server, and presentation server. Each server is, of course, a computer and subject to the risks given earlier. In addition, performance can degrade due to poor or non-scalable database design, network bottlenecks, and inadequate bandwidth or capacity on any single server.

—ISTQB_CTFL_PT

Any multi-tier system will always perform at the speed of the slowest component or tier that is used. Initially, after identifying poor system performance, the job will be to identify the component or tier causing the problem. The next step is to focus effort to identify the root cause of that component or tier bottleneck. One point to consider is the inclusion of load balancing. If load balancing is a part of the production system, it is often not included in the test environment. It is also not a coincidence that load balancing often is a problem in production, a component not tested.

As would be thought, a multi-tier system is made up of multiple single computer systems talking to each other. Inevitably, the same rules apply from the single computer systems mentioned earlier.

Summary   Systems of systems running on multiple servers (database/application/presentation server), each of which is a computer and subject to the risks given earlier, as well as poor or nonscalable database design, network bottlenecks, and inadequate bandwidth or capacity on any single server.

Distributed Systems

These are systems of systems, similar to a multi-tier architecture, but the various servers may change dynamically, such as an e-commerce system that accesses different inventory databases depending on the geographic location of the person placing the order. In addition to the risks associated with multi-tier architectures, this architecture can experience performance problems due to critical workflows or dataflows to, from, or through unreliable or unpredictable remote servers, especially when such servers suffer periodic connection problems or intermittent periods of intense load.

—ISTQB_CTFL_PT

Distributed systems can be compared with multiple single computer systems that are a long way apart, so once again the same rules apply. Issues relating to the network (bandwidth, packet loss, and latency) can play havoc with distributed systems, especially if the system shares LAN/WAN where traffic can vary. Limitations on the test environment can hamper performance testing this system type. A test environment can always use WAN emulation, where software or hardware switches allow the network bandwidth/latency/packet loss conditions to be replicated. The downside of WAN emulation however is although the real network is being emulated, it may not produce the variable conditions that might occur in production. If testing is done on the production network, the performance engineer will not have control of the network traffic and may get test results that cannot be replicated due to possibly variable network traffic.

Summary   Distributed systems are like multi-tier architecture, but servers can change dynamically (such as geolocation). In addition to multi-tier architectures, performance problems due to critical workflows or dataflows to/from/through unreliable or unpredictable remote servers (periodic connection problems or intermittent periods of intense load) can lead to performance issues.

Virtualized Systems

These are systems where the physical hardware hosts multiple virtual computers. These virtual machines may host single-computer systems and applications as well as servers that are part of a multi-tier or distributed architecture. Performance risks that arise specifically from virtualization include excessive load on the hardware across all the virtual machines or improper configuration of the host virtual machine resulting in inadequate resources.

—ISTQB_CTFL_PT

Virtualization is an option many organizations take for both production and test environments and is a much-valued addition. Virtualization has a downside though. If a test environment needs to be "production like," virtualization can introduce problems. For functional testing, the environment needs to be functionally the same as the production environment. Virtualization can achieve this without question.

When it comes to performance testing, the environment needs to perform the same as the production environment. An important difference with a virtualized environment is the architecture. Many production environments are virtualized, so the architecture will be similar. One difference might be significant however – the use of dynamic resource allocation. As load increases on an environment with dynamic resource allocation activated, more resources (CPU/memory/disk) are added for the resource pool. In this instance, it's better to fix the resources for the initial performance testing to get a measured set of results on a standard environment.

On the other hand, if the test environment is virtualized to represent a distributed or multi-tier system, it may behave differently due to it being virtualized. It needs to be noted that any virtual environment is different from a physical environment:

- A physical environment has the application installed directly on the base operating system.

- A virtual environment on the base operating system is an application (e.g., VMware or VirtualBox), within which an entire operating system executes (which may or may not think it's the only operating system on the machine).

A discrepancy may exist between a virtualized environment and a physical environment. Arif et al.[2] conducted a study on this difference and found

We conducted the same performance tests in both virtual and physical environments and compare the performance testing results based on the three aspects that are typically examined for performance testing results:

1. *single performance metric (e.g. CPU time from virtual environment vs. CPU time from physical environment)*

2. *the relationship among performance metrics (e.g. correlation between CPU and IO) and*

3. *performance models that are built to predict system performance.*

Our results show that:

1. *a single metric from virtual and physical environments do not follow the same distribution, hence practitioners cannot simply use a scaling factor to compare the performance between environments,*

2. *correlations among performance metrics in virtual environments are different from those in physical environments,*

---

[2] [Arif et al] M.M. Arif, W. Shang & E. Shihab, "Empirical Study on the Discrepancy Between Performance Testing Results from Virtual and Physical Environments," Empirical Software Engineering, June 2018, Volume 23, Issue 3, pp1490–1518

3. *statistical models built based on performance metrics from virtual environments are different from the models built from physical environments suggesting that practitioners cannot use the performance test results across virtual and physical environments.*

—Arif et al.

Summary   Virtual machines host single computer systems/applications/servers. Performance risks include excessive load on the hardware across all the virtual machines or inadequate resources from improper configuration of the host virtual machine.

Dynamic/Cloud-Based Systems

These are systems that offer the ability to scale on demand, increasing capacity as the level of load increases. These systems are typically distributed and virtualized multitier systems, albeit with self-scaling features designed specifically to mitigate some of the performance risks associated with those architectures. However, there are risks associated with failures to properly configure these features during initial setup or subsequent updates.

—ISTQB_CTFL_PT

So, by this point, a pattern should be detected. If we combine virtualized systems with distributed systems, we end up with dynamic/cloud-based systems. Along with the previous issues, cloud-based systems have some extra considerations.

The first highlights an issue in getting information from the cloud environment. Because some monitoring requires certain ports to be open to conduct monitoring, it might be difficult to gather information from a virtual environment on the cloud. Communicating with the cloud provider might help mitigate this problem.

The second relates to security. The nature of a performance test (many users accessing the system from a limited number of IP addresses) might be mistaken by the cloud provider as a denial-of-service attack. The cloud provider should be notified performance testing is being undertaken, both to allow monitoring and notify security to allow the performance test.

151

Summary   Cloud systems (typically distributed and virtualized multi-tier systems) can scale on demand, increasing capacity as the level of load increases. Performance risks include failures to properly configure self-scaling features and loss of network.

Client-Server Systems

These are systems running on a client that communicate via a user interface with a single server, multi-tier server, or distributed server. Since there is code running on the client, the single computer risks apply to that code, while the server-side issues mentioned above apply as well. Further, performance risks exist due to connection speed and reliability issues, network congestion at the client connection point (e.g., public Wi-Fi), and potential problems due to firewalls, packet inspection and server load balancing.

—ISTQB_CTFL_PT

An important characteristic of a client-server (or "thick client") system is the processing that is passed to the client. Going back to the 1960s and 1970s, most machines used were dumb terminals connected to a mainframe or minicomputer. These machines were basic input/output devices, with no real processing capability. All the processing was done on the mainframe/minicomputer. After the birth of the microcomputer, the capabilities of these end-user machines began to increase. This meant the server (whether a mainframe/minicomputer/microcomputer) could now pass some processing off to the client. This changed the communication behavior – the mainframe/dumb terminal model had small amounts of information sent and received very frequently. Client-server communication changed this by the server passing much larger amounts of data back to the client for processing (Figure 3-8).

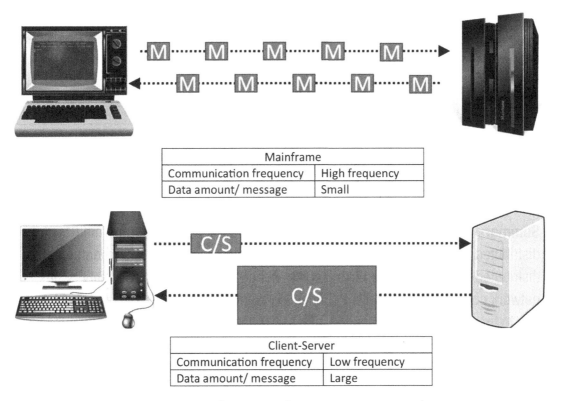

Figure 3-8. *Traffic flow – mainframe vs. client-server*

The importance of this in terms of performance means:

- Processing load is passed from the server to the client, meaning potentially more users can be served with the same server resource utilization.

- Client resource utilization now must be considered as part of the performance testing.

- The network must now support larger dataflows less frequently than the mainframe environment.

Another issue to be considered with client-server is the type of connection between the client and the server. In almost every instance, a stateful connection is created. This is important for two reasons:

1. The number of connections now becomes a consumable resource that requires both inclusion in the performance test and monitoring.

2. Virtual users sitting idle consuming a connection must be taken into consideration.

Summary   Client-server systems (client user interface with a single/multi-tier/ distributed server). Performance risks include single computer risks (client) and the distributed/multi-tier server risks (server), connection speed and reliability issues, network congestion at the client connection point (e.g., public Wi-Fi), and problems due to firewalls, packet inspection, and server load balancing.

Mobile Applications

These are applications running on a smartphone, tablet, or other mobile device. Such applications are subject to the risks mentioned for client-server and browser-based (web apps) applications. In addition, performance issues can arise due to the limited and variable resources and connectivity available on the mobile device (which can be affected by location, battery life, charge state, available memory on the device and temperature). For those applications that use device sensors or radios such as accelerometers or Bluetooth, slow dataflows from those sources could create problems. Finally, mobile applications often have heavy interactions with other local mobile apps and remote web services, any of which can potentially become a performance efficiency bottleneck.

—ISTQB_CTFL_PT

Mobile environments introduce an added layer of complexity. Because of their very nature, communication with mobile devices may be intermittent. The means of communication may also change – the network might switch from GPRS or EDGE to 3G, to 4G, to 5G (if available), to Wi-Fi.

Based on this, mobile applications operate in one of three modes:

1. **Never Connected**, for stand-alone applications. All required data and information becomes available upon installation of the application. For example, the calculator on Android OS is a stand-alone application that does not need any network connection.

2. **Partially Connected**, normally used for ad hoc updates to the application. Updates can be full updates of data back to the server or just changes to data. An example is the game *Candy Crush Saga*, where users can play the game without a connection, and once a network connection is available, data is uploaded to Facebook.

3. **Always Connected**, like an enterprise wireless network and a set of applications and servers allowing employees to connect to the organization's network. This could allow employees to use their mobile devices within the organization's network connections to Microsoft Teams to make audio and video calls. A good example of this always connected mode is WhatsApp.

These connection types determine the way in which data is synchronized between the mobile device and the back-end system. Data synchronization can be done in two ways using two methods:

- **"Store-and-forward" synchronization** allows users to store and transmit information. Initially, the application stores the data locally, and when a connection is established, the mobile app forwards the locally stored data onto the server.

- **Continuous synchronization** is achieved either synchronously or asynchronously when the connectivity between the client and server is continuous.

- **Synchronous method** requires both the sender and receiver to have a synchronized clock before data transmission commences.

- **Asynchronous method** does not require a clock synchronization but adds a parity bit to the data before transmission.

These factors add a level of complexity to any performance test environment.

Summary   Mobile applications are subject to the risks for client-server and browser-based (web apps) applications and performance issues due to the limited/variable resources and connectivity available on the mobile device (location, battery life, charge state, available memory on the device, temperature), slow dataflows from internal components (accelerometers or Bluetooth), and interactions with other local mobile apps/remote web services.

Embedded Real-Time Systems

These are systems that work within or even control everyday things such as cars (e.g., entertainment systems and intelligent braking systems), elevators, traffic signals, Heating, Ventilation and Air Conditioning (HVAC) systems, and more. These systems often have many of the risks of mobile devices, including (increasingly) connectivity-related issues since these devices are connected to the Internet. However, the diminished performance of a mobile video game is usually not a safety hazard for the user, while such slowdowns in a vehicle braking system could prove catastrophic.

—ISTQB_CTFL_PT

Embedded real-time systems can once again combine the technology of a single computer system with mobile. The real difference here is the operating system the device uses. A single computer or a mobile device will have a full operating system (Microsoft/Linux/OS X or Android/iOS). An embedded real-time system will only have a basic "as needed" OS to do a specific job. These devices could include simple PCBs with embedded software, up to complex Internet of Things (IoT – in effect embedded system) devices. The moment these devices connect online or operate within a larger "system of systems," the issue of performance vs. security comes into play (especially in recent times in industries like automotive and manufacturing). Previously, security was left out or minimal because of the impact on performance. As could be well understood, these devices were limited in terms of processing and memory. As the hardware became more capable (and more connected), the need to secure these devices increased.

To highlight this, an interesting event occurred on September 20, 2016, against the website krebsonsecurity.com. A distributed denial-of-service attack was launched against the site, and the attack included several unique characteristics, these being:

- The size of the attack – 620 gigabits of traffic per second, the largest DDoS attack traffic detected at the time.

- The nature of the attack – Most of the attack consisted of simple methods (SYN floods, GET and POST floods), with the addition of GRE traffic.[3]

- The dispersed nature of the attack – Many DDoS attacks are region based, whereas this attack used a botnet dispersed around the globe.

The botnet used in this attack possessed a new set of capabilities, using slave IoT devices to generate a proportion of the malicious traffic.

Another consideration is the fact that embedded real-time systems show the essence of the answer to the question, "What is load?"

Changes to the code could have a dramatic effect on the performance of these systems due to the limited amount of resources available.

Summary   Embedded systems have the risks of mobile devices, including (increasingly) connectivity-related issues. As these systems can be safety critical, both performance and security can be an issue.

Mainframe Applications

These are applications—in many cases decades-old applications—supporting often mission-critical business functions in a data center, sometimes via batch processing. Most are quite predictable and fast when used as originally designed, but many of these are now accessible via APIs, web services, or through their database, which can result in unexpected loads that affect throughput of established applications.

—ISTQB_CTFL_PT

---

[3]Generic routing encapsulation (GRE) is a communication protocol used to establish a direct, point-to-point connection between network nodes (`www.incapsula.com/blog/what-is-gre-tunnel.html`).

Historically, the users of mainframe environments interfaced with these systems using a "dumb terminal." A dumb terminal is an input/output device with no processing resources available. It basically sends a request to the mainframe; the mainframe processes the request to derive a response which is then sent back to the dumb terminal. This principle has been moved forward to today with remote desktop emulation and applications such as Citrix mimicking this behavior. In both cases, the only things sent to the server are mouse movements, mouse clicks, and typing.

Mainframes are designed to handle a large volume of input and output data by including several subsidiary computers called channels or peripheral processes. This leaves the mainframe CPU free to deal only with high-speed data handling. Today, mainframe systems consist mainly of databases and files of considerable size, and their primary job is data handling.

It was typical to partition a mainframe to handle various tasks simultaneously. In this way, it is closely related to virtual machines sharing a limited resource pool.

Any mainframe system that still exists runs code written in legacy languages (e.g., COBOL). The mainframe may also run an old operating system which may be difficult to monitor with modern tools.

Summary   Legacy mainframe systems support mission-critical business functions in a data center (sometimes via batch processing) and are accessible today via APIs, web services, or through their database. Risks come from unexpected loads that affect throughput of applications.

Note that any particular application or system may incorporate two or more of the architectures listed above, which means that all relevant risks will apply to that application or system. In fact, given the Internet of Things and the explosion of mobile applications—two areas where extreme levels of interaction and connection is the rule—it is possible that all architectures are present in some form in an application, and thus all risks can apply.

—ISTQB_CTFL_PT

The preceding quote explains the issues today with performance testing. Because many of these environments can be combined into a larger system of systems, the relevant risks of all the constituent components will certainly apply. The combination of these risks could also create new risks not considered.

Summary   Systems of systems combine the risks from the individual constituent parts.

While architecture is clearly an important technical decision with a profound impact on performance risks, other technical decisions also influence and create risks. For example, memory leaks are more common with languages that allow direct heap memory management, such as C and C++, and performance issues are different for relational versus non-relational databases. Such decisions extend all the way down to the design of individual functions or methods (e.g., the choice of a recursive as opposed to an iterative algorithm). As a tester, the ability to know about or even influence such decisions will vary, depending on the roles and responsibilities of testers within the organization and software development lifecycle.

—ISTQB_CTFL_PT

Memory Leaks

memory leak

A memory access failure due to a defect in a program's dynamic store allocation logic that causes it to fail to release memory after it has finished using it.

—ISTQB Glossary

Memory leaks were a common problem, especially when computers had very little memory and developers fundamentally oversaw memory management. This problem today has been reduced with languages like Java having "garbage collection," or automatic memory management. Both C and C++ have no such built-in memory management. Systems built with these languages can still have memory leak problems.

Be warned however, memory leaks can still occur in Java. A Java object being referenced (but not used) wouldn't be removed by garbage collection and could allow multiple objects to be created, consuming memory.

Even with working garbage collection, issues can still occur. As it consumes resources, inefficient garbage collection can have effect on the overall performance, even stalling the system until the operation is complete. A primary choice relating to this is the frequency of garbage collection. If the garbage collectors were to come to your house every day, they wouldn't have much rubbish to take away, but you would need to put the bin out each night. If your garbage pickup was every two weeks, there would be a lot more rubbish, but you must only put the bins out once. Garbage collection from memory works the same. It can be done frequently, with lots of short stalls, or infrequently with much fewer long stalls. Garbage collection also requires more memory and is slower than explicit memory management.

Relational vs. Nonrelational Databases

Relational vs. nonrelational databases are a fascinating area, becoming more relevant in the "Age of Data" we are just entering. Basically put, the hint to defining these both is in the name:

- Relational DBs define a structure (tables, fields, and rows) into which the data is placed to allow it to be easily sorted, filtered, and combined ("joined") with other stored data. Think of a relational DB as a set of index cards stored within a filing cabinet. It allows data to be consistent, easily categorized, and navigated, with clearly defined relationships between elements.

- Nonrelational DBs don't have a clear structure to allow unorganized data to be stored. All the data is added into something much like a journal, into which people write their thoughts. There is a basic structure (dates or page numbers), with the journal getting longer and longer. If you need to find something, there's a rough index based on dates/page numbers; otherwise, you start reading at page one. This greater flexibility for changing datasets, with analysis being more dynamic.

Relational DBs are good for complex queries against a finite dataset. Nonrelational DBs are good for storing large amounts of nonstructured data for dynamic analysis. There is no defined performance standards for these, as there are too many variables (the size of the dataset, data read/writes per second, available bandwidth/machine resources/etc.). Suffice to say, data storage and retrieval can become a bottleneck in any system.

Recursive and Iterative Algorithms

Finally, the difference between recursive and iterative algorithms (and no, they're not quite the same – Figure 3-9). The main difference between recursion and iteration is a recursion is a process applied to a function. An iteration is a set of instructions which we want to get repeatedly executed:

- A recursive function calls itself until a control variable condition is met, leading to less code being executed, but possibly taking longer to run. Because the recursive functions are continuously called, it can put a performance overhead on this method.

- An iterative function loops until a condition is met, leading to more code executed, but that code being simpler.

Importantly, if there's an issue, infinite recursion can crash the system, while infinite iteration can consume resources.

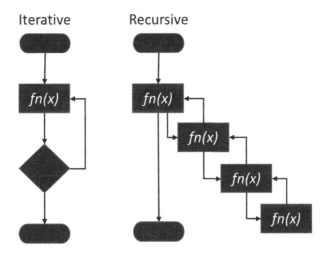

Figure 3-9. *Iterative vs. recursive algorithm*

Summary   More than architecture influences and creates risks, such as

- Memory leaks with languages that allow direct heap memory management (C and C++)

- Relational vs. nonrelational databases

- Recursive as opposed to an iterative algorithm

The ability to know about or even influence such decisions will vary, depending on the roles and responsibilities of performance engineers within the organization and development lifecycle.

3.3 Performance Risks Across the Software Development Lifecycle

PTFL-3.3.1 (K4) Analyze performance risks for a given product across the software development lifecycle

> *The process of analyzing risks to the quality of a software product in general is discussed in various ISTQB syllabi (e.g., see [ISTQB_FL_SYL] and [ISTQB_ALTM_SYL]). You can also find discussions of specific risks and considerations associated with particular quality characteristics (e.g., [ISTQB_UT_SYL]), and from a business or technical perspective (e.g., see [ISTQB_ALTA_SYL] and [ISTQB_ALTTA_SYL], respectively). In this section, the focus is on performance-related risks to product quality, including ways that the process, the participants, and the considerations change.*
>
> —ISTQB_CTFL_PT

risk

> *a factor that could result in future negative consequences*
>
> —ISTQB Glossary

> *the combination of the probability of an event and its consequence*
>
> —ISO 16085

> *the effect of uncertainty on objectives*
>
> —ISO Guide 73

Today, there exist many definitions for risk. The preceding definitions each look at an aspect that should be considered:

1. The glossary definition includes important components on the definition of risk – probability (*"could" result*) and impact (*future negative consequences*). When assessing risks, an area of concern is determining accurate levels for both probability and impact (more on this shortly).

2. The ISO 16085 definition covers an important point about defining risk. One of the major problems with risk is very similar to another favorite of performance engineers – defining non-functional requirements. Both suffer from similar issues in that they can both be poorly defined. As this definition comes from an ISO standard, there are some notes that accompany this definition:

    a. The term "risk" is generally used only when there is at least the possibility of negative consequences.

    b. In some situations, risk arises from the possibility of deviation from the expected outcome or event.

3. This ISO guide tries to unify the many definitions around risk. Accordingly, there are several notes that accompany this definition:

    a. An effect is a deviation from the expected – positive and/or negative.

    b. Objectives can have different aspects (such as financial, health and safety, and environmental goals) and can apply at different levels (such as strategic, organization-wide project, product, and process).

    c. Risk is often characterized by reference to potential events and consequences, or a combination of these.

d. Risk is often expressed in terms of a combination of the consequences of an event (including changes in circumstances) and the associated likelihood of occurrence.

e. Uncertainty is the state, even partial, of deficiency of information relating to understanding or knowledge of an event, its consequence, or likelihood.

We should also consider the relationship between the different risk categories (Figure 3-10).

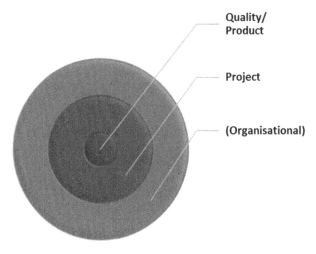

Figure 3-10. *Risk relationship model*

quality risk

a product risk related to a quality characteristic

project risk

a risk that impacts project success

—ISTQB Glossary

Although not included in the glossary, organizational risk relates to the damage to an organization's reputation and profitability.

The relationship between each of these risk categories can be both simple and complex. There is a defined relationship between quality, project, and organizational risk. No risk exists in a vacuum. A mistake people often make is to consider a risk as a single entity. Risks exist in the context of a larger cause-effect chain – one risk becoming a problem could indeed be triggering events for further risks to change probability.

The 2010 Deepwater Horizon explosion serves as a good example to consider each risk level and the relationship between them:

- At the product level, there were several failures (the safety history of the oil rig was poor), leading to an increased probability of a catastrophic accident.

- At the project level, because operations were already running five weeks late, the operators appear to have chosen riskier procedures to save time, even disregarding the safety advice of the rig staff and contractors.

- At the organizational level, the explosion led to the deaths of 11 people with 16 others injured. It went on to become the largest environmental disaster in US history, leaking an estimated 4.9 million barrels of oil into the Gulf of Mexico. The disaster cost BP $54 billion for the clean-up, environmental and economic damages, and penalties, along with BP pleading guilty to 11 criminal counts of manslaughter, two misdemeanors, and a felony count of lying to the US Congress. BP was also temporarily banned from contracts with the US government until March 2014.

This is a dramatic example of how both quality and project risks can have an effect at the organizational level.

Performance engineers, once again like non-functional requirements, need to know how to define a risk. Most risks (like non-functional requirements) are poorly defined. A correctly defined risk is made up of three parts (Figure 3-11):

Cause – A description of the source of the risk. The event or situation that gives rise to the risk

Event – A description of the area of uncertainty in terms of the threat or the opportunity

Effect/impact – A description of the impact that the risk would have on the organizational activity should the risk materialize

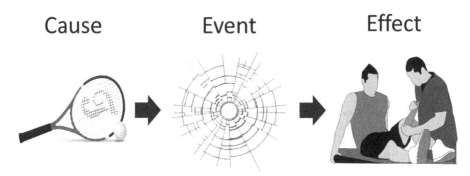

Figure 3-11. *Components of a well-defined risk*

For performance-related risks to the quality of the product, the process is:

1. *Identify risks to product quality, focusing on characteristics such as time behavior, resource utilization, and capacity.*

2. *Assess the identified risks, ensuring that the relevant architecture categories (see Section 3.2) are addressed. Evaluate the overall level of risk for each identified risk in terms of likelihood and impact using clearly defined criteria.*

3. *Take appropriate risk mitigation actions for each risk item based on the nature of the risk item and the level of risk.*

4. *Manage risks on an ongoing basis to ensure that the risks are adequately mitigated prior to release.*

—ISTQB_CTFL_PT

The process listed earlier is encompassed within risk management:

risk management

The coordinated activities to direct and control an organization with regards to risk.

—ISTQB Glossary

A continuous process for systematically identifying, analyzing, treating and monitoring risk throughout the lifecycle of a product or service.

—ISO 16085

Coordinated activities to direct and control an organization with regards to risk.

—ISO Guide 73

Once again, each of the three definitions deals with the slightly different version of risk management:

- ISTQB emphasizes coordinated activities – risk management is like any other process. It doesn't just happen but needs to be formalized.

- ISO 16085 looks at risk management as a continuous process, additionally mentioning monitoring – a forgotten but important risk management component.

- ISO Guide 73 describes risk management as an organization-wide process.

Risk management is a combination of all three definitions.

risk analysis

The overall process of risk identification and risk assessment.

—ISTQB Glossary

risk identification

The process of finding, recognizing and describing risks.

—ISTQB Glossary

By calling on a broad sample of stakeholders, the risk identification process is most likely to identify risks. A range of techniques exist for identifying risk, broadly grouped in techniques that "look backward" (a risk checklist), identifying historic risks that could occur, and "look forward" (a brainstorming exercise) to identify new, undiscovered risks. As mentioned earlier, these identified risks must consist of cause/event/effect. Countless times on projects, there is a risk in the risk register that states

There is a risk the project could run late.

The format to follow to define the risk:

There is a risk that [the cause] which could cause [the event] leading to [the effect].

The risk above (the project running late) is not a risk based on the risk format. It could be the effect of a risk, or it could be the event. It certainly isn't the cause and isn't all three. The cause is the important, as this is the focus to attempt to mitigate the risk. The first question to ask would be what event could lead the project to run late? There might be many events:

- The test environment failed the environment acceptance test.

- A third-party supplier delayed delivery of code.

- Performance requirements were not quantifiable.

- The performance tool was incompatible with the new system.

Following that, if we take the event of the test environment failing the acceptance test, what could cause this? It might be:

- The specification for the environment wasn't defined.

- The required hardware wasn't available in time.

- The specification was defined but not followed.

- The person tasked with preparing the environment went on extended sick leave.

Each of these could then be a separate project risk, one of which is:

There is a risk that the test environment specification isn't defined which could cause the test environment to fail the environment acceptance test, leading to the project running late.

Risk identification is complete once the risks have been properly identified and defined. It must be stressed that risks identified may be a mix at this point and may not relate to performance. But this nonperformance risk should not be discarded, as it still could be a risk to the project.

risk assessment

The process to examine identified risks and determine the risk level.
risk level

The qualitative or quantitative measure of a risk defined by impact and likelihood.

—ISTQB Glossary

The next step is to categorize the identified risks in our case into performance and nonperformance risks (as nonperformance risks should be out of scope). These could then be further categorized into quality (product), project, and organizational risks. Examples of each of these:

- Quality (product) – There is a risk that hard disk IO delays could cause business process delays leading to data processing transaction failure.

- Project – There is a risk that the performance test environment specification isn't defined which could cause environment acceptance test failure leading to a project delay.

- Organizational – There is a risk that performance failure due to a load spike after go-live could cause a system failure leading to a regulatory fine.

Notice that with the quality risk the mitigation would be running a performance test to check the hard disk IO. The project risk would require steps taken to ensure the test environment specification is written to allow the performance test environment to be built to specification. The simple view on both risks is to return to the time-cost-quality-scope-risk diagram. The quality risk looks at the quality corner and can be mitigated with testing. The project risk considers the time-cost part – it could take longer or cost more if any risk becomes an issue. Scope can also affect this relationship – the more things against which we need to consider quality, the more time and money (project risk) it might take. And, of course, the more overall risk we are faced with (both quality and project), the higher the overall organizational risk the organization might face.

The organizational risk is interesting, in that conducting spike testing could mitigate the quality risk of a performance failure due to a load spike but could also reduce the cost of a fine were this risk to become an issue. This is also a good example of how risks do not exist in a vacuum. The organizational risk links back to quality risks relating to a spike in load. Often, a risk becoming an issue could become the triggering event for the probability of other risks becoming an issue changing.

Next is to determine the risk level. The risk level is a product of both the impact (how bad the risk will be if it becomes an issue) and the probability (how likely is this risk to become an issue). One of the biggest problems with risk assessment is the qualitative perception of risk that stakeholders tend to rely on over the recorded facts.

We don't see things as they are, we see them as we are....

—Anais Nin

As the quote says, people tend to see things based on our own perception rather than on objective data (whether it is available or not). Of course, the illustration shows a person holding the sun. We know the person isn't really holding it, but the perception we have can show otherwise! It is interesting to consider the relationship between actual risk which could have an adverse effect on an organization and the perception of risk. Different individuals will have different perceptions of risk, just as will different teams, departments, and even organizations.

On this, Bruce Schneier wrote:

We over-react to intentional actions, and under-react to accidents, abstract events, and natural phenomena (if two aircraft had been hit by lightning and crashed into a New York skyscraper, few of us would be able to name the date on which it happened)

We over-react to things that offend our morals (moral emotions are the brain's call to action).

We over-react to immediate threats and under-react to long-term threats.

We under-react to changes that occur slowly and over time.

—schneier.com, 2008

The main consideration is the difference between qualitative and quantitative assessment.

Quantitative (Actual)	Qualitative (Perceived)
Impact and likelihood are calculated from **known facts**	Impact and likelihood are assigned using **subjective judgment**
Can be accurately replicated	Cannot be accurately replicated

The preference would be to use quantitative analysis. Unfortunately, the facts required to perform quantitative analysis are rarely available.

Therefore, performance engineers are forced to use qualitative assessment. If this is the case, it's a good idea to involve a range of different knowledgeable stakeholders to help assess the risk. Even relying on subjective judgment, an attempt should be made to conduct the assessment as "objectively" as possible. When quantitative assessments of risk levels are used inappropriately, the results mislead the stakeholders about the extent to which one understands and can manage risk. This is a dangerous area as so much risk assessment is done relying on qualitative assessment to conduct the assessment (recall inductive reasoning from earlier). Stakeholders will guess both the probability and impact of a particular risk. It's much better to try and be quantitative – basing the probability and impact on known calculable values. Unfortunately, no risk assessment can be 100% quantitative, so the challenge will be to make risk assessment as quantitative as possible. An excellent standard from the US National Institute of Standards and Technology (NIST) Special Publication 800-30 Revision 1 "*Guide for Conducting Risk Assessments*" gives a great outline of risk assessment. Although the standard was written for information security, the method can be applied to any risk assessment. This standard is available for free online at `https://nvlpubs.nist.gov/nistpubs/Legacy/SP/nistspecialpublication800-30r1.pdf`.

To determine the quantitative value associated with both the likelihood and impact, objective criteria must be defined. For example, an individual might score the impact from 1 to 5 (1 the lowest, 5 the highest). But how can it be decided what a "3" is?

Impact criteria might relate to the cost of the loss if the risk becomes an issue. For an example, see Table 3-7.

Table 3-7. *Impact Criteria – Cost of Loss*

Impact Value	Cost of Loss
1	$1–10,000
2	$10,001–100,000
3	$100,001–1,000,000
4	$1,000,001–10,000,000'
5	$10,000,001+

More than one single criterion should be used. This could be combined with the number of customers affected (Table 3-8).

Table 3-8. *Impact Criteria – Customer Exposure*

Impact Value	Customer Exposure
1	No exposure
2	<5%
3	5–10%
4	11–24%
5	25%+

The overall risk impact could then be the average of the combined criteria impact values.

NIST has a well-structured methodology for assessing both the impact and likelihood. From NIST Publication 800-30, the following tables for the risk likelihood are used.

Table 3-9. *Probability Criteria*

Qualitative Values	Semi-qualitative Values		Description – If the Threat Event Is Initiated or Occurs
Very high	96–100	5	It is **almost certain** to have adverse impacts
High	80–95	4	It is **highly likely** to have adverse impacts
Moderate	21–79	3	It is **somewhat likely** to have adverse impacts
Low	5–20	2	It is **unlikely** to have adverse impacts
Very low	0–4	1	It is **highly unlikely** to have adverse impacts

Although not quite appropriate, the table shows how probability levels could be calculated. The risk level can be determined using a risk matrix (Table 3-10).

Table 3-10. *Risk Matrix*

Risk Matrix

		Risk Likelihood				
		1	2	3	4	5
Risk Impact	5	Medium	High	High	Critical	Critical
	4	Medium	Medium	High	High	Critical
	3	Low	Medium	Medium	High	High
	2	Low	Low	Medium	Medium	High
	1	Low	Low	Low	Medium	Medium

Once the risk has been categorized and assessed, mitigation is the next step.

risk mitigation

The process through which decisions are reached and protective measures are implemented for reducing or maintaining risks to specified levels.

—ISTQB Glossary

Risk management differs depending on the type of risk. Mitigation for quality risk involves testing, whereas project risk requires management to make decisions regarding the time, cost, or scope of the performance project.

Mitigation will lower either the probability, the impact, or maybe both. The question that remains is by how much was the risk probability and/or impact reduced by the mitigation steps. There can be three factors to consider:

1. **Was the original risk mitigated?** Occasionally, mitigation steps are put in place that mitigate risk, but not the identified risk. A good example is a warning sign. The sign may not be effective in discouraging risky behavior, and people might continue doing things they are warned about. In most cases, however, the sign is more to protect the organization or person posting the sign from liability.

2. **Could mitigation introduce new risks?** Occasionally, the mitigation selected can introduce new risks. For example, if a decision is made to run more performance test than initially planned, it could introduce a new risk regarding more testing taking longer and increasing the probability of the project running late.

3. **Is the mitigation effective?** Even putting mitigation into place may only reduce the original risk probability and/or impact by a small amount. The misnomer for some stakeholders is that the risk will be removed once mitigated. The task of mitigation is to reduce the risk level to the risk appetite defined for this risk.

risk appetite

The amount of risk the organization, or subset of it, is willing to accept.

—M_o_R

To reduce the risk to zero for a quality risk, exhaustive testing would be required. Exhaustive testing, as per Principle 2 of the general testing principles, is impossible.

Summary   Identify risks to product quality. Assess the identified risks, and evaluate the overall level of risk for each identified risk in terms of likelihood and impact using clearly defined criteria. Take risk mitigation actions for each risk based on the nature of the level of risk. Manage risks on an ongoing iterative basis.

As with quality risk analysis in general, the participants in this process should include both business and technical stakeholders. For performance-related risk analysis the business stakeholders must include those with a particular awareness of how performance problems in production will actually affect customers, users, the business, and other downstream stakeholders. Business stakeholders must appreciate that intended usage, business-, societal-, or safety-criticality, potential financial and/or reputational damage, civil or criminal legal liability and similar factors affect risk from a business perspective, creating risks and influencing the impact of failures.

—ISTQB_CTFL_PT

An interesting point between both the technical and business stakeholders is their joint understanding of a risk, but from different points of view. The technical stakeholders are better placed to determine on the probability of a performance risk – the probability of the system not achieving the desired performance goals. The business stakeholders are better to determine the impact, whether this be in lost productivity or lost revenue, if the risk becomes an issue in production.

Summary Both business and technical stakeholders should be involved in risk management. Business stakeholders must understand risk factors to the business processes such as intended usage; business, societal, or safety criticality; potential financial and/or reputational damage; and civil or criminal legal liability can affect risk.

Further, the technical stakeholders must include those with a deep understanding of the performance implications of relevant requirements, architecture, design, and implementation decisions. Technical stakeholders must appreciate that architecture, design, and implementation decisions affect performance risks from a technical perspective, creating risks and influencing the likelihood of defects.

—ISTQB_CTFL_PT

The technical definition of the system was covered previously in Chapter 3.1 (technical overview/requirements definition/volumetric analysis/environment analysis and specification/test data planning).

Summary   Technical stakeholders must understand the requirements, architecture, design, and implementation decisions of the system and that they can affect risk.

The specific risk analysis process chosen should have the appropriate level of formality and rigor.

—ISTQB_CTFL_PT

The process can be drawn from international or national standards (such as NIST SP 800-37 or ISO 16085), industry standards (PCI DSS[4] or DO-178C/ED-12C[5]), or the organization's internal standards. These can be mandatory regulatory processes (DO178C, for example) or optional (ISO 16085) depending on the requirements of the organization, the legal jurisdiction, and the project.

Summary   Risk management should have the relevant formality.

For performance-related risks, it is especially important that the risk analysis process be started early and is repeated regularly. In other words, the tester should avoid relying entirely on performance testing conducted towards the end of the system test level and system integration test level. Many projects, especially larger and more complex systems of systems projects, have met with unfortunate surprises due to the late discovery of performance defects which resulted from requirements, design, architecture, and implementation decisions made early in the project. The emphasis should therefore be on an iterative approach to performance risk identification, assessment, mitigation, and management throughout the software development lifecycle.

—ISTQB_CTFL_PT

---

[4]The Payment Card Industry Data Security Standard (PCI DSS) is an information security standard for organizations handling credit cards from the major card schemes.

[5]DO-178C/ED-12C – Software Considerations in Airborne Systems and Equipment Certification is the primary document by which certification authorities such as the US FAA, the European EASA, and Transport Canada approve all commercial software-based aerospace systems.

The two keywords mentioned earlier are **early** and **continuous**. Risk management begins on day one of any project and continues until the system is finally decommissioned, never to be used again. The principle of *Performance by Design* should be adhered to, meaning performance engineering (and the associated risks) should be the goal throughout the system life span.

Summary   Risk management should be iterative throughout the software development lifecycle project.

For example, if large volumes of data will be handled via a relational data-base, the slow performance of many-to-many joins due to poor database design may only reveal itself during dynamic testing with large-scale test datasets, such as those used during system test. However, a careful technical review that includes experienced database engineers can predict the problems prior to database implementation. After such a review, in an iterative approach, risks are identified and assessed again.

—ISTQB_CTFL_PT

The above is a good example, as it starts to demonstrate a move from performance testing to performance engineering. Something that's been made popular by such problems as data security and privacy is the "by design" concept. Often, people believe performance can be "tested" into a system. Certainly, when the organization starts performance testing, this will be the case. But this will be limited in scope and can only remediate known defects. As performance data is built up over time, performance engineers can give more information on the various bottlenecks and issues the organization may have and allow these to be designed out of the system.

Summary   Iterative risk management will regularly conduct risk analysis.

In addition, risk mitigation and management must span and influence the entire software development process, not just dynamic testing. For example, when critical performance-related decisions such as the expected number of transactions or simultaneous users cannot be specified early in the project,

*it is important that design and architecture decisions allow for highly vari-
able scalability (e.g., on-demand cloud-based computing resources). This
enables early risk mitigation decisions to be made.*

—ISTQB_CTFL_PT

Techniques such as FMEA[6] can be an important method for removing performance
quality risks early in the lifecycle, aligning with the *Performance by Design* principle.

Summary   Iterative risk management starts at the beginning of any project.

---

*Good performance engineering can help project teams avoid the late dis-
covery of critical performance defects during higher test levels, such as system integration testing or user acceptance testing. Performance defects
found at a late stage in the project can be extremely costly and may even
lead to the cancellation of entire projects.*

—ISTQB_CTFL_PT

In 2004, Stecklein et al. wrote the paper "Error Cost Escalation Through the Project Life
Cycle" looking at the error cost escalation. Although not directly related to performance
(the paper covered both hardware and software errors), the results are telling:

*The results show the degree to which costs escalate, as errors are discovered
and fixed at later and later phases in the project life cycle. If the cost of fixing
a requirements error discovered during the requirements phase is defined
to be 1 unit, the cost to fix that error if found during the design phase
increases to 3 — 8 units; at the manufacturing/build phase, the cost to fix
the error is 7 — 16 units; at the integration and test phase, the cost to fix the
error becomes 21 — 78 units; and at the operations phase, the cost to fix the
requirements error ranged from 29 units to more than 1500 units.*

—Stecklein et al., 2004

---

[6]Failure mode and effect analysis (FMEA) is a proactive method developed to identify, evaluate,
and prevent product and/or process failures early in the design stage, to design risk out of a
system.

178

Summary   Performance defects identified late can be more expensive than defects found earlier.

> *As with any type of quality risk, performance-related risks can never be avoided completely, i.e., some risk of performance-related production failure will always exist. Therefore, the risk management process must include providing a realistic and specific evaluation of the residual level of risk to the business and technical stakeholders involved in the process. For example, simply saying, "Yes, it's still possible for customers to experience long delays during check out," is not helpful, as it gives no idea of what amount of risk mitigation has occurred or of the level of risk that remains. Instead, providing clear insight into the percentage of customers likely to experience delays equal to or exceeding certain thresholds will help people understand the status.*

> *—ISTQB_CTFL_PT*

In accordance with the definition supplied by ISO Guide 73, the relationships between the risk level, risk tolerance, and risk appetite (Figure 3-12) are:

- The risk level faced by many organizations is usually distributed over a wide continuum – simplified in this instance from low to high risk levels.

- The risk tolerance specifies the level of risk the organization is aiming to reduce the risk level of the identified performance risk either to or below.

- The risk appetite is the range of risk that the organization is targeting with mitigation to reduce the risk level of each.

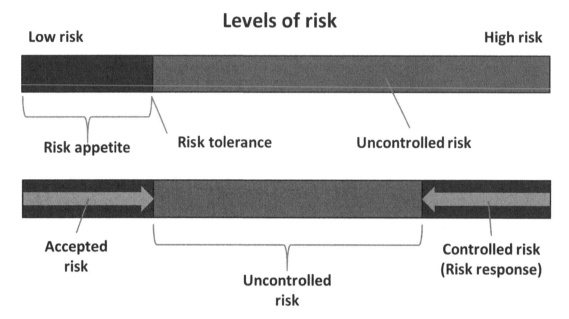

Figure 3-12. *Risk terminology*

The diagram represents the ideal – all risks above the risk tolerance are targeted. As testing is performed, the mitigated risk lowers the level of quality risk. Sometimes, the tolerance may not be achieved, and a decision would need to be made on whether the tolerance should be raised or time/cost extended to allow more quality risk mitigation (i.e., testing) to continue. An easy way to remember this relationship is:

- Risk level is a measure.
- Risk tolerance is a threshold.
- Risk appetite is a range.

risk appetite

> *The amount of risk the organization, or subset of it, is willing to accept.*
>
> —M_o_R

risk tolerance

> *The threshold levels of risk exposure that, with appropriate approvals, can be exceeded, but which when exceeded, will trigger some form of response (e.g. reporting the situation to senior management for action).*
>
> —M_o_R

The final point to note is this risk model defines that acceptable risk is not zero risk. Zero risk is unachievable, as it falls into the realm of exhaustive testing. There will always be some residual risk even after the risk has been mitigated. But because the residual risk is below the risk tolerance, it has been accepted by the organization.

Summary   Performance risk cannot be eliminated. Accurate, quantified risk levels should be reported to stakeholders to enable them to make informed decisions.

3.4 Performance Testing Activities

PTFL-3.4.1 (K4) Analyze a given project to determine the appropriate performance testing activities for each phase of the software development lifecycle

> *Performance testing activities will be organized and performed differently, depending on the type of software development lifecycle in use.*
>
> —ISTQB_CTFL_PT

Performance testing activities will be organized and performed differently depending on the type of software lifecycle in use.

Sequential Development Models

> *The ideal practice of performance testing in sequential development models is to include performance criteria as a part of the acceptance criteria which are defined at the outset of a project. Reinforcing the lifecycle view of testing, performance testing activities should be conducted throughout the software development lifecycle. As the project progresses, each successive performance test activity should be based on items defined in the prior activities as shown below.*
>
> —ISTQB_CTFL_PT

Sequential methodologies are less used today as organizations select agile-based methodologies. It doesn't mean these sequential methodologies will never be used however. To refresh your memory (especially if you've never worked in a non-agile-based project), the V-model is covered in Figure 3-13.

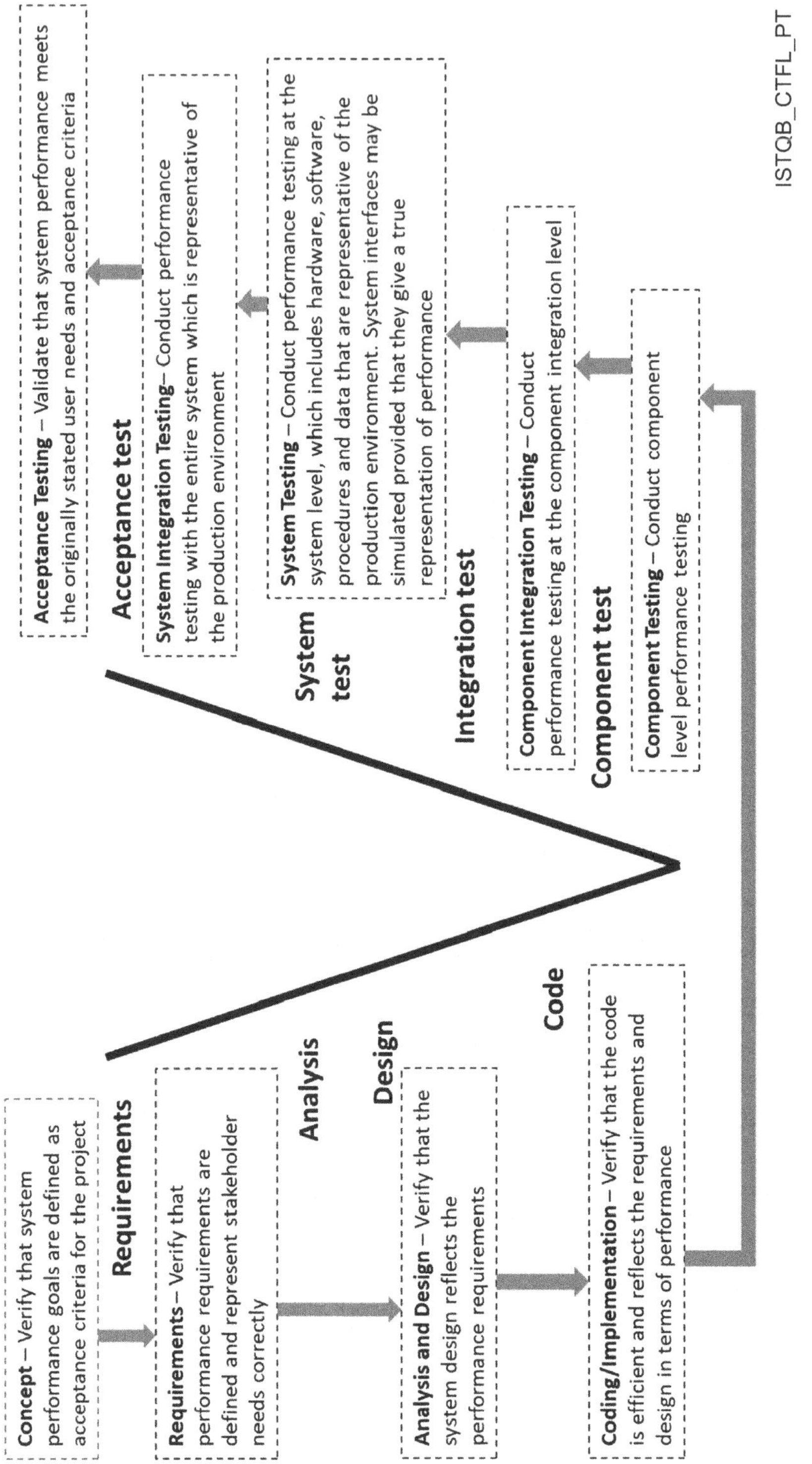

Figure 3-13. V-model development methodology

Summary   Performance criteria should be included as part of the acceptance criteria and should be included throughout sequential methodology–based projects.

Iterative and Incremental Development Models

In these development models, such as Agile, performance testing is also seen as an iterative and incremental activity (see [ISTQB_FL_AT]). Performance testing can occur as part of the first iteration, or as an iteration dedicated entirely to performance testing. However, with these lifecycle models, the execution of performance testing may be performed by a separate team tasked with performance testing.

—ISTQB_CTFL_PT

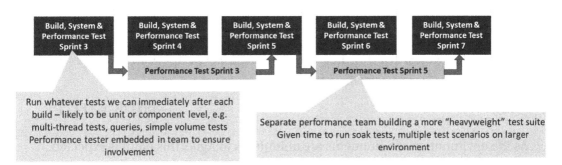

Figure 3-14. *Iterative/incremental sprint–based development methodology*

Performance testing within the iterative/incremental methodologies is interesting (Figure 3-14). It's important to note a full end-to-end performance test in almost all situations cannot be created and executed within the sprint due to a lack of time (most sprints are two weeks in length). The trade-off tends to be new features encoded are performance tested, and a limited amount of regression testing can be done within the sprint. Larger end-to-end performance tests are normally conducted outside of the sprint on a fixed snapshot of the code. Any information gathered at the end of this run is then fed back into a subsequent sprint for defect repair, refactoring, and/or development process improvement.

Summary   Performance criteria should be included as part of the acceptance criteria and should be included throughout iterative and incremental methodology–based projects. Performance testing may consist of small tests within the sprint and larger end-to-end tests run outside the sprints.

The following list from the syllabus (the bulleted list inside the syllabus references) includes sections added to the syllabus points:

Continuous Integration (CI) is commonly performed in iterative and incremental software development lifecycles, which facilitates a highly automated execution of tests. The most common objective of testing in CI is to perform regression testing and ensure each build is stable. Performance testing can be part of the automated tests performed in CI if the tests are designed in such a way as to be executed at a build level. However, unlike functional automated tests, there are additional concerns such as the following:

- *The setup of the performance test environment – This often requires a test environment that is available on demand, such as a cloud-based performance test environment.*

—ISTQB_CTFL_PT

As the environment requirements are ubiquitous to Agile, this point is expected. Of course, in earlier sprints the code base may not be adequate to create a full end-to-end performance test, hence end-to-end testing happens later. But it could be (and is actually happening more and more) a performance testing requirement that each component is tested to a production-like level.

Summary   CI relies on automated regression test execution as part of the iterative development. Test environments need to be available on demand for execution.

- *Determining which performance tests to automate in CI – Due to the short timeframe available for CI tests, CI performance tests may be a subset of more extensive performance tests that are conducted by a specialist team at other times during an iteration.*

—ISTQB_CTFL_PT

Risk and user story prioritization can help with this decision.

Summary   Prioritizing performance tests to automate are a subset due to limited execution time.

- *Creating the performance tests for CI – The main objective of performance tests as part of CI is to ensure a change does not negatively impact performance. Depending on the changes made for any given build, new performance tests may be required.*

—ISTQB_CTFL_PT

regression testing

A type of change-related testing to detect whether defects have been introduced or uncovered in unchanged areas of the software.

—ISTQB Glossary

A great deal of testing in Agile is predicated on regression testing. Sometimes (and often mistakenly) functional testing is the basis for regression. It must be noted that ALL test types – including performance testing – must be considered when establishing a regression test suite.

Summary   CI performance tests mainly check regression, with tests created for new features.

Executing performance tests on portions of an application or system – This often requires the tools and test environments to be capable of rapid performance testing including the ability to select subsets of applicable tests.

—ISTQB_CTFL_PT

This can be a major limiting factor for many CI/CD environments. Often, the tool isn't the issue, but the way the performance test scripts are created. Programming disciplines like modularization can help mitigate this. As well, returning to the business process model, breaking the scripts into the business process/task/step model can also be useful in modularizing the script.

Summary   CI performance tests are often executed on a subset of the system.

Although the test process is similar, Agile does not change things. As mentioned, test environments are needed much earlier, and regression testing is a continuous activity. It is usually a question not of what is needed with Agile, but when will it be needed.

The answer is it's usually needed early!

CI/CD processes rely on Agile-based methodologies as shown in Figure 3-15.

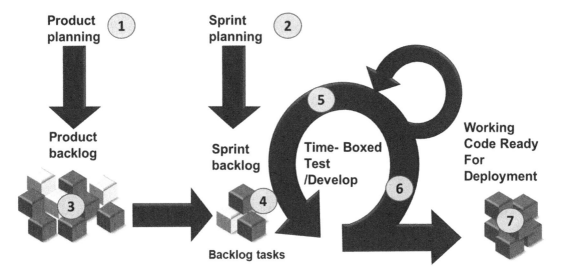

Figure 3-15. *Iterative/incremental sprint–based development methodology*

Performance testing in the iterative and incremental software development lifecycles can also have its own lifecycle activities:

1. **Release Planning** *–In this activity, performance testing is considered from the perspective of all iterations in a release, from the first iteration to the final iteration. Performance risks are identified and assessed, and mitigation measures planned. This often includes planning of any final performance testing before the release of the application.*

2. **Iteration Planning** *– In the context of each iteration, performance testing may be performed within the iteration and as each iteration is completed. Performance risks are assessed in more detail for each user story.*

3. **User Story Creation** – *User stories often form the basis of performance requirements in Agile methodologies, with the specific performance criteria described in the associated acceptance criteria. These are referred to as "non-functional" user stories.*

4. **Design of Performance Tests** – *performance requirements and criteria which are described in particular user stories are used for the design of tests (see section 4.2)*

5. **Coding/Implementation** – *During coding, performance testing may be performed at a component level. An example of this would be the tuning of algorithms for optimum performance efficiency.*

6. **Testing/Evaluation** – *While testing is typically performed in close proximity to development activities, performance testing may be performed as a separate activity, depending on the scope and objectives of performance testing during the iteration. For example, if the goal of performance testing is to test the performance of the iteration as a completed set of user stories, a wider scope of performance testing will be needed than that seen in performance testing a single user story. This may be scheduled in a dedicated iteration for performance testing.*

7. **Delivery** – *Since delivery will introduce the application to the production environment, performance will need to be monitored to determine if the application achieves the desired levels of performance in actual usage.*

—ISTQB_CTFL_PT

Although this breakdown looks different from the earlier diagram for sequential methodologies, the actual activities performance testers complete are similar. The biggest difference between the two is WHEN these activities are done within the iterative/incremental methodologies and how often these are done.

Summary   Iterative and incremental methodologies have the following lifecycle activities:

1. Release Planning   3. User Story Creation   5. Coding/Implementation   7. Delivery

2. Iteration Planning   4. Design of Performance Tests 6. Testing/Evaluation

Commercial Off-the-Shelf (COTS) and Other Supplier/Acquirer Models

Many organizations do not develop applications and systems themselves, but instead are in the position of acquiring software from vendor sources or from open-source projects. In such supplier/acquirer models, performance is an important consideration that requires testing from both the supplier (vendor/developer) and acquirer (customer) perspectives.

—ISTQB_CTFL_PT

This creates an interesting paradigm. Many reasons exist for a system performing poorly. A system could perform poorly due to architectural issues or code bottlenecks. Irrelevant of the environment the system is installed upon, these issues will exist. A system with good performance however could be installed onto an environment inadequate for the resource demand the system needs. And, not to point fingers at software vendors, the customer must realize the vendor may be reluctant to speak about poor performance...

Summary   Built software (COTS/open source) acquisition is typical, with the need for performance test from both the vendor and acquirer.

Regardless of the source of the application, it is often the responsibility of the customer to validate that the performance meets their requirements. In the case of customized vendor-developed software, performance requirements and associated acceptance criteria which should be specified as part of the contract between the vendor and customer. In the case of COTS applications, the customer has sole responsibility to test the performance of the product in a realistic test environment prior to deployment.

—ISTQB_CTFL_PT

Hence, the requirement that the customer tests the product in a realistic test environment. It could be required that some performance criteria be added to the requirements list when purchasing software.

It may not always be the vendor's fault. The author has had experience when working as a consultant performance engineer; both the vendor and the customer were blaming each other for failed performance.

The vendor blamed the poor client infrastructure for the performance issues.

The customer blamed the inefficient server client communication being used.

 "This is indeed a mystery", I remarked. "What do you imagine that it means?"

"I have no data yet. It is a capital mistake to theorize before one has data. Insensibly one begins to twist facts to suit theories instead of theories to suit facts…"

—Conan Doyle, 1892sb

It was an interesting job, as both the vendor and client had a very limited dataset to prove that they were correct. Both were twisting the data to suit their own theory. After performance testing, it was proved that both were correct in this case – both the inefficient protocol (taking more bandwidth than was stated) and the poor infrastructure (a limited WAN network with high latency) were to blame.

Another complication today is systems supplied as Software as a Service (SaaS). There are challenges for multitenant systems (and indeed single tenant) as the acquirer has little control over the infrastructure the system runs on or the code versions and upgrade/change control managed by the vendor. The vendor may give broad performance SLAs, but these are often from production experience or testing a vanilla version and not the real version the customer is using. In this case, custom configuration to the customer's needs (and therefore changing the system characteristics from vanilla) or even adding customizations and integrations. Access to test systems are also an issue as they are hard to recreate, and the customer testing in production is usually impractical and even contractually banned by the vendor.

Summary   COTS – The acquirer is responsible for performance testing in a realistic environment to check it meets the performance acceptance requirements.

Customized, vendor-developed –The acquirer tests to accept the product; the vendor can also be contracted to provide performance requirement data.

Chapter 3 Questions

1. When applying the principal performance testing activities, when should defining the scope occur?

   A. Test planning, monitoring, and control

   B. Test analysis and design

   C. Test implementation and execution

   D. Test closure

2. When applying the principal performance testing activities, when should performance test cases be assembled into performance test procedures?

   A. Test planning, monitoring, and control

   B. Test analysis and design

   C. Test implementation and execution

   D. Test closure

3. When applying the principal performance testing activities, when should analysis of test objectives, SLAs, IT architecture, process models, and other items that comprise the test basis occur?

   A. Test planning, monitoring, and control

   B. Test analysis and design

   C. Test implementation and execution

   D. Test closure

4. When applying the principal performance testing activities, when should action plans be provided in case issues be encountered?

    A. Test planning, monitoring, and control

    B. Test analysis and design

    C. Test implementation and execution

    D. Test closure

5. When applying the principal performance testing activities, when should results be expressed through metrics which are often aggregated to simplify the meaning of the results?

    A. Test planning, monitoring, and control

    B. Test analysis and design

    C. Test implementation and execution

    D. Test closure

6. When applying the principal performance testing activities, when should performance test cases be devised?

    A. Test planning, monitoring, and control

    B. Test analysis and design

    C. Test implementation and execution

    D. Test closure

7. Consider the following technical environments:

1. Single computer	4. Virtualized	7. Mobile
2. Multi-tier system	5. Dynamic/cloud-based	8. Embedded
3. Distributed	6. Client/server and browser-based	9. Mainframe

Which of these is likely to have a performance risk due to excessive resource consumption?

    A. 1

    B. 1,2,3,6,7

    C.   1,2,4,5,6,7,8,9

    D.   1,2,3,4,5,6,7,8,9

8. Which of these is most likely to cause a performance risk due to a by-product of using a development language which allows direct heap management?

    A.   Memory leak

    B.   Stack overflow

    C.   Garbage collection

    D.   Increased CPU utilization

9. A company is changing the data it collects on customers to include statistical information on racial and/or ethnic origin and trade union membership and, to improve security, biometric data. As this company has operations in Europe, the General Data Protection Regulations will apply to this data. Furthermore, this data falls into the special category data (personal data that needs more protection because of its sensitive nature). Which of the following performance test product risk characteristics should NOT apply when identifying risks?

    A.   Time behavior

    B.   Capacity

    C.   Performance risk impact

    D.   Resource utilization

10. A company is reengineering an in-house system to move into a cloud environment. A product risk was identified relating to systems running in a cloud environment not performing to the expected level. Stakeholders are unsure the system will perform with an adequate response time. The first development iteration is about to begin – what steps could be conducted to help reduce the risk?

A. Test from the UI with the full dataset loaded to ensure the response time will be adequate when the full API set has been migrated to the cloud.

B. Conduct a network assessment to ensure there are no latency or bandwidth issues between the cloud environment and the client machines.

C. Test via the web services at the API level to ensure access to the data is fast enough without having the testing complicated by the UI.

D. Conduct a technical review of the database implementation and conduct a performance test from the UI with the full dataset loaded.

11. A project stakeholder has contacted you to begin planning for the performance testing of a new project. You have a vague description of the system and business processes to be built, and the project is about to begin. The stakeholder has a template performance planning document but doesn't understand which SDLC will be used.

Release Planning	Performance Test Design	Performance Testing/
Sprint Planning	Coding/Implementation	Evaluation
User Story Creation		Delivery

Can you identify the SDLC?

A. Sequential

B. Test-driven development

C. Iterative/incremental

D. Commercial off the shelf

12. The following relate to key characteristics of performance testing in the listed software development methodologies:

i. Performance tests are automated to be run automatically with each build, focusing on regression testing the stability of each build.

ii. Performance testing can be conducted as small tests within each cycle, as well as larger, end-to-end performance tests outside the cycle.

    iii. As the project progresses, each successive performance test activity should be based on items defined in the prior activities to achieve the acceptance criteria developed at the project outset.

    iv. Acceptance testing is the test level performance testing is conducted, executed in a production-like environment by representatives of the end users.

Which of the following combination is correct?

A. (i) Sequential; (ii) CI; (iii) iterative/incremental; (iv) COTS

B. (i) CI; (ii) iterative/incremental; (iii) sequential; (iv) COTS

C. (i) Iterative/incremental; (ii) CI; (iii) COTS; (iv) sequential

D. (i) CI; (ii) COTS; (iii) iterative/incremental; (iv) sequential

CHAPTER 4

Performance Testing Tasks

ISTQB Keywords

concurrency

The simultaneous execution of multiple independent threads by a component or system.

load generation

The process of simulating a defined set of activities at a specified load to be submitted to a component or system.

load profile

Documentation defining a designated number of virtual users who process a defined set of transactions in a specified time period that a component or system being tested may experience in production.

operational profile

An actual or predicted pattern of use of the component or system.

ramp-down

A technique for decreasing the load on a system in a measurable and controlled way.

ramp-up

A technique for increasing the load on a system in a measurable and controlled way.

system of systems

Multiple heterogeneous, distributed systems that are embedded in networks at multiple levels and in multiple interconnected domains, addressing large-scale interdisciplinary common problems and purposes, usually without a common management structure.

© Keith Yorkston 2021
K. Yorkston, *Performance Testing*, https://doi.org/10.1007/978-1-4842-7255-8_4

system throughput

The amount of data passing through a component or system in a given time period.

test plan

Documentation describing the test objectives to be achieved and the means and the schedule for achieving them, organized to coordinate testing activities.

think time

The amount of time required by a user to determine and execute the next action in a sequence of actions.

virtual user

A simulation of activities performed according to a user operational profile.

4.1 Planning

Planning is an important part of the performance test process. Traditionally, it was often neglected or minimalized for the simple reason that the performance engineer "knew what they were doing...."

Today, the importance of planning is seen at the completion of the project. The performance testing process must work within the wider software development lifecycle, and the plan creates the "expected result" for the performance testing project, process, and tasks.

4.1.1 Deriving Performance Test Objectives

PTFL-4.1.1 (K4) Derive performance test objectives from relevant information

> *Stakeholders may include users and people with a business or technical background. They may have different objectives relating to performance testing. Stakeholders set the objectives, the terminology to be used and the criteria for determining whether the objective has been achieved.*
>
> —ISTQB_CTFL_PT

Stakeholders can be considered according to the following four categories:

- Internal stakeholders – An obvious definition to an internal stakeholder is someone internal to a project/department/ organization.

- External stakeholders – Users, third-party suppliers, or people outside of the "internal" stakeholder group.

- Neutral stakeholders – Auditors/regulators/law enforcement who are more interested in ensuring the organization "follows the rules."

- Anti-stakeholders – Rarely, some stakeholders want the project to fail (e.g., users of a legacy system being replaced, who could lose their job as a result).

The primary stakeholder groups performance engineers deal with are the internal and external stakeholders. It would be wrong to assume either business or technical knowledge in any stakeholder group. In fact, individuals could possess either or, in the rare occasion, both business and technical knowledge.

Summary   Stakeholders include technical and business backgrounds, each with different objectives, terminology, and acceptance criteria.

Objectives for performance tests relate back to these different types of stakeholders. It is a good practice to distinguish between user-based and technical objectives. User-based objectives focus primarily on end-user satisfaction and business goals. Generally, users are less concerned about feature types or how a product gets delivered. They just want to be able to do what they need to do.

—ISTQB_CTFL_PT

One of the main communication tasks for performance engineers is to act as a translator between business and technical stakeholders. A knowledgeable performance engineer can help convert business requirements into technical performance objectives. The communication goes back the other way, with the translation of technical details back to the business stakeholders.

Communication is an important skill for all performance engineers. One of the tasks required is to explain exactly what performance is. Stakeholders some of the time imagine that performance testing is purely stress testing – loading the system until failure. Or only focused on response time. It's the job of performance engineers to let stakeholders know the methodology, the tasks, and the analysis and interpretation of results.

Summary   Business stakeholders focus on user-based objectives (end-user satisfaction and business goals), allowing users to do what they need to do.

Technical objectives, on the other hand, focus on operational aspects and providing answers to questions regarding a system's ability to scale, or under what conditions degraded performance may become apparent.

—ISTQB_CTFL_PT

Once again, the need for an interpreter is evident. It does raise the point that to be a good interpreter a performance engineer can be great technically, but without a knowledge of the business, you're only halfway to the objective of becoming a great performance engineer.

The following list includes *[italics]* added to the syllabus points.

Summary   Technical stakeholders focus on operational aspects (resource utilization/capacity/scalability).

Key objectives of performance testing include identifying potential risks, finding opportunities for improvement, and identifying necessary changes.

When gathering information from the various stakeholders, the following questions should be answered:

- *What transactions will be executed in the performance test and what average response time is expected?* *[**Business**]*

- *What system metrics are to be captured (e.g., memory usage, network throughput) and what values are expected?* *[**Technical**]*

- *What performance improvements are expected from these tests compared to previous test cycles?* *[**Both**]*

—ISTQB_CTFL_PT

The preceding list is a generic (and very short) list of questions to ask. The "Art of Questioning" can be vital for performance engineers as many performance test objectives and even the types of performance test needed come from the questions the organization stakeholders ask. Especially when prompted by experience performance engineers. Clarification of stakeholder needs is a necessary skill. For example, a stakeholder might make the statement, "The system needs to be faster."

A good question a performance engineer might ask is, "Why?"

It can even be better (as found by Toyota) to ask why five times:

> *The basis of* Toyota*'s scientific approach is to ask why five times whenever we find a problem... By repeating why five times, the nature of the problem as well as its solution becomes clear.*[1]

Why does the system need to be faster? How much faster? If you require a 2-second response time, what would happen if the response time was 2.1 seconds?

That level of performance test translation (business to technical and technical to business) can help stakeholders understand the ramifications of objectives and more importantly the time and cost of achieving them. The system can always be faster, but it might be very expensive to achieve...

Summary   Key performance objectives include

- Identifying potential risks

- Identifying improvements and changes needed

- Business transactions and expected response times

- Technical system metrics and expected values

---

[1]5 Whys: The Ultimate Root Cause Analysis Tool – https://kanbanize.com/lean-management/improvement/5-whys-analysis-tool

4.1.2 The Performance Test Plan

PTFL-4.1.2 (K4) Outline a performance test plan which considers the performance objectives for a given project

> *The Performance Test Plan (PTP) is a document created prior to any performance testing occurring. The PTP should be referred to by the Test Plan (see [ISTQB_FL_SYL]) which also includes relevant scheduling information. It continues to be updated once performance testing begins.*
>
> —ISTQB_CTFL_PT

As a side note, the standard ISO29119-3 also has a slightly more comprehensive document hierarchy with the contents of test plans included. This standard speaks of two types of test plan – the higher-level project or master test plan and the subprocess test plan which the PTP falls under. It also has test plan examples for both sequential and iterative/incremental methodologies.

An important practical note is the size of the PTP. Performance engineers should try to limit the size of the PTP document to less than 30 pages. This is based on the premise that the larger the document, the fewer people are likely to read and understand it. If there is generic information repeated in the document taken from the glossaries (like the performance test type definitions) or the test strategy (like the PTP objectives), they can be cross-referenced rather than repeated ad nauseam.

Summary   The performance test plan is created prior to performance testing occurring, refers to the project test plan, and will be updated as needed during performance testing.

The following information should be supplied in a PTP.

Objective

> *The PTP objective describes the goals, strategies and methods for the performance test. It enables a quantifiable answer to the central question of the adequacy and the readiness of the system to perform under load.*
>
> —ISTQB_CTFL_PT

Note this information on strategies and methods can often be taken from the relevant test strategy. Often, a simple reference to the relevant strategy section will suffice, but it can be helpful to copy these into the PTP for easy reference.

Summary   Objectives describe the quantifiable goals, strategies, and methods.

Test Objectives

Overall test objectives for performance efficiency to be achieved by the System Under Test (SUT) are listed for each type of stakeholder (see Section 4.1.1).

—ISTQB_CTFL_PT

As mentioned previously, these performance test objectives must be quantifiable and clearly state under what load conditions the objective is to be achieved.

Summary   Test objectives describe the quantifiable system under test business and technical objectives.

System Overview

A brief description of the SUT will provide the context for the measurement of the performance test parameters. The overview should include a high-level description of the functionality being tested under load.

—ISTQB_CTFL_PT

As well as describing the functionality, a simple architecture diagram should also be included at this point – further details are included in the following System Configuration.

Summary   System overview includes the high-level functions and brief system description.

Types of Performance

The types of performance testing to be conducted are listed (see Section 1.2) along with a description of the purpose of each type.

—ISTQB_CTFL_PT

The purpose of the PTP is to create an "expected result" for the planned performance testing that can act to inform stakeholders. As mentioned earlier, this could be cross-referenced from the test strategy rather than repeated in the PTP. Not all types will be used in every performance test project, so only the relevant performance test types need be included.

Summary   Types to be tested (load/stress/scalability spike/endurance/concurrency/capacity).

Acceptance Criteria

Performance testing is intended to determine the responsiveness, through-put, reliability and/or scalability of the system under a given workload. In general, response time is a user concern, throughput is a business concern, and resource utilization is a system concern. Acceptance criteria should be set for all relevant measures and related back to the following as applicable:

- *Overall performance test objectives*

- *Service Level Agreements (SLAs)*

- *Baseline values – A baseline is a set of metrics used to compare current and previously achieved performance measurements. This enables particular performance improvements to be demonstrated and/or the achievement of test acceptance criteria to be confirmed. It may be necessary to first create the baseline using sanitized data from a database, where possible.*

—ISTQB_CTFL_PT

Performance engineers can sometimes fall into the trap of describing an end solution with acceptance criteria. We must remember that acceptance criteria should state the intent, not a solution. This stands true for all types of acceptance criteria, both functional and non-functional. A good acceptance criteria checklist to follow is:

- Clear

- Concise

- Testable

- Understandable

- User perspective based

These could be measured as a response time or other such performance criteria. They should also be stated as a desired outcome (e.g., "2–3 seconds to save a form") which could be investigated and quantified to define expected results. Of course, having "a number" to work toward is helpful. The danger can be to make up a number (seven seconds?) for the sake of a number. A better approach is to give a range to work toward, then investigate this to narrow the range.

Summary   Acceptance criteria should be based on response time (user), throughput (business), and resource utilization (system) and relate back to the performance test objectives, SLAs, and/or baseline values.

Test Data

Test data includes a broad range of data that needs to be specified for a performance test. This data can include the following:

- *User account data (e.g., user accounts available for simultaneous log in)*

- *User input data (e.g., the data a user would enter into the application in order to perform a business process)*

- *Database (e.g., the pre-populated database that is populated with data for use in testing)*

—ISTQB_CTFL_PT

Much was written in Chapter 3.1 on test data. Remember the three types of test data required:

- Master data – Data in the system before execution that may or may not be used directly in the performance test

- User-defined data – Data that is input at runtime as part of the performance test

- Transactional data – Data created at runtime that should be captured as part of the results of the performance test

To use the preceding examples:

- Database = master data

- User accounts = master data (not directly used in the test)/user-defined data (used in the test)

- User input data = user-defined data

Summary   Test data includes master/user-defined/transactional data.

The test data creation process should address the following aspects:

- *data extraction from production data*

- *importing data into the SUT*

- *creation of new data*

- *creation of backups that can be used to restore the data when new cycles of testing are performed*

- *data masking or anonymizing. This practice is used on production data that contains personally identifiable information and is mandatory under General Data Protection Regulations (GDPR). However, in performance testing, data masking adds risk to the performance tests as it may not have the same data characteristics as seen in real-world use.*

—ISTQB_CTFL_PT

It's also essential that any data used comply with local data privacy regulations. This point cannot be emphasized enough, but not for the reason most people think. From a security point of view, test systems are a tempting target. Sometimes, they contain production data, and security can quite often be very lax (e.g., users with elevated privileges and/or simple-to-guess passwords). An example of this type of hack was the Equifax data breach experienced in the UK in 2017. Initially, the company stated 400,000 records were lost, before the number jumped to over 15.2 million. Disturbingly, the following line in the press release from Equifax (October 10, 2017) stated about the lost data:

> *Regrettably this file contained data relating to actual consumers as well as sizeable test datasets, duplicates and spurious fields.*
>
> —www.equifax.co.uk/about-equifax/press-releases/en_gb/-/
> blog/equifax-ltd-uk-update-regarding-the-ongoing-
> investigation-into-us-cyber-security-incident

This is a primary reason (especially for organizations affected by the provisions of the General Data Protection Regulations) to ensure that test data is not in danger of releasing private information. Even allowing performance engineers access to organization information (such as personnel records or payroll information) could be a breach of the privacy regulations.

Summary   Test data creation can be extracted production data/ SUT imported data/ new data/ restored backup data. Personal data must be masked or anonymized to comply with privacy regulations.

System Configuration

The system configuration section of the PTP includes the following technical information:

- *A description of the specific system architecture, including servers (e.g., web, database, load balancer)*

- *Definition of multiple tiers*

- *Specific details of computing hardware (e.g., CPU cores, RAM, Solid State Disks (SSD), Hard Drive Disks (HDD)) including versions*

- *Specific details of software (e.g., applications, operating systems, databases, services used to support the enterprise) including versions*

- *External systems that operates with the SUT and their configuration and version (e.g., Ecommerce system with integration to NetSuite)*

- *SUT build/version identifier*

—ISTQB_CTFL_PT

Another consideration is the mechanism through which any changes to configuration are made. In fact, any changes to the software, hardware, or the configuration for either must be tracked. It can be wise to capture a "before and after" for the system configuration and the related performance test results. This can show a direct benefit of performance testing to the stakeholders.

Summary   System configuration includes the system build and version, architecture, tier definitions, hardware details, software details, and external system integration.

Test Environment

*The test environment is often a separate environment that mimics production, but at a smaller scale. This section of the PTP should include how the results from the performance testing **will be extrapolated** to apply to the larger production environment. With some systems, the production environment becomes the only viable option for testing, but in this case the specific risks of this type of testing must be discussed.*

Testing tools sometimes reside outside the test environment itself and may require special access rights in order to interact with the system components. This is a consideration for the test environment and configuration.

Performance tests may also be conducted with a component part of the system that is capable of operating without other components. This is often cheaper than testing with the whole system and can be conducted as soon as the component is developed.

—ISTQB_CTFL_PT

Test environments can become a massive issue, and yet they can also be a performance engineer's best friend. Processes must be put in place for the creation, management, configuration changes, and the eventual monitoring, reporting, and archiving of this environment. The environment includes the test data and tools as well as the SUT.

An important rule that all performance engineers and project staff must understand is The Golden Rule of Test Environments During Performance Test Development and Execution:

We work as a team, and we do what the performance engineer says!

Having control of the performance test environment is vital, as small configuration changes, code drops, OS tweaks, and even "extra users" can have a significant effect on the results of a performance test. The author once spent two days diagnosing a performance issue – during a load test, there were strange peaks in the resource utilization on the system. After spending time diagnosing this, it was discovered the performance testing environment was simultaneously being used for performance testing and the end-user training! The system under test behaved as expected for about an hour, until the training users started an exercise, and the performance dropped. (Still not happy about this...)

Extrapolation is highlighted in the syllabus quote because it is fraught with danger. Important to this is the definition of extrapolation:

Extrapolation is an estimation beyond the original observation data range.

The key parts of this definition are the fact that it's an estimate, beyond the range of collected data. Two schools of thought exist on extrapolation:

1. Extrapolation is a valid scientific approach, often used in engineering simulations.

2. There are lies, d*mn lies, and extrapolations.

There is truth in both statements, but in terms of performance testing, extrapolation can be dangerous. Engineering simulations can extrapolate based on known behavior – we can extrapolate upon the tensile strength of concrete because engineers have experimented enough to have a basis for known behavior. This data is then converted into an equation or algorithm to allow calculations based on the observed behavior. But engineers are always aware that this extrapolation could be subject to outside environment variables.

In the case of IT system performance, it can almost be guaranteed we do not have enough data on which to base an assumption. Most systems we test are complex with many varying factors involved. Extrapolation, as a result, tends to oversimplify the questions being asked. For example, a system can support 500 concurrent users with two application servers. If another three application servers are added, will the system be able to host 1250 concurrent users?

The danger performance engineers can be subject to is almost all systems do not scale linearly. At some point, the system will reach a bottleneck limit affecting the overall performance of the system.

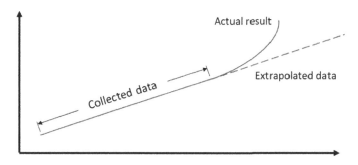

Figure 4-1. *A possible pitfall in extrapolating beyond a data sample*

 And, at that point, measurements tend to change from the near lin-ear to the unpredictable. Once again, Holmes gives the best advice:

I never guess. It is a shocking habit – destructive to the logical faculty.

—Conan Doyle, 1890

The more data performance engineers gather, the more assured we can be on a conclusion. More data points can give a better indication of the actual path the data will take – only plotting two points will always give a straight line!

The reasons why we might need to extrapolate include:

- Production hardware is expensive or cannot be supplied in time leading to a less capable test environment.

- Certain types of performance testing (stress or capacity planning) which might encourage extrapolation.

In conclusion, extrapolation can be performed, but both the performance engineer and the stakeholders must be aware of the risks.

Summary   The test environment can be a smaller version of production (although production can be used with risks), include tool access (with access rights), and can be performed on components of the system. Results may need extrapolation to suit behavior in production.

Test Tools

This section includes a description of which test tools (and versions) will be used in scripting, executing and monitoring the performance tests (see Chapter 5). This list normally includes:

- *Tool(s) used to simulate user transactions*
- *Tools to provide load from multiple points within the system architecture (points of presence)*
- *Tools to monitor system performance, including those described above under system configuration*

—ISTQB_CTFL_PT

As briefly mentioned earlier, the tools themselves form part of the performance test environment. An essential part of the performance test project is to conduct a proof of concept on the SUT to ensure the tool will be adequate to create virtual user scripts, generate an adequate load, and gather monitoring data and results.

Something that could be added to the PTP or included in the test strategy or as a separate document is a set of test tool guidelines. These could include:

- The points mentioned in Chapter 3.1 around scripting and scenario creation

- Procedures to follow when installing and setting up the tool

- Procedures for execution and results capture

- Information on data creation and management

- Notes on the maintenance of scripts, scenarios, and data

- Procedures for maintaining and updating the tools

Summary   Performance tools include scripting (tools to simulate and monitor transactions), test execution (applying load from multiple points of presence), and monitoring.

Profiles

Operational profiles provide a repeatable step-by-step flow through the application for a particular usage of the system. Aggregating these operational profiles results in a load profile (commonly referred to as a scenario). See Section 4.2.3 for more information on profiles.

—ISTQB_CTFL_PT

operational profile

An actual or predicted pattern of use of the component or system.

—ISTQB Glossary

Operational profiles have been mentioned previously in Chapter 1.2. Operational profiles are a result of the volumetric analysis, following the mantra of who/what/where/when/how. On the information derived from this, linked to the performance test requirements, an operational profile can be derived. The operational profile becomes the basis for any subsequent performance testing; it becomes imperative for performance engineers to "think outside the box" when considering what actual users would do when using the system. The load profile then goes on to document the performance test.

Summary   Operational profiles describe the business process path through the system. These combine to form the load profile (scenario) to include further details on ramp-up and ramp-down, duration, and virtual user numbers.

Relevant Metrics

A large number of measurements and metrics can be collected during a performance test execution (see Chapter 2). However, taking too many measurements can make analysis difficult as well as negatively impact the application's actual performance. For these reasons, it is important to identify the measurements and metrics that are most relevant to accomplish the objectives of the performance test.

—ISTQB_CTFL_PT

Performance testing can suffer from an effect known to quantum physics as the observer effect:

The observer effect is the theory that the observation of a quantum phenomenon inevitably changes that phenomenon.

The same can be said of the monitoring performance engineers set up during performance testing. The more data from multiple sources the performance engineer gathers during the test, the more resources and bandwidth are required to perform this monitoring. As well, the more data gathered means more data for the performance engineer to filter through to find the significant results.

In the same token, merely monitoring response time would be wholly inadequate. A good rule to follow with monitoring goes back to the standard set of metrics. Following this model allows stakeholders to understand the metrics gathered (as they are standard), along with giving a basic set of information to guide further analysis if an issue is discovered.

Summary   Relevant metrics and measures are defined for capture during test execution. Too much monitoring can affect system performance.

The following table, explained in more detail in Section 4.4, shows a typical set of metrics for performance testing and monitoring. Test objectives for performance should be defined for these metrics, where required, for the project:

Performance Metrics	
Type	**Metric**
Virtual User Status	# Passed
	# Failed
Transaction Response Time	Minimum
	Maximum
	Average
	90% Percentile
Transactions Per Second	# Passed/second
	# Failed/second
	# Total/second
Hits (e.g., on database or web server)	Hits/second
	• Minimum
	• Maximum
	• Average
	• Total
Throughput	Bits/second
	• Minimum
	• Maximum
	• Average
	• Total

(continued)

Performance Metrics	
Type	**Metric**
HTTP Responses Per Second	Responses/second
	• Minimum
	• Maximum
	• Average
	• Total
	Response by HTTP response codes
CPU usage	% of available CPU used
Memory usage	% of available memory used

—ISTQB_CTFL_PT

From the monitoring list earlier, items from Chapter 2.1 could include disk input/output and queueing. Other monitoring could be protocol specific (such as hits and HTTP responses listed earlier), environment specific (database read/writes), or application or system specific (SAP background/batch jobs or ABAP processes).

At this point, it's worth thinking about sampling rate. How much data will be captured as part of the performance test? The sampling rate is the time period between each sample for that particular monitor. There's a balancing act between the amount of data captured and the granularity of the sampling rate. A good example could be a performance test might show a banking system has a CPU problem when the staff logs in between 0915 and 0945 each morning. The administrators were monitoring the CPU constantly (sampling continuously), but averaging the results in 30-minute blocks – 09:00 to 09:30 and 09:30 to 10:00 (low granularity). Because of this averaging, the administrators were seeing no issue in the CPU monitoring data. After removing the averaging and looking at the raw sample data, the CPU issue became evident.

The sampling rate should be frequent enough to resolve the details of changes in the data. If however we capture measures every second for a 48-hour endurance test, we will see every change, but the dataset captured will take up a lot of disk space! A good way of thinking about this is to apply the Shannon-Nyquist sampling rate[2] – the minimum sample rate that captures the "essence" of the information.

Summary   Typical metrics include virtual user status, transaction response times, transactions per second, hits per second, throughput, HTTP response per second (if applicable), and CPU and memory usage.

Risks

Risks can include areas not measured as part of the performance testing as well as limitations to the performance testing (e.g., external interfaces that cannot be simulated, insufficient load, inability to monitor servers). Limitations of the test environment may also produce risks (e.g., insufficient data, scaled down environment). See Sections 3.2 and 3.3 for more risk types.

—ISTQB_CTFL_PT

A main role of the PTP is the mitigation of both performance project risk relating to the performance testing and performance -related quality risk. Although specific performance risks can be included in the PTP, often it's more efficient to link to these risks in a project or organization risk register. It should always be remembered that the PTP should act as the "performance risk mitigation manual."

Summary   Risks include quality/project risks not covered, including limitations to testing or the environment.

---

[2]There's an excellent video available on the Shannon-Nyquist sampling theorem – www.youtube. com/watch?v=FcXZ28BX-xE. Although it doesn't ever mention performance test monitoring, it's a sound basis onto which to build monitoring sampling.

4.1.3 Communicating About Performance Testing

PTFL-4.1.3 (K4) Create a presentation that enables various stakeholders to understand the rationale behind the planned performance testing

> *The tester must be capable of communicating to all stakeholders the rationale behind the performance testing approach and the activities to be undertaken (as detailed in the Performance Test Plan). The subjects to be addressed in this communication may vary considerably between stakeholders depending on whether they have a "business/user-facing" interest or a more "technology/operations-facing" focus.*
>
> *—ISTQB_CTFL_PT*

ISO29119 Part 3 deals directly with issues surrounding communication. It has long been an area many organizations could improve in general, let alone the QA team and more specifically performance testing. The following are taken from the communication-related test plan section:

6.2.4.5 Stakeholders

Lists the stakeholders and their relevance to the testing. Describes how the communication with each stakeholder is to be performed.

> *—ISO29119-3*

This section should outline the "who's who" in the project and how these people can keep in touch via meetings/stand-ups/team chat/etc. The stakeholders will include both technical- and business-focused staff to enable a broad range of expertise be available to the performance engineer.

6.2.5 Testing communication

Describes the lines of communication between testing, other lifecycle activities, and within the organization.

EXAMPLE This could include the authority for resolving issues raised as a result of the testing activities and the authority for approving test products and processes. This information may be represented visually.

NOTE A visual representation could include an organization chart or a figure that illustrates the flow of information and data.

—ISO29119-3

This section helps fit performance testing into the wider communication between the project staff (developers/other testers/project management staff), business staff (business analysts and frontline business staff), and technical staff (system admins/network admins/DBAs). All are important for performance testing to allow performance engineers the full end-to-end information set for the system under test.

6.2.7.2 Test deliverables

Identifies all documents that are to be delivered from the testing activity or equivalent information to be recorded electronically, for example in databases or dedicated test tools.

EXAMPLE The following documents could be included:

- *Test Plan;*

- *Test Design Specification;*

- *Test Case Specification;*

- *Test Procedure Specification;*

- *Test Data Readiness Report;*

- *Test Environment Readiness Report;*

- *Incident Reports;*

- *Test Status Reports; and*

- *Test Completion Report.*

Test input data and test output data may be identified as deliverables. Test tools created as part of the testing activity may also be included. If documents have been combined or eliminated, then this list will be modified accordingly.

This subsection may include when the document(s) should be delivered, and to/from whom (preferably by position, not name).

—ISO29119-3

Test deliverables are the written form of communication. And, just like other project members, performance engineers must think about what is needed to adequately document the project.

6.2.9.1 Roles, activities, and responsibilities

Provides an overview of the primary (they are the activity leader) and secondary (they are not the leader, but providing support) people filling the test-related roles and their corresponding responsibilities and authority for the testing activities. In addition, identifies those responsible for providing the test item(s). They may be participating either full- or part-time.

EXAMPLE The responsible parties could include the project manager, the test manager, the developers, the test analysts and executors, operations staff, user representatives, technical support staff, data administration staff, and quality support staff.

For each testing person, specify the period(s) when the person is required.

—ISO29119-3

Roles, activities, and responsibilities give the job description for project members. Once again, the performance engineer needs to understand not only their own role and, importantly, how to communicate this role to other project members. As well, performance engineers must understand other roles and how they can help in the work we do.

Before proceeding, a few notes on this standard. There are a few in the software testing realm that heartily disagree with this standard, for a host of valid reasons. Rather than revisit this argument that began in 2014 and continues today, there is an anecdote that might help put this in context:

Many years ago, a colleague of mine ran an ISEB Practitioner course for a large insurance company in the UK. One attendee on the course had an interesting background, they were now managing UAT but had come from the business not from the IT department – so had considerable experience of management, but none of software development and testing. Part of this course covered methods of test process improvement – specifically a method called TPI (test process improvement!) This individual could see the benefit in the method – so much so they bought the book (Test Process Improvement: A step-by-step guide to structured testing by Tim Koomen and Martin Pol). This individual began implementing TPI in their test team within the organization and found that it helped fill in the gaps in their knowledge. A few years later, my colleague met this individual at a conference – who just so happened to now be the Head of Quality within this multinational insurance firm. In that time, this individual had progressed from just using TPI, to understanding the flaws in the method and knowing how to improve them.

ISO29119 is a tool. If a performance engineer has limited experience in test planning, it can be very useful to help establish the document hierarchy (including the PTP), the types of documents needed, and their content.

But, inevitably, the gaps will start to show. It's OK to stop using it! It's OK to change, remove, or add to the PTP template, the hierarchy, types, or content.

The moral of the story is – if a tool is useful, use it. If it's not, then please don't.

What should be added to the PTP (and even the test strategy if it's continuously used) is a communications plan. This section isn't as important if all stakeholders, project staff, and performance engineers are based in one location. If the aforementioned are distributed (whether across town or around the world), formal planned communication becomes more important. The communications plan should include:

- The documents required, including who will write them, when they are to be completed, and to whom they are distributed (roles, not names).

- The lines of communication, including scheduled meetings/emails/ instant messaging, including the communication schedule and/or frequency, who prepares them, and once again to whom they are distributed (roles, not names).

- The lines of authority, including to whom issues are raised (whether they be performance defects, environment issues, or the like).

- Any nonformal communication conducted during the project – that is, the performance engineer working in the server room with the administrators probably won't need formal meetings with each other.

Summary   Performance engineers communicate to all stakeholders (business/ user-facing and technology/operations-facing) the rationale behind the performance testing approach and the activities to be undertaken.

The following stakeholder lists include sections added to the syllabus points.

Stakeholders with a Business Focus

The following factors should be considered when communicating with stakeholders with a business focus:

- *Stakeholders with a business focus are less interested in the distinctions between functional and non-functional quality characteristics.*

—ISTQB_CTFL_PT

Part of the reason why business stakeholders don't care about the non-functional aspects comes down to the misunderstanding that it's not their concern. Much of the time, the technical aspects are out of scope for this group because, "It's a technical thing, we should leave it to IT to worry about."

- *Technical issues concerning tooling, scripting and load generation are generally of secondary interest.*

—ISTQB_CTFL_PT

Much the same as the previous point, these technical issues can be compared to the "mobile phone magic" of making a phone call – the end user only wants to make a successful call and doesn't think of the technology and infrastructure needed to do this. Of course, it could become a primary interest if the ability to generate the required load comes at a high cost.

- *The connection between product risks and performance test objectives must be clearly stated.*

—ISTQB_CTFL_PT

Performance objectives describe the overall desired outcome. These objectives are derived from both performance testing requirements (describing the positive aspects) and performance quality risks (defining the negative). It has been likened to the requirements telling performance engineers what to test and the risk telling them how much to test.

- *Stakeholders must be made aware of the balance between the cost of planned performance tests and how representative the performance testing results will be, compared to production conditions.*

—ISTQB_CTFL_PT

Describing the limitations to the planned performance testing is vital. Understanding the cost of exposure metric will be a great help to understanding the return on investment for performance testing. The cost of exposure involves determining, for each performance risk item, three factors:

1. The probability of a failure relating to the performance risk

2. The cost of loss (expressed as an average cost for each occurrence of the performance risk) associated with a typical failure related to the performance risk should it occur in production

3. The cost of mitigating (performance testing) such failures

For example, a small bank is about to go live with a new payment processing system. The project stakeholders were handed a quote for £50,000 for performance testing this system, which they think is a high cost and are hesitant to pay for this.

This system, if it fails, will cost $1 million per day in revenue (impact) for every day it isn't servicing clients (impact). It was calculated there is a 10% probability the system will fail under high processing load (probability), typical on the last working day each month. Initially, there's a calculation called expected monetary value (EMV – Figure 4-2) that can be used to estimate the cost of the risk occurring (covering points 1 and 2):

$1 000 000 x 10% = $100 000 (for a 24-hour outage);

or

$41 666.67 per hour (for simplicity, a linear progression can be assumed)

$1 000 000 x 10% = $100 000 (for a 24-hour outage);

or

$41 666.67 per hour (for simplicity, a linear progression can be assumed)

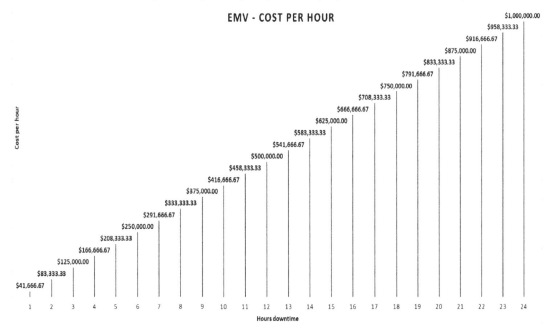

Figure 4-2. *Expected monetary value progression per hour*

As well, this could happen each month. If performance testing is estimated to cost $50,000 to reduce the probability to 1%, the calculation changes:

$1 000 000 x 1% = $10 000 (for a 24-hour outage);

or

$4 166.67 per hour

This is a coarse calculation, but demonstrative as to the benefit the bank might get from performance testing. The end result may be to convince the bank it's a wise investment to pay for about an hour of downtime to avoid the direct loss of revenue, and at this point the uncalculated effect any occurrence this outage might have on the reputation and future profitability of the bank (organizational risk).

- *The repeatability of planned performance tests must be communicated. Will the test be difficult to repeat, or can it be repeated with a minimum of effort?*

  —ISTQB_CTFL_PT

This is vital for performance tests used in regression testing. In many organizations, regression testing is a key component of the testing work conducted. Unfortunately, the regression test set for many organizations only contain functional tests. Any change might indeed introduce functional defects, but they can also introduce performance defects as well.

- *Project risks must be communicated. These include constraints and dependencies concerning the setup of the tests, infrastructure requirements (e.g., hardware, tools, data, bandwidth, test environment, resources) and dependencies on key staff.*

  —ISTQB_CTFL_PT

The PTP should also state how these performance project risks could be mitigated – a key requirement for any test plan. If, for example, an organization continuously has problems with test environments, the risks associated with this should be identified, assessed, and mitigated within the next PTP or even promoted into the test strategy to be used by all projects. Mitigating project risks often means changing the way the process runs to exclude the cause. If test environments are problematic (as they often are), performance engineers should get better at specifying the environment, along with justifying the expense of creating the desired environment against the cost and probability of system failure.

- *The high-level activities must be communicated (see Sections 4.2 and 4.3) together with a broad plan containing costs, time schedule and milestones.*

  —ISTQB_CTFL_PT

Summary   Communication with business stakeholders includes highlighting

- The distinction between function and non-functional requirements

- Technical issues impacting performance project success

- Demonstration of return on investment

- The importance of repeatable tests for regression

- The balance between time, cost, risk, quality, and performance project scope

---

And now for those techy nerds...

Stakeholders with a Technology Focus

The following factors must be considered when communicating with stake-holders with a technology focus:

- *The planned approach to generating required load profiles must be explained and the expected involvement of technical stakeholders made clear.*

—ISTQB_CTFL_PT

Using the phone call analogy from the earlier point – these are the phone company staff who ensure calls can be completed. They don't care what the call is about, just that it is completed successfully.

- *Detailed steps in the setup and execution of the performance tests must be explained to show the relation of the testing to the architectural risks.*

—ISTQB_CTFL_PT

Another important point once again. The translation between the business process steps and the impact these steps have on the SUT and related infrastructure is an important analysis step upon which the performance engineer should focus. As an example, a performance engineer was to create a set of performance tests required over 80 different individual business reports, each to be run by a virtual user. After studying the underlying architecture, it was found that all 80 reports would fit into seven different report categories against the back-end architecture – each category taking a different path through the infrastructure tiers. The individual reports within each category were simply variations on the data being selected. Thus, the scripting job went from 80 record-and-playback scripts to 7 slightly more capable scripts.

- *Steps required to make performance tests repeatable must be communicated. These may include organizational aspects (e.g., participation of key staff) as well as technical issues.*

—ISTQB_CTFL_PT

Performance engineers must create repeatable performance tests to enable their addition to the regression set. This could mean involving both business and technical stakeholders to achieve repeatability (running a certain business path through the system or having custom performance test API or functions created).

- *Where test environments are to be shared, the scheduling of performance tests must be communicated to ensure the test results will not be adversely impacted.*

—ISTQB_CTFL_PT

Once again, The Golden Rule of Test Environments During Performance Test Development and Execution applies (do what the performance engineer says, especially when changing anything). We really need to come up with a better name for this rule!

Scheduling can become an issue, as the performance environment is now a well-specified environment, populated with production-like data that everyone would like to use. It can mean performance testing is often run outside of normal work hours (as previously mentioned).

- *Mitigations of the potential impact on actual users if performance testing needs to be executed in the production environment must be communicated and accepted.*

—ISTQB_CTFL_PT

Occasionally, conducting performance tests in the production environment is the only alternative. The primary advantage of using the production environment is the environment will be realistic. On the negative side, results can be unpredictable based on the network conditions. Any other traffic on this network can adversely affect reproducible results. Also, certain types of performance testing (such as stress and spike testing) can put the production system at greater risk of failing.

- *Technical stakeholders must be clear about their tasks and when they are scheduled.*

—ISTQB_CTFL_PT

It's important that performance engineers inform technical stakeholders they aren't required for the full duration of performance testing. In most cases, technical resources will be required while preparing the performance tests. Once execution commences and results are available, it will be important for the technical stakeholders to be available during analysis to help decide the next steps in the performance test.

Summary   Communication with technical stakeholders includes highlighting

- The load profile and the technical stakeholder's tasks and involvement
- How the detailed steps relate to the environment architecture
- How the performance test can be repeatable
- How the environment can be shared
- Possible risks of performance testing in production

4.2 Analysis, Design, and Implementation

4.2.1 Typical Communication Protocols

PTFL-4.2.1 (K2) Give examples of typical protocols encountered in performance testing

> *Communication protocols define a set of communications rules between computers and systems. Designing tests properly to target specific parts of the system requires understanding protocols.*
>
> *—ISTQB_CTFL_PT*

A performance engineer must understand both how performance testing is done and the key characteristics of a system or application under test. How APIs, applications, and systems communicate is an important facet of a performance engineer's knowledge (Table 4-1).

Table 4-1. *OSI Layers*

Open Source Interconnection (OSI) Layers			
7	**Application**	Data	Presents the data to the users
6	**Presentation**	Data	Formats the data to be presented to the Application layer
5	**Session**	Data	Allows the establishment of sessions between processes
4	**Transport**	Segment/ Datagram	Ensures the message is delivered error-free, in sequence, with no duplication or data losses
3	**Network**	Packet	Controls the physical part the data takes
2	**Data link**	Frame	Provides the data frame transfer from one node to another
1	**Physical**	Bit	Provides the transmission and reception of the unstructured raw data bitstream over some physical means (ethernet/wireless)

Communication protocols are often described by the Open Systems Interconnection (OSI) model layers (see ISO/IEC 7498-1), although some protocols may fall outside of this model. For performance testing, protocols from Layer 5 (Session Layer) to Layer 7 (Application Layer) are most commonly used for performance testing. Common protocols include:

- *Database – ODBC, JDBC, other vendor-specific protocols*

- *Web – HTTP, HTTPS, HTML*

- *Web Service – SOAP, REST*

—ISTQB_CTFL_PT

The syllabus refers to the following protocols as being typical for performance testing today (Table 4-2). These protocols relate to web-based applications and systems. Note these are a good target for questions in the exam!

Table 4-2. *Protocols from the Syllabus*

Protocols	
HTML	Hypertext Markup Language – the standard markup language of the Web. Browsers use HTML for font, color, graphic, and hypertext effects on web pages. In its latest iteration (HTML5), pages are built using less HTML (as HTML5 uses cascading style sheets (CSS3) or JavaScript), with dynamic elements created server-side using PHP ("Hypertext Pre-processor" – PHP code is transformed into HTML before the page is loaded) or ASP ("Active Server Page" – similar to PHP, ASP is run server-side to generate dynamic pages).
HTTP	Hypertext Transfer Protocol – describes the formatting and transmission of messages. HTTP is called a stateless protocol because each command is executed independently, without any knowledge of the commands that came before it.
HTTPS	Hypertext Transfer Protocol Secure – the secure version of HTTP. Communications between the browser and website are encrypted by Transport Layer Security (TLS) or its predecessor Secure Sockets Layer (SSL).
JDBC	Java Database Connectivity – similar in function to ODBC, JDBC uses Java API to connect and execute database queries, being part of Java SE (Java Standard Edition).
ODBC	Open Database Connectivity – a standard API to connect to and execute database queries.
REST	Representational State Transfer – a messaging protocol for web service interfaces like SOAP. REST allows a greater variety of data formats (SOAP only allows XML) and performs better than SOAP.
SOAP	Simple Object Access Protocol – a messaging protocol for web service interfaces using XML (eXtensible Markup Language).

Summary   Performance testing normally uses protocols from OSI layers 5 to 7 for databases (ODBC, JDBC), the Web (HTTP, HTTPS, HTML), and web services (SOAP, REST).

> *Generally speaking, the level of the OSI layer which is most in focus in performance testing relates to the level of the architecture being tested. When testing some low level, embedded architecture for example, the lower numbered layers of the OSI model will be mostly in focus.*

—ISTQB_CTFL_PT

This is an interesting area to consider. There can be many reasons why a performance engineer might select an OSI level in which to create virtual user scripts. A good example is to record the same script at different recording levels – in this case, recording opening the website www.bbc.co.uk at the network layer (Figure 4-3) and the application layer (Figure 4-4).

Figure 4-3. *A winsock script recorded at the network layer*

At the network layer, the contents of individual packets were recorded literally, ending in hundreds of packets captured.

Figure 4-4. *An HTTP/HTML script recorded at the application layer*

At the application layer, a single (albeit large) function captures the page request.

Why use the lower level? It might be that some information is missed in the higher level that needs capturing, or the higher-level protocol isn't able to be recorded – resulting in the lower-level protocol being the alternative.

Summary   Performance testing focuses on the OSI layer of the architecture being tested.

Additional protocols used in performance testing include:

- *Network – DNS, FTP, IMAP, LDAP, POP3, SMTP, Windows Sockets, CORBA*

- *Mobile – TruClient, SMP, MMS*

- *Remote Access – Citrix ICA, RTE*

- *SOA – MQSeries, JSON, WSCL*

—ISTQB_CTFL_PT

Of course, even though a lot of performance testing relates to web-based systems, other protocols are important. It may be that a selection of protocols is needed - HTTPS at the front end using REST with data passed using JSON, with JDBC interacting with the back-end database. Further protocols are included in Table 4-3.

Table 4-3. *More Syllabus Protocols*

Protocols	
CORBA	Common Object Request Broker Architecture – a messaging protocol allowing objects distributed over a network to communicate with each other irrespective of the platform and language used to develop those objects.
Citrix ICA	Independent Computing Architecture – a proprietary protocol for an application service system designed by Citrix Systems for thin client, transporting keystrokes and mouse coordinates and clicks from the client and screen updates from the server.
DNS	Domain Network System – a protocol that converts a website's numeric IP address into human-readable host names.
FTP	File Transfer Protocol – a protocol for the transfer of computer files between a client and a server.
IMAP	Internet Message Access Protocol – an Internet standard protocol used by email clients to retrieve email messages from a server over a TCP/IP connection.
JSON	JavaScript Object Notation – an open standard file format using human-readable text to transmit data objects (attribute-value pairs and array data types or any other serializable value).
LDAP	Lightweight Directory Access Protocol – a protocol used for directory services authentication, providing a communication language that applications use to communicate with other directory service servers.
MMS	Multimedia Messaging Service – a standard mobile messaging protocol including multimedia content to and from a mobile device.
MQSeries	Message Queue (also known as WebSphere MQ and IBM MQ) – a messaging protocol allowing independent and potentially nonconcurrent applications on a distributed system to securely communicate with each other.
POP3	Post Office Protocol 3 – the latest version of a client/server standard communication protocol for **receiving** email.

(continued)

Table 4-3. (*continued*)

Protocols

RTE	Remote Terminal Emulation – a protocol passing individual keystrokes to a server via a terminal emulator.
SMP	Session Multiplex Protocol – a protocol providing session management capabilities between a database client and server. The protocol enables multiple logical client connections to connect to a single server over a single physical connection.
SMTP	Simple Mail Transfer Protocol – a standard communication protocol for **transmitting** email.
TruClient	A technology patented by HP (now Micro Focus, formerly Mercury/Mercury Interactive) for LoadRunner VuGen scripting, making scriptwriting easier but making the actual virtual user scripts more memory hungry.
Windows Sockets	A Microsoft network protocol describing how software should access network services.
WSCL	Web Services Conversation Language – made up of the document type descriptions (the XML schema), the interactions (Send/SendReceive/ReceiveSend/Receive/Empty), the transitions (the ordering relationship), and the conversations (the transactions) of a web service.

Summary   Additional protocols for network (DNS, FTP, IMAP, LDAP, POP3, SMTP, Windows Sockets, CORBA), mobile (TruClient, SMP, MMS), remote access (Citrix ICA, RTE), and SOA (MQSeries, JSON, WSCL).

It is important to understand the overall system architecture because performance tests can be executed on an individual system component (e.g., web server, database server) or on a whole system via end-to-end testing. Traditional 2-tier applications built with a client-server model specify the "client" as the GUI and primary user interface, and the "server" as the back-end database. These applications require the use of a protocol such as ODBC to access the database. With the evolution of web-based applications and multi-tiered architectures, many servers are involved in processing information that is ultimately rendered to the user's browser.

—ISTQB_CTFL_PT

Consider the architecture in Figure 4-5.

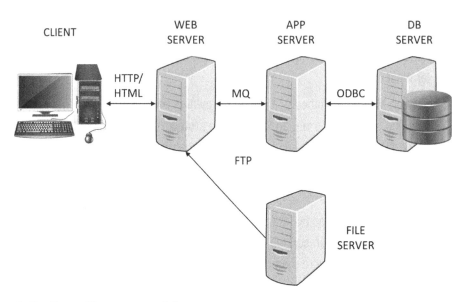

Figure 4-5. *Overall system architecture*

Figure 4-5 tends to be a typical diagram (minus the cute little server and client graphics) presented to performance engineers. But it should be argued it isn't complete! Remember, the test environment may include other devices (firewalls, switches/routers, or load balancers), so it's always a good idea to check! Other things might be the link between the client and web server – will this be using TLS or SSL? But for this example, it will suffice...

To perform end-to-end performance testing, it would be natural to script virtual users from the GUI point of view from the client. That way, the requests sent from the user would pass through the infrastructure as it would in production. Vusers would be created to simulate the end users.

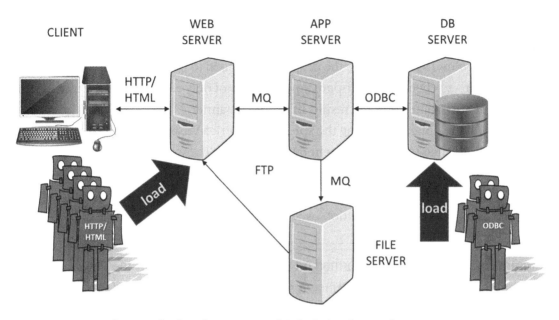

Figure 4-6. *Splitting the load across multiple injection points*

But, the database in this case is shared by another system. The performance test cannot push more load through the front end, as this wouldn't create the correct performance test conditions. In this case, the load coming from the other system (which is out of scope for this test) could be simulated using ODBC Vusers (Figure 4-6).

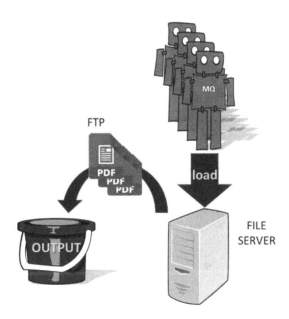

Figure 4-7. *Testing a single tier*

Another use is testing an individual tier within the system (Figure 4-7). If this system is being built, it may be that the file server is a third-party application being integrated into the end-to-end system. Thus, the project might need to performance test this individual tier – to check the third-party application not only can handle the input load requests but also can retrieve the results in a timely manner.

This could be done by creating the specific MQSeries Vusers. In this case, the output isn't returned to the source generating the load. These .pdf files could be forwarded to a machine simulating the web server – these results could then be captured as part of the test.

Once again, this is a typical action used by performance engineers.

Summary   Tests can be performed on individual components or the end-to-end system, broken into the client (GUI) and server (web/database server(s)), with different protocols used between the client and web server (HTML/HTTP) and web and database server (ODBC).

Depending on the part of the system that is targeted for testing, an understanding is required of the appropriate protocol to be used. Therefore, if the need is to perform end-to-end testing emulating user activity from the browser, a web protocol such as HTTP/HTTPS will be employed. In this way, interaction with the GUI can be bypassed and the tests can focus on the communication and activities of the backend servers.

—ISTQB_CTFL_PT

This refers to the point made in Chapter 1.4 regarding load generation (Figure 4-8).

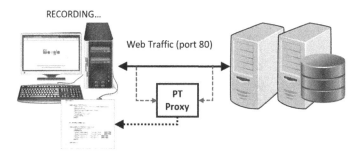

Figure 4-8. *Performance script recording*

As the tool records the script, it creates a proxy through which all the specific protocol traffic passes, and the script is generated. On playback, the load is generated by the scripts executing the protocol calls – thus avoiding the overhead of running the browser and rendering the GUI (Figure 4-9).

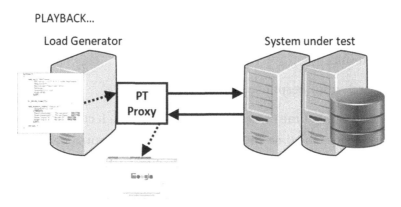

Figure 4-9. *Performance script playback*

Summary   Knowledge of the protocol for the part of the system being tested is essential. Recording from the GUI, the protocol calls are captured and replayed to bypass the need for the GUI.

4.2.2 Transactions

PTFL-4.2.2 (K2) Understand the concept of transactions in performance testing

> *Transactions describe the set of activities performed by a system from the point of initiation to when one or more processes (requests, operations, or operational processes) have been completed. The response time of transactions can be measured for the purpose of evaluating system performance. During a performance test these measurements are used to identify any components that require correction or optimization.*
>
> —ISTQB_CTFL_PT

Transaction can be simplified to an interaction between an actor/client and the target server. For example, a user can use amazon.co.uk to search for The Proclaimers album *Sunshine on Leith*. This involves:

- A request from the user sent to amazon.co.uk for "Sunshine on Leith CD"

- Processing by the Amazon website to retrieve and assemble the search results

- The search result response received by the user

The transaction would time this end-to-end interaction. It could be then broken down further to consider the time spent in transit on the network between the client and server, time taken to complete the operation among the various Amazon servers, and the response time traveling back to the client from Amazon.

Using Micro Focus LoadRunner Virtual User Generator (VuGen), the following statement sends the request to the server:

```
web_url("ref=nb_sb_noss",
    "URL=https://{host_www_amazon_co_uk}/s/ref=nb_sb_noss?url=search-alias%3Daps&field-keywords=sunshine+on+leith+cd",
    "Resource=0",
    "RecContentType=text/html",
    "Referer=https://{host_www_amazon_co_uk}/",
    "Snapshot=t10.inf",
    "Mode=HTML",
    LAST);
```

To time this transaction, statements are added to the code to time the user request and server response:

```
lr_start_transaction("Search");

web_url("ref=nb_sb_noss",
    "URL=https://{host_www_amazon_co_uk}/s/ref=nb_sb_noss?url=search-alias%3Daps&field-keywords=sunshine+on+leith+cd",
    "Resource=0",
    "RecContentType=text/html",
    "Referer=https://{host_www_amazon_co_uk}/",
    "Snapshot=t10.inf",
    "Mode=HTML",
    LAST);

lr_end_transaction("Search", LR_AUTO);
```

These times are then captured as part of the execution:

```
Action.c(214): Notify: Transaction "Search" started.
Action.c(216): web_url("ref=nb_sb_noss") started    [MsgId: MMSG-26355]
...
```

```
Action.c(216): web_url("ref=nb_sb_noss") was successful, 285540 body bytes,
9497 header bytes      [MsgId: MMSG-26386]
Action.c(225): Notify: Transaction "Search" ended with a "Pass" status
(Duration: 0.8170 Wasted Time: 0.0874).
```

Summary   Transactions describe a set of activities from initiation to process completion, to be measured as part of the performance test to identify issues.

Simulated transactions can include think time to better reflect the timing of a real user taking an action (e.g., pressing the "SEND" button). The transaction response time plus the think time equals the elapsed time for that transaction.

—ISTQB_CTFL_PT

It could be easy to misinterpret the preceding statement. Think time is a concept used to represent the time during the test when no activity is taking place between the client and the server. To use the previous example, before a user submits the Amazon search, the user might take a few seconds to look at the page and type in the initial search string (in this case, 14 seconds). This was the time recorded that it took the performance engineer to record the step with no requests being sent to the server. Hence, that is represented in the script as the think time (like a wait method – execution pauses):

```
lr_think_time(14);

lr_start_transaction("Search");

web_url("ref=nb_sb_noss",
    "URL=https://{host_www_amazon_co_uk}/s/ref=nb_sb_noss?url=search-alias%3Daps&field-keywords=sunshine+on+leith+cd",
    "Resource=0",
    "RecContentType=text/html",
    "Referer=https://{host_www_amazon_co_uk}/",
    "Snapshot=t10.inf",
    "Mode=HTML",
    LAST);

lr_end_transaction("Search", LR_AUTO);
```

Currently, this think time is fixed. This is useful at the beginning of performance testing as it allows the test to be replicated if a problem occurs. Once any initial issues have been rectified, this think time can be set as randomized (e.g., between 50% and 150% of the recorded think time – the think time for that statement would now be a random value between 7 and 21 seconds), to allow the script to run in a realistic manner.

The placement of both transaction time and think time steps is important, as the last thing a script needs is to have a think time embedded within a transaction, corrupting the recorded time.

Summary   Think time is used to simulate a real user performing actions. The response time plus the think time is the elapsed time.

The transaction response times collected during the performance test show how this measurement changes under different loads imposed on the system. Analysis may show no degradation under load while other measurements may show severe degradation. By ramping up load and measuring the underlying transaction times, it is possible to correlate the cause of degradation with the response times of one or more transactions.

—ISTQB_CTFL_PT

As mentioned previously, the first sign a system could have a potential performance issue can be transaction times increasing. Transaction time usually is the end effect – from this point, we can start to derive the cause/effect relationship.

There is nothing like first-hand evidence.

—Conan Doyle, 1887

Slow transaction times could in fact be the first evidence of the crime of poor performance.

Summary   Transaction time changes dependent on load, with some measurements varying more than others. Transactions with severe degradation can be the effect source for diagnosing the cause.

Transactions can also be nested so that individual and aggregate activities can be measured. This can be helpful, for example, when understanding the performance efficiency of an online ordering system. The tester may want to measure the discrete steps in the order process (e.g., search for item, add item to cart, pay for item, confirm order) as well as the order process as a whole. By nesting transactions, both sets of information can be gathered in one test.

—ISTQB_CTFL_PT

Although transaction times can be nested, the statement earlier stands true. If any think times are included with a transaction time, it will give an incorrect measurement. The use of nested transaction times can aid in the breakdown of an entire web page. Some tools (LoadRunner among them) allow a lower-level recording still at the application layer. This would allow individual transactions to be created against elements of the page, as well as an overall transaction for the page request/response.

Summary   Transactions can also be nested so that individual and aggregate activities can be measured within one test.

4.2.3 Identifying Operational Profiles

PTFL-4.2.3 (K4) Analyze operational profiles for system usage

Operational profiles specify distinct patterns of interaction with an application such as from users or other system components. Multiple operational profiles may be specified for a given application. They may be combined to create a desired load profile for achieving particular performance test objectives (see Section 4.2.4).

—ISTQB_CTFL_PT

operational profile

An actual or predicted pattern of use of the component or system.

—ISTQB Glossary

The representation of a distinct set of tasks performed by the component or system, possibly based on the behavior of users when interacting with the component or system, and their probabilities of occurrence. A task is logical rather than physical and can be executed over several machines or be executed in non-contiguous time segments.

—Bath and McKay, 2014

operational profile testing

Statistical testing using a model of system operations (short duration tasks) and their probability of typical use.

—Bath and McKay, 2014

Summary   Operational profiles describe a user's interaction with the system. Multiple operational profiles are combined to form a load profile (scenario) to fulfill a test objective.

The following principal steps for identifying operational profiles are described in this section:

1. *Identify the data to be gathered*

2. *Gather the data using one or more sources*

3. *Evaluate the data to construct the operational profiles*

—ISTQB_CTFL_PT

As spoken of in Chapter 1.2, the operational profile is based on the following volumetric questions:

- Who – Who are the users?

- What – Which business processes are they using?

- Where – Where is the load coming from?

- When – Which time of the day does the load represent?

- How – What are the users doing to complete the transaction?

As mentioned in the previous paragraph, operational profiles can be defined at the user group level (focusing on the who) rather than focusing on the system under test (focusing on the what).

The example to follow with the syllabus points is as follows.

A mid-sized savings bank (Min Lille Bank) is consolidating their business offering in the mortgage market. The bank has 4500 employees and 150,000 mortgage customers. They have 87 branches, spread through all major towns and cities in the country. The bank has €39 billion in mortgage assets, with an annual turnover of €924 million. Being an early adopter of online services, they are known in the country as online mortgage specialists, with 70% of their mortgages coming from online applications. A new CEO has set some new business objectives of growing their mortgage market by 5% per annum for the next four years (growth total of 20% on today's success number – added pressure for marketing and sales). The bank uses both internal branch staff, who use an internal client to complete 20% in branch, and mortgage brokers using the online system for the remaining 10%.

Currently, the bank has 3000 successful mortgage applications per year, with a current mortgage closure rate of 1100 per year (lower than the current mortgage success rate, due to market growth). The bank CEO is concerned only 40% of applications are successful and wants to increase that.

Potential customers can access the web front end on the new system to complete their mortgage application (Figure 4-10).

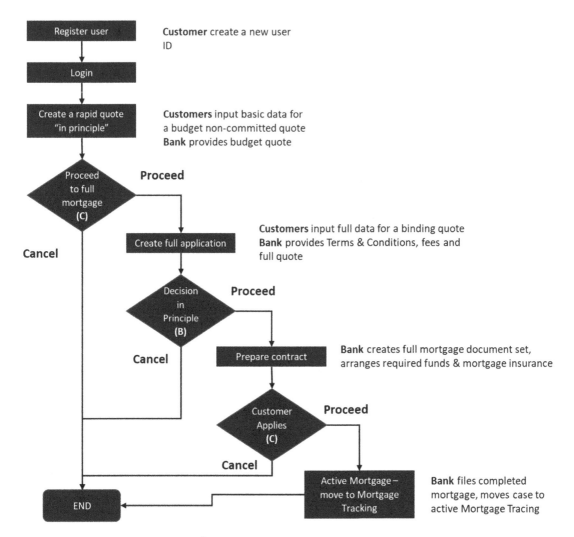

Figure 4-10. *Mortgage application process*

There is a requirement that the *prepare contract* step is 100% successful under load – these documents are legally binding, and early in the bank's online mortgage experience, some mortgages were created with a 0% interest rate that were legally binding if the customer signed (and all the customers presented a 0% interest mortgage did sign!)

The application can be halted and returned to if interrupted (like not having that important piece of paper I thought was in the shoebox with the other papers…).

Once the mortgage is created, active mortgages can be viewed (Figure 4-11). A concern was raised by the business – if the base mortgage rate changes, they are afraid of a spike in active mortgage users viewing their new mortgage rates. A recent rate change had 60% of total active mortgages customer log in within 12 hours of the country's central bank changing the base rate, with the mortgage system subsequently crashing.

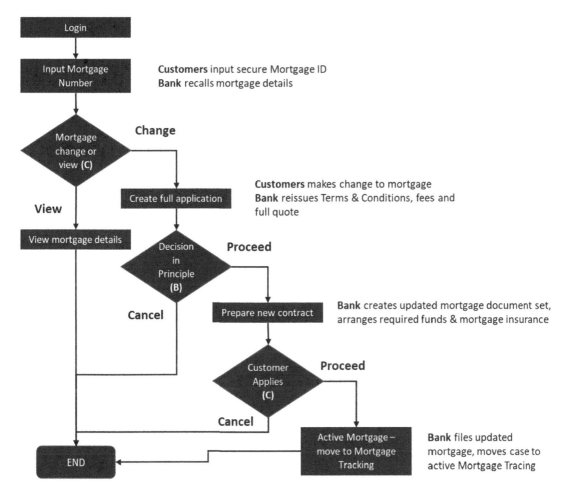

Figure 4-11. *Adding the view mortgage process*

On an average day, 1500 customers view their mortgage, with an average peak day viewing of 20,000 customers.

This is an opportunity to work through the scenario, based on the following syllabus points. Develop an operational profile, to compare with the model answer. Gaps have been left – it will be good practice to also consider further questions to be asked.

Identify Data

Earlier, three types of performance test data were covered.

Master Data

Master data is contained within the system before the performance test is executed. It includes existing user accounts, the product catalogue, existing user orders, and so on.

User-Defined Data

User-defined data is data to be input by the test during execution. Some of this will be existing master data (user accounts/product codes/etc.) with some being added to the test (order quantities, delivery addresses, etc.). It's this data that forms the input data during the performance test.

Transactional Data

Transactional data is created dynamically as part of execution by the system under test (order numbers/delivery docket numbers/etc.). To correlate the input data with the results, transactional data will be captured as part of the test execution results.

Although these will be useful for creating tests, the syllabus looks at this not as the data used during performance testing earlier, however. To avoid confusion, the section refers to data relating to volumetrics and the creation of operational profiles. From earlier, volumetrics consider:

- Who – who are the users?

- What – which business processes are they using?

- Where – where is the load coming from?

- When – which time of the day does the load represent?

- How – what are the users doing to complete the transaction?

This then goes on to help develop the operational profiles and eventual load profiles.

> *Where users interact with the system under test the following data is gathered or estimated in order to model their operational profiles (i.e., how they interact with the system):*

- *Different types of user personas and their roles (e.g., standard user, registered member, administrator, user groups with specific privileges).*

- *Different generic tasks performed by those users/roles (e.g., browsing a web site for information, searching a web site for a particular product, performing role-specific activities). Note that these tasks are generally best modelled at a high level of abstraction (e.g., at the level of business processes or major user stories).*

- *Estimated numbers of users for each role/task per unit of time over a given time period. This information will also be useful for subsequently building load profiles (see Section 4.2.4).*

—ISTQB_CTFL_PT

If we consider the preceding scenario, let's break this down using the syllabus points (be prepared to flip back a few pages):

Different Types of User Personas and Their Roles

- From the preceding scenario, the user personas include users creating mortgages:

  - Internal bank staff – In branch completing mortgages with customers

  - Mortgage brokers – Independent agents using the website to complete mortgages for clients

  - Online customers – Completing the application online

- The user persona for viewing an active mortgage.

What other users might there be? Could we include internal staff running sales reports or administrators running admin tasks as part of the user personas within this performance testing?

Different Generic Tasks Performed by Those Users/Roles

The two main business processes are:

- The mortgage application process (Figure 4-10)

- The view mortgage process (Figure 4-11)

Could other business processes be included? As mentioned before, could there be sales reports or admin tasks added to the process list? Reporting might be a consideration, as any business intelligence reporting can sometimes add a large amount of load to the database.

Estimated Numbers of Users for Each Role/Task

So far, we have the percentage breakdown from the scenario:

- Internal bank staff – 20%

- Mortgage brokers – 10%

- Online customers – 70%

If we look at successful applications, there's 3000 per year (so just over 8 per day average). But earlier, there was a line where the "bank CEO is concerned only 40% of applications are successful." Thus, those 3000 successful mortgages are only 40% of applications. We could then look at:

- Successful transactions – 3000 (40%)

- Unsuccessful transactions – 4500 (60%)

So far, so good. We can now also add the customers viewing mortgages:

- On an average day, 1500 customers view their mortgage, with an average peak day viewing of 20,000 customers.

Note there's a difference here. In the first example, we only have a total number of transactions per year. We would need to ask about the distribution of the 3000 transactions – ideally, "when do they happen?" Even with the view mortgages, we would need to determine when during the day these transactions would occur.

And, once again, the question to ask relates to "anything else." Any other reports/ admin tasks/business processes would also be included into the role/task breakdown.

We have covered the who and the what, but what about the other three?

Where the users come from are two places. There are internal users working in bank branches or offices, who might be taking a different network path to the server than the external, distributed web users. Thus, any performance test might need to take these into account when considering the source of load.

When these transactions occur was highlighted earlier. The way these transactions are distributed over the days of the week and the hours of each day. It might be generalized, for example, that almost all the external web users will create their online mortgage applications on a weekday night after 19:00. Business report, on the other hand, might be needed for the board meeting the next day. So these might be run before 17:00.

How the users complete their transactions will differ. For example, the internal staff and mortgage brokers might complete the transactions much faster than external online applications.

All of these characteristics must be considered when building the operational profiles.

Gather Data

It should always be remembered the source of performance test information may not always be in the expected spot. Sometimes, performance information will come from databases or server logs. It may come from individual expert users or from a survey of a wide range of different users. Or it might come from an unexpected location – a train company once needed to find out how many people might access their website in adverse weather. They determined this by counting the number of passengers departing the stations via the ticket gates. From this, they assumed that if a major storm hit Sunday night, the number of people hitting the website to see if the trains are still running would be the Monday morning number of exits from the station.

The data mentioned above can be gathered from a number of different sources:

- *Conducting interviews or workshops with stakeholders, such as product owners, sales managers and (potential) end users. These discussions often reveal the principal operational profiles of users and provide answers to the fundamental question "Who is this application intended for".*

- *Functional specifications and requirements (where available) are a valuable source of information about intended usage patterns which can also help identify user types and their operational profiles. Where functional specifications are expressed as user stories, the standard format directly enables types of users to be identified (i.e., As an X, I want Y so that Z). Similarly, UML Use Case diagrams and descriptions identify the "actor" for the use case.*

- *Evaluating usage data and metrics gained from similar applications may support identification of user types and provide some initial indications of the expected numbers of users. Access to automatically monitored data (e.g., from a web master's administration tool) is recommended. This will include monitoring logs and data taken from usage of the current operational system where an update to that system is planned*

- *Monitoring the behavior of users when performing predefined tasks with the application may give insights into the types of operational profiles to be modelled for performance testing. Coordinating this task with any planned usability tests (especially if a usability lab is available) is recommended.*

—ISTQB_CTFL_PT

All information gathered can be useful to a performance engineer who considers a wide source of performance information. Even down to the way users might think while using the system, this point alone has served well in creating operational profiles. Small changes to the way the transactions are done can have a big influence on how "lifelike" the performance test actually is. The desire should always be to create "real" performance scripts and scenarios that behave like real users. Thus, the operational profile too must match the users.

Construct Operational Profiles

The following steps are followed for identifying and constructing operational profiles for users:

- *A top-down approach is taken. Relatively simple broad operational profiles are initially created and only broken down further if this is needed to achieve performance test objectives (see Section 4.1.1)*

- *Particular user profiles may be singled out as relevant for performance testing if they involve tasks which are executed frequently, require critical (high risk) or frequent transactions between different system components, or potentially demand large volumes of data to be transferred.*

- *Operational profiles are reviewed and refined with the principal stakeholders before being used for the creation of load profiles (see Section 4.2.4).*

—ISTQB_CTFL_PT

Based on the preceding points, our operational profiles might begin to look as follows:

1. Internal staff creating mortgage applications – 600 successful transactions (20% of 3000), determined to occur between banking business hours (1000–1600), with the application completed quickly to simulate experienced staff, from a more centralized load source (to simulate staff within branches) via the WAN.

2. Mortgage brokers creating mortgage applications – 300 successful transactions (10% of 3000) determined to occur throughout the day (08:00 to 21:00) to reflect brokers visiting customers at their workplace or at home, with the application completed quickly to simulate experienced staff, from a distributed load source accessing the server via an external-facing web server.

3. External customers creating successful mortgage applications – 2100 successful transactions (70% of 3000) determined to occur in the evening (19:00 to 22:00) to reflect customers completing the application after dinner, with the application completed slowly to simulate customers inexperienced with the process, from a distributed load source accessing the server via an external-facing web server.

4. External customers creating unsuccessful mortgage applications – 4500 unsuccessful transactions completed during the evening (19:00 to 22:00) to represent customers failing the mortgage criteria for the amount being borrowed/mistakes in the online application, completed slowly to simulate inexperienced customers accessing the server from a distributed source through the external web server.

5. Viewing active mortgages

   a. 1500 active mortgage views, completed in the evening (19:00–22:00)

   b. 22,000 active mortgage views within a four-hour period to simulate a change in central bank interest rates and mortgage holders viewing their updated mortgage amounts

Of course, there's still quite a bit missing. For example, we still don't know how many of the transactions will look as part of a performance test, but that will come later as part of the load profile.

Now you might think, "Well, why not give us the full information to work it out in the notes above?!?"

You very rarely get the full set of volumetric information when you start to look at establishing operation profiles (and if you do, I hope you stay at that organization – your job will be much easier). Much of the time, it's better to know which questions to ask (the right combination of who/what/where/when/how) to get the information you need.

Summary   Identify data to gather – user roles, user tasks, estimated number of users. Gather the data – interviews, functional specifications/requirements, evaluate usage data, monitor user behavior. Evaluate the data to create the operational profile – top-down approach to create broad operational profiles, single out relevant user profiles, review and approval by stakeholders.

The system under test is not always subjected to loads imposed by the user. Operational profiles may also be required for performance testing of the following types of system (please note this list is not exhaustive).

—ISTQB_CTFL_PT

Some buzzwords – robotic process automation (RPA) and digital transformation can be distilled into the generated load mentioned earlier. Both terms are marketing spin for getting the system to do more of the business legwork itself.

What was once the work of genius soon becomes the work of tinsmiths...

Or, in our case, the work of a server tier.

Summary   Load can also be generated by automated system processes.

Off-line Batch Processing Systems

The focus here lies principally on the throughput of the batch processing system (see Section 4.2.5) and its ability to complete within a given time period. Operational profiles focus on the types of processing which are demanded of the batch processes. For example, the operational profiles for a stock trading system (which typically includes online and batch-based transaction processing) may include those relating to payment transactions, verifying credentials, and checking compliance of legal conditions for particular types of stock transactions. Each of these operational profiles would result in different paths being taken through the overall batch process for a stock. The steps outlined above for identifying the operational profiles of online user-based systems can also be applied in the batch processing context.

—ISTQB_CTFL_PT

An example implementation of this process is the separation between an online transaction processing system (OLTP) and an online analytical processing system (OLAP). Consider the trading system mentioned earlier to which OLTP/OLAP is applied. OLTP would be used for day trading, capturing the details of trades done that day. Based on the nature of trading in today's world, these transactions need processing as rapidly as possible. Thus, OLTP queries should be short and simple and hence require less processing time and less memory and disk space.

OLAP holds archived data – passed to it from the OLTP system. It allows a user to view different summaries of multidimensional data. Using OLAP, information can be extracted from the much larger structured database for analysis. OLAP queries can be much more complex, as time is less of a factor and they run much less frequently (Figure 4-12).

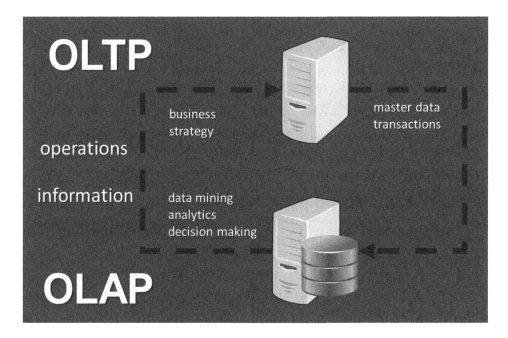

Figure 4-12. *OLAP vs. OLTP*

Summary   Offline batch processes are automated processes that are triggered with the requirement to complete in an expected time. Multiple operational profiles may be included.

Systems of Systems

Components within a multi-system (which may also be embedded) environment respond to different types of input from other systems or components. Depending on the nature of the system under test, this may require modelling of several different operational profiles to effectively represent the types of input provided by those supplier systems. This may involve detailed analysis (e.g., of buffers and queues) together with the system architects and based on system and interface specifications.

—ISTQB_CTFL_PT

The system of systems concept is more common than most realize. Even legacy systems today are being incorporated into interconnected systems of systems. As systems of systems grow larger with more interconnected tiers, the performance challenge also grows larger. And, with more interconnected tiers, the more difficult it will be to find the performance bottleneck.

Another consideration that's becoming more relevant is the integration of IoT devices. IoT devices can complicate tracking bottlenecks as they can be difficult to monitor as part of a wider performance test.

One of the performance factors is the choice of middleware. A good example is the use of XML to pass data. XML is wonderfully useful in that it can be formatted to suit any situation – so long as the message receiver can understand it. The downside of XML is that the protocol is insecure plain text that is often used to send more information than is needed – a typical performance issue.

This is one of the requirements of using a system of systems – a common communication method. A wide range of middleware options exists to act as a translator between disparate systems – database, application server, message-oriented, and web and transaction processing monitors, along with messaging frameworks like XML, REST, SOAP, and JSON.

Summary   Systems of systems are multiple systems linked together, running different operational profiles to simulate load from these systems.

4.2.4 Creating Load Profiles

PTFL-4.2.4 (K4) Create load profiles derived from operational profiles for given performance objectives

> *A load profile specifies the activity which a component or system being tested may experience in production. It consists of a designated number of instances that will perform the actions of predefined operational profiles over a specified time period. Where the instances are users, the term "virtual users" is commonly applied.*
>
> —ISTQB_CTFL_PT

operational profile

> *An actual or predicted pattern of use of the component or system.*

load profile

> *Documentation defining a designated number of virtual users who process a defined set of transactions in a specified time period that a component or system being tested may experience in production.*
>
> —ISTQB Glossary

Earlier in Chapter 1, the difference between the operational profiles (Figure 4-13) and load profiles (Figure 4-14) was defined. Several possible operational profiles could make up a single load profile, from which the performance test can be built.

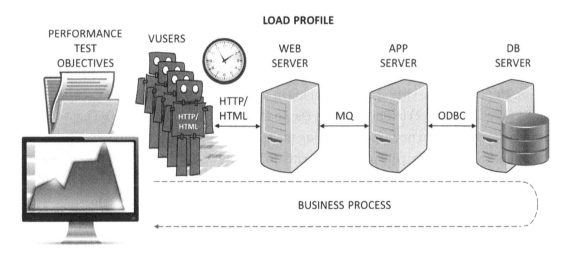

Figure 4-13. *An operational profile*

Figure 4-14. *A load profile*

The principal information required to create a realistic and repeatable load profile is:

- The performance testing objective (e.g., to evaluate system behavior under stress loads)

- Operational profiles which accurately represent individual usage patterns (see Section 4.2.3)

- Known throughput and concurrency issues (see Section 4.2.5)

- The quantity and time distribution with which the operational profiles are to be executed such that the SUT experiences the desired load. Typical examples are:

  - Ramp-ups – Steadily increasing load (e.g., add one virtual user per minute)

  - Ramp-downs – Steadily decreasing load

  - Steps – Instantaneous changes in load (e.g., add 100 virtual users every five minutes)

  - Predefined distributions (e.g., volume mimics daily or seasonal business cycles)

A point of clarification is required. It's important to distinguish the difference between a user and a transaction. A user can perform many transactions (depending on the business process being executed).

As well, the concept of a virtual user isn't to represent a single person. For example, an online betting site might be conducting performance testing around placing bets on a horse or dog race. The operational profile states the user logs in, places a bet before the event, then 2% of the users log out. It takes the average user 20 seconds to complete this action. Hence, a single virtual user might log in with a single user ID and place a bet on Duffel Coat Supreme (2) in Race 4 of the Dapto Dogs (yes – it's a real place). That same virtual user might then not log out (leaving the stateless session ID running on the server to simulate a user leaving the page open with no activity or browsing to a different site) and begin the next iteration with a new user ID.

So, in the space of one minute, the same virtual user might have logged in three times (login transactions) with three separate user IDs, placed three bets (bet transactions), and left two session IDs running (one logout transaction).

Summary   A load profile combines operational profiles with groups of virtual users ramping up, running for a duration, and ramping down to replicate production load.

The following example shows the construction of a load profile with the objective of generating stress conditions (at or above the expected maximum for a system to handle) for the system under test.

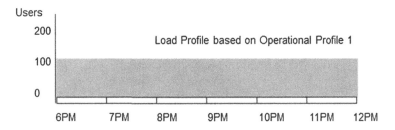

At the top of the diagram a load profile is shown which consists of a step input of 100 virtual users. These users perform the activities defined by Operation Profile 1 over the entire duration of the test. This is typical of many performance load profiles that represent a background load.

—ISTQB_CTFL_PT

The real load would include the ramp-up and ramp-down to effectively add to the overall test time. It would look like the one in Figure 4-15.

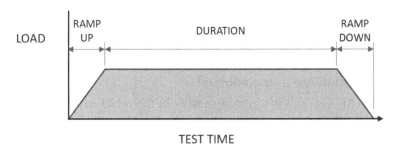

Figure 4-15. *Ramp-up, duration, and ramp-down*

It's always worth thinking of the entire end-to-end test as the end product.

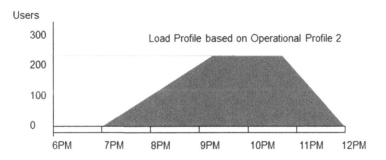

The middle diagram shows a load profile that consists of a ramp-up to 220 virtual users that is maintained for two hours before ramping down. Each virtual user performs activities defined in Operational Profile 2.

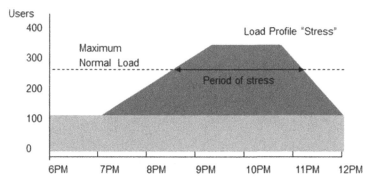

Diagram 1: Example of constructing a "stress" load profile

The lower diagram shows the load profile that results from the combination of the two described above. The system under test is subjected to a three-hour period of stress. For further examples, refer to [Bath & McKay 2014].

—ISTQB_CTFL_PT

Combining tests together in the preceding manner can save time in the ramp-up and ramp-down of large numbers of users – it's not unusual to have multiple load/stress/ spike tests or even endurance tests combined.

From Bath and McKay, this is a good example of the relationship between the volumetric analysis and the derived operational profile for a vacation booking website. This operational profile is like many online transaction sites – a smaller midday peak, followed by a much higher peak later in the day after everyone is home from work/ school, *Pointless*[3] has been watched, and dinner is done. Note as well we have different "user groups" – one group browsing and the other booking.

---

[3] A very British gameshow, where the object is not to just get the question right but to come up with an answer no one else has thought of! Lowest number of points win – question points are from when asking 100 random people the question, how many out of 100 got that answer. Zero points (or "pointless") are the best answers!

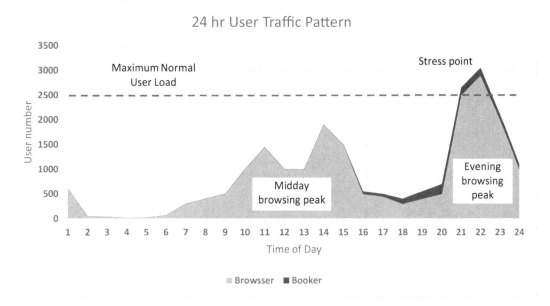

Figure 4-16. *User traffic pattern over 24 hours (from Bath & McKay 2014)*

The number of transactions/minute is the next example (Figure 4-17). Note that from the y-axis, in combination with the preceding example, we could say between 1400 and 1900 the running users ramp up from 100 transactions/minute to 1000 transactions/minute.

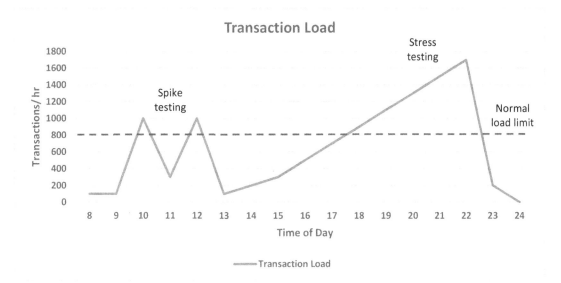

Figure 4-17. *Transaction traffic pattern (from Bath & McKay 2014)*

The above is a good example of the comparison between the number of transactions (Figure 4-17) and the number of users (Figure 4-16). The syllabus referred to load as the running virtual users, whereas Bath and McKay look at the measure of load as both users and transactions, highlighting the difference between the two.

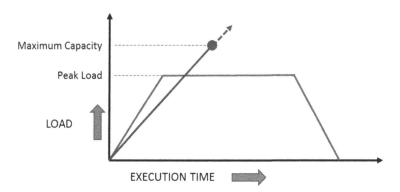

Figure 4-18. *Stress/capacity test*

Finally, although the examples refer to stress testing, it might be the tests are closer to capacity tests. Stress testing (Figure 4-18) tends to have an "open end" – load increases until a point of failure is reached. Capacity testing is looking to see if the maximum limits of a component or system meet the requirements.

Efficiency should always be a consideration when planning and creating performance tests. The ability to include multiple operational and load profiles within one scenario can save a lot of time ramping up virtual users. Other efficiencies (data refresh/reuse; after-hours execution) can also aid execution efficiency.

As an example, three load profiles are to be run – one test with 1000 virtual users, one with 1500, and one with 1900, with a legacy system that can only support the ramp-up of 1 virtual user every four seconds. Thus, if running each load profile individually, the ramp-ups on three separate tests would be

	Vusers	Ramp-Up Time
Level 1 load	1000	4000 sec = 1hr 6min 40s
Level 2 load	1500	6000 sec = 1hr 40min
Level 3 load	1900	7600 sec = 2hrs 6min 40s

Of course, it will still take over two hours to log in the 1900 virtual users, but it makes sense to "stop on the way" to test at 1000 and 1500 virtual users as shown in Figure 4-19.

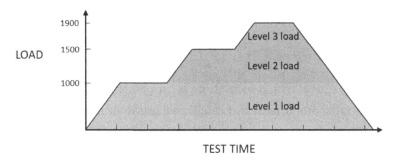

Figure 4-19. *Load profile breakdown*

4.2.5 Analyzing Throughput and Concurrency

PTFL-4.2.5 (K4) Analyze throughput and concurrency when developing performance tests

> *It is important to understand different aspects of workload: throughput and concurrency. To model operational and load profiles properly, both aspects should be taken into consideration.*
>
> —ISTQB_CTFL_PT

Simply put, throughput is **how much** is being done; concurrency is **when** it's being done.

System Throughput

> *System throughput is a measure of the number of transactions of a given type that the system processes in a unit of time. For example, the number of orders per hour or the number of HTTP requests per second. System throughput should be distinguished from network throughput, which is the amount of data moved over the network (Section 2.1).*
>
> —ISTQB_CTFL_PT

system throughput

> *The amount of data passing through a component or system in a given time period.*
>
> —ISTQB Glossary

Throughput is the rate at which something is processed. In the case of a system, throughput can be both categorized and calculated as the number of transactions completed (either total or successful/unsuccessful).

Summary System throughput is the amount of transactions processed in a given time. System throughput differs from network throughput (data passing the network in a given time).

> *System throughput defines load on the system. Unfortunately, quite often the number of concurrent users is used to define the load for interactive systems instead of throughput. This is partially true because that number is often easier to find, and partially because it is the way load testing tools define load. Without defining operational profiles – what each user is doing and how intensely (which also is throughput for one user) – the number of users is not a good measure of load. For example, if there are 500 users running short queries each minute, we have a throughput of 30,000 queries per hour. If the same 500 users are running the same queries, but one per hour, the throughput is 500 queries per hour. So there are the same 500 users, but a 60x difference between loads and at least a 60x difference in the hardware requirements for the system.*
>
> —ISTQB_CTFL_PT

Although system throughput can be used to **define** load, actual load is code executing in an environment (including all the code execution outcomes such as messages sent/received, files created/read/updated/deleted, etc.).

As mentioned earlier (and later in the preceding syllabus quote), one user can perform more than one transaction. Another consideration is the rate at which these transactions are done.

Summary   System throughput defines load on the system, as it links to the operation profile to describe the rate at which users are performing actions.

Workload modelling is usually done by considering the number of virtual users (execution threads) and the think time (delays between user actions). However, system throughput is also defined by processing time, and that time may increase as load increases.

$$system\ throughput = \frac{\left[number\ of\ virtual\ users\right]}{\left(\left[processing\ time\right]+\left[think\ time\right]\right)}$$

So when the processing time increases, throughput may significantly decrease even if everything else stays the same.

System throughput is an important aspect when testing batch processing systems. In this case, the throughput is typically measured according to the number of transactions that can be accomplished within a given time frame (e.g., a nightly batch processing window).

—ISTQB_CTFL_PT

An example of the system throughput equation could be a system with 500 users, a transaction processing time of 30 seconds, and a think time of 20 seconds. According to the equation

$$system\ throughput = \frac{500}{\left(30+20\right)}$$

$$= 10\ transactions/second$$

It's important to note that this transaction rate is an average. Were a performance test to be run, for the first 50 seconds of the test, there would be zero transactions. As the performance test ramps up, the transaction rate would increase until the full 500 virtual users are running. This is the reasoning behind the test "not starting" until the ramp-up has completed.

Using the scenario from earlier in the chapter, let's say the central bank has changed the base interest rate (meaning the upper rate will apply):

On an average day, 1500 customers view their mortgage, with an average peak day viewing of 20,000 customers.

We can also use the distribution suggested by Bath and McKay for the rate at which over a day the mortgage viewing will be spread (Figure 4-20).

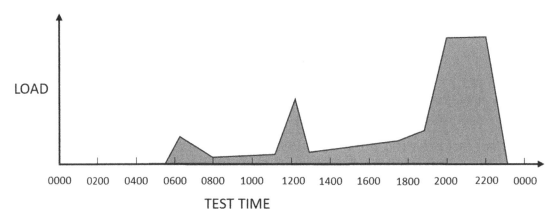

Figure 4-20. *Mortgage viewing distribution breakdown*

From this, we have an approximation of the distribution of the performance test numbers. But, how would these relate to the preceding graph? If we were considering the upper peak of 20,000 **transactions**, we would need to consider how many virtual users would be required to generate this transaction rate. It will depend on a few factors:

- How long it takes for a user to complete the view mortgage business process (web logs have shown on average, users take 180 seconds for the end-to-end view mortgage business process).

- How many transactions are needed per hour (to cover the average of 20,000 transactions in 18 hours as above, 1100 transactions per hour are needed).

- How many transactions are done by each user (in this case, it's a bit easier, as each user will log in, view their mortgage with the new interest rate, and log out).

- Which transactions have a higher organization importance (in the example, it could be argued that all have importance, but from a performance point of view, login and view mortgage are more resource intensive).

- Which key transaction is being tested (as per the requirement, the view mortgage is the key based on the customer requirement of viewing the effect of a base rate change on their mortgage payments).

Initially, transaction rate can be calculated for a planned test. For each user taking 180 seconds to complete the business process, 20/hour can be completed. It was decided that each of the first two peaks will take 1 hour, and the third peak will ramp up in 15 minutes, run for 1 hour, then ramp down (about 4 hours in total). To break this down further, calculations can be done for each of the load profile components – the base load and the three peaks (Figure 4-21).

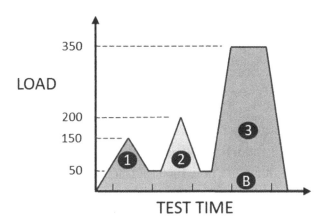

Figure 4-21. *User profile breakdown*

BASE LOAD – Over 4 hours, with a 50-user group, 4000 transactions will be completed.

PEAK 1 – Over 1 hour, with a 100-user peak over base, 1000 transactions will be completed.

PEAK 2 – Over 1 hour, with a 150-user peak over base, 1500 transactions will be completed.

PEAK 3 – Over 1 hour, with a 300-user peak over base, 6000 transactions will be completed, plus 1500 for ramp-up and ramp-down (Figure 4-22).

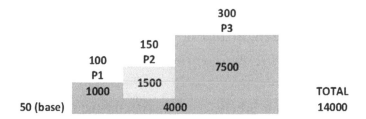

Figure 4-22. Transaction profile breakdown

Thus, in the 4-hour performance test, with a peak of 350 virtual users, a total of 14,000 transactions will be completed.

To determine these numbers, use area calculations:

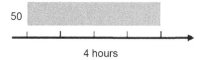

BASE – 50 (users) x 4 (hours) = 200 user-hours;

with 20 transactions/hour = 20 x 200 = 4000 transactions[4]

PEAK 1 – 100 (users) x 1 (hour)/ 2 = 50 user-hours

with 20 transactions/hour = 20 x 50 = 1000 transactions

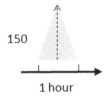

PEAK 2 – 150 (users) x 1 (hour)/ 2 = 75 user-hours

with 20 transactions/hour = 20 x 75 = 1500 transactions

---

[4]Note the ramp-up and ramp-down were excluded from the calculation, as the test hasn't officially "begun" until the base 50-user load was running.

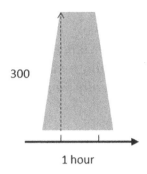

300

1 hour

PEAK 3 – 300 (users) x 0.5 (hour)/ 2 = 75 user-hours (15 minutes ramp-up, 15 minutes ramp-down)

with 20 transactions/hour = 20 x 75 = 1500 transactions

Plus

300 (users) x 1 (hour) = 300 user-hours

with 20 transactions/hour = 20 x 300 = 6000 transactions

TOTAL = 7500 transactions

If you ever said while doing geometry at school, "When will I ever use this stuff?" – question answered!

It should also be noted that each virtual user will log in with different user credentials each iteration to simulate different users querying the relevant mortgage documents.

Summary Workload modeling is the combination of the number of virtual users, the transaction, and think times to calculate the system throughput:

$$system\ throughput = \frac{\left[number\ of\ virtual\ users\right]}{\left(\left[processing\ time\right] + \left[think\ time\right]\right)}$$

System throughput is important for batch processing systems (the number of transactions completed within a given timeframe).

Concurrency

Concurrency is a measure of the number of simultaneous/parallel threads of execution. For interactive systems, it may be a number of simultaneous/parallel users. Concurrency is usually modelled in load testing tools by setting the number of virtual users.

—ISTQB_CTFL_PT

concurrency

The simultaneous execution of multiple independent threads by a component or system.

—ISTQB Glossary

Bear in mind that idle users in a system might also represent concurrency – either stateless sessions being maintained by the server or a stateful session consuming a connection.

Concurrency is an important measure. It represents the number of parallel sessions, each of which may use its own resources. Even if throughput is the same, the amount of resources used may differ depending on concurrency. Typical test setups are closed systems (from the queuing theory point of view), where the number of users in the system is set (fixed population). If all users are waiting for the system's response in a closed system, no new users can arrive. Many public systems are open systems – new users are arriving all the time even if all the current users are waiting for the system's response.

—ISTQB_CTFL_PT

Queueing theory is the study of the formation, function, and congestion of waiting lines (queues).

The theory is built on two components:

- One or more servers supplying a service

- Several clients requesting a service

Queueing theory studies the queue (the client arrival rate, number of servers, number of clients, the maximum queue capacity, average service completion time, and queuing rules – first-in-first-out, last-in-first-out, prioritized, or random-order service). It's an interesting area that can directly impact performance engineers from both the technical side (read/write queueing on a hard drive) and the business side (a bank teller system response time affecting the length of the queue at the bank at lunchtime).

The concept of a closed system is relevant to queueing theory. Closed systems have a fixed client number that move between the internal system queues but never leave the system. This relates to many test environment, as the environment (and in fact many internal organization systems) have a fixed number of users. This may be unrealistic in terms of the production system – if the system is a web-based public system, it will be an open system (or more accurately a worldwide closed system with a client number in the billions). This should be considered, as many web systems are tested with an estimated peak load, but that might be below the number of users the system could spike to.

A company called Click Frenzy (ClickFrenzy.com.au) discovered this in 2012. Click Frenzy was an online sales site, where manufacturers and large retailers could join a shopping event called a flash sale (like "Cyber Monday") that has become popular. The first "Click Frenzy" date was announced to begin on November 20, 2012, with a large amount of marketing leading up to the event. The company was confident they could handle the anticipated load, convinced they had created a "user-friendly online marketplace built to withstand enormous concurrent traffic volumes."[5] Having signed up hundreds of retailers and thousands of users, the sale began at 19:00 AEST, November 20. Within the first minute, the site crashed due to the spike in load. This then had a cascading effect to the retailer's websites, as users who couldn't gain access to the sale went from ClickFrenzy.com.au to the retailer's sites. After the dust settled, the following lessons were proposed:

1. It's vital the servers can handle a massive and rapid increase in load while running a flash sale. If the servers cannot, be prepared for reputational and financial loss (remember organizational risks can become issues!).

2. If your site is covered in the media (especially if the flash sale gets news coverage), refer to point 1.

---

[5] www.digitalpulse.pwc.com.au/click-frenzy-fail-learnings/

3. If competitors run a flash sale, ensure your servers can handle overflow load to your website in the event of the competitor's site failing.

4. Your site will get a large traffic spike, so cloud services offering automatic resource scaling (AWS Auto Scaling/Azure Autoscale/Google Cloud Managed Instance Groups Autoscaling) are a must.[6]

From the perspective of a user/virtual user, concurrency can be considered at three levels. Consider the vacation site used by Bath and McKay earlier:

1. Application level – How many users are active on the site (searching for holidays, viewing destination information, booking vacations, checking booked vacation details)

2. Business process level – How many users are in the booking vacation process (selecting flights/hotels/car rentals/insurance/inputting payment information)

3. Transaction level – How many users are clicking on purchase RIGHT NOW (clicking the "Purchase" button in the last second)

Concurrency, at whatever level, can place specific performance conditions onto the system under test. In many performance situations, a sub-objective may be to, "under load," determine the system's ability to handle simultaneous business process/transaction events. Different issues can be explored:

- Race conditions – At a low level, two threads simultaneously access a shared variable. The first thread reads the variable, and the second thread reads the same value. The first thread and second thread then perform operations on the value, and they "race" to see which thread writes its values last is preserved because of the thread is writing over the value that the previous thread wrote. This can cause functional defects directly. If one of the threads is delayed due to performance issues, a race condition can be a functional defect dependent on the amount of load on the system. It can also be one of the intermittent defects found by functional testers that are very difficult to diagnose.

---

[6]http://littleredjet.com/click-frenzy-crazy-fail-all-of-the-above-of-2012/

- Semaphoring – In programming, a semaphore can be used as a thread stoplight. Depending on the value of a variable or data type, it might allow or disallow execution of a designated thread to continue. Semaphoring can be used to avoid a race condition, but it can also cause operations to take much longer to complete.

- Load spikes – Imagine a sales website has run a marketing campaign advertising next Monday at 08:00 GMT the online store will open, and "amazing savings can be had for a limited time while stocks last." It would be safe to predict a spike in load at 08:00 based on business process and transaction concurrency could overload the system's ability to complete customer sales.

- Resource exhaustion – Consumable resources such as available threads or connections from a connection pool might be exhausted, leading to a drop in performance. Or it could be the system servers simply run out of memory.

Summary   Concurrency represents parallel sessions consuming resources. Consider the nature of the production system (closed – fixed user number vs. open – web-based public system) when considering how concurrency is determined.

4.2.6 Basic Structure of a Performance Test Script

PTFL-4.2.6 (K2) Understand the basic structure of a performance test script

> *The differences between theory and practice are smaller in theory than they are in practice...*

> —Unknown

A performance test script should simulate a user or component activity that contributes to the load on the system under test (which may be the whole system or one of its components). It initiates requests to the server in a proper order and at a given pace.

—ISTQB_CTFL_PT

It is imperative that the script:

- Performs the business process as the user would perform it (within reason, of course. An approval, e.g., might be scripted to be completed immediately as part of a performance test rather than wait for hours for an authorizer to see the email...)

- Uses a range of both positive and negative test data (as if there is a possibility a user will perform a transaction the right way or the wrong way, someone will always choose the wrong way)

- Is created in a modular, easy-to-maintain form (as you will be changing it in the future, so make it easy both for yourself and fellow performance engineers)

- Can perform error handling (as it will need to deal with both negative and positive data as well as error conditions)

Summary   Performance scripts should simulate the real system user, in the same order and at the same speed.

The best way to create performance test scripts depends on the load generation approach used (Section 4.1):

- *The traditional way is to record communication between the client and the system or component on the protocol level and then play it back after the script has been parameterized and documented. The parameterization results in a scalable and maintainable script, but the task of parameterization may be time consuming.*

- *Recording at the GUI level typically involves capturing GUI actions of a single client with a test execution tool and running that script with the load generation tool to represent multiple clients.*

- *Programming may be done using protocol requests (e.g., HTTP requests), GUI actions, or API calls. In the case of programming scripts, the exact sequence of requests sent to and received from the real system must be determined, which may be not trivial.*

—ISTQB_CTFL_PT

Script creation isn't as clear-cut as the preceding bullet points. It would be rare that a single method on its own would be used, unless limited by the tool itself.

As an example, Fiddler is a proxy server tool used to log, inspect, and (potentially) alter HTTP and HTTPS traffic. It captures the web traffic by diverting the web ports (80 and 443) through the tool proxy. Although you cannot script using Fiddler, the captured output log can be imported into other tools (such as Micro Focus LoadRunner or Performance Center) to automatically create a script from the captured log.

LoadRunner and Performance Center both use the same tool – the Virtual User Generator, or VuGen – to create scripts. This tool uses the GUI to record the script, but predominantly doesn't record this from the front-end GUI. Once again, it diverts ports through the tool proxy to capture the protocol calls to create the scripts. VuGen also has TruClient – a patented recording method that creates a GUI-based script which, like the Fiddler log, can be converted to a protocol-based script for execution in a load test.

JMeter is an open source tool that also uses the proxy recording method. Like Fiddler and VuGen, the proxy captures the user actions and the corresponding protocol calls to the server.

Again, both VuGen and JMeter can also run API and custom protocol functions. Almost every script created uses a similar combination today. It would be extremely rare to program a full script for a load test, but there are specific instances where this might be the only alternative.

Summary   Performance scripts can be created with

1. Capturing the protocol request/response (avoiding the GUI interaction)

2. Recording the GUI and playing this back

3. Programming protocol/GUI/API calls

Usually a script is one or several sections of code (written in a generic pro-gramming language with some extensions or in a specialized language) or an object, which may be presented to a user by the tool in a GUI. In both cases the script will include server requests creating load (e.g., HTTP requests) and some programming logic around them specifying how exactly these requests would be invoked (e.g., in what order, at what moment, with what parameters, what should be checked). The more sophisticated the logic, the more need for using powerful programming languages.

—ISTQB_CTFL_PT

Most scripting tools today are based on either Java or a C-based language (C, C++, C#). Allowing programming logic to be added to the base recording helps add run logic, error handling, and custom methods/functions to the script.

Summary   Performance scripts are written in code sections/ functions/ objects and methods in a generic language (C-based, Java), with programming logic to decide how the requests are run.

Overall Structure

Often the script has an initialization section (where everything gets pre-pared for the main part), main sections that may be executed multiple times, and a clean-up section (where necessary steps are taken to finish the test properly).

—ISTQB_CTFL_PT

This is based on the earlier premise that for legacy client/server systems (with a stateful connection and no timeout set), a user logs in once, performs many tasks, and logs off in the evening. This has been carried forward to today in many areas – an ERP user would recognize this as a standard workday (Figure 4-23).

Figure 4-23. *Run logic for a client-server type system*

It's important to note that, as mentioned before, an idle user may still be a consideration in such a test. Any connected user, whether they are performing a task or not, still consumes a connection.

Another point to note on this type is the logout process. Occasionally, these systems capture users' states at logout – meaning the logout transaction does not merely terminate the session. In the example illustration, the login is contained within the *vuser_init*, the tasks contained within the *PlaceBet* action, and the logout in the *vuser_end*. It's important to note the *vuser_init* and *vuser_end* only execute once.

Figure 4-24. *Run logic for a web-based system*

User behavior can change depending on the environment. A browser-based application may still require a user to login. However, this will be either a stateful connection with a timeout or a stateless connection. But the nature of the transaction may change. It may be the user only wishes to perform a discrete task. Hence, they log in, perform the task, and either log out or the session eventually times out (Figure 4-24).

Many systems today follow this pattern – even the web-equivalent ERP that have taken over from the client/server versions.

In this example, both *vuser_init* and *vuser_end* are empty. The actions within the *Run* section contain the tasks the user would perform. Further, the *Logout* action has been randomized to mimic the behavior of real users – in this system, only 2% of users manually log out. The others rely on the session ID expiring. The *BLANK* action contains no code to allow that user session to stay running.

Summary   Performance scripts have an initiation section (run once to "to log in"/start the test), a main section (run multiple times to perform user actions), and a clean-up section ("log out").

Data Collection

To collect response times, timers should be added to the script to measure how long a request or a combination of requests takes. The timed requests should match a meaningful unit of logical work–for example, a business transaction for adding an item to an order or submitting an order.

It is important to understand what exactly is measured: in the case of protocol-level scripts it is server and network response time only, while GUI scripts measure end-to-end time (although what exactly is measured depends on the technology used).

—ISTQB_CTFL_PT

Another consideration is that of transactional data. As stated, transactional data is created at runtime by the system. This could be status bar messages, order numbers, and even mortgage contract documents. These could be used as actual results for checkpoints added to the script, to be compared with some predetermined expected result. This is an important consideration, as this will be proof that the business process was completed satisfactorily or could be the starting point for remediation.

Summary   Performance scripts collect response times via tool functions to measure the time a transaction takes. Protocol-level scripts exclude GUI rendering times (hence not end-to-end).

Result Verification and Error Handling

An important part of the script is result verification and error handling. Even in the best load testing tools, default error handling tends to be minimal (such as checking the HTTP request return code), so it is recommended to add additional checks to verify what the requests actually return. Also, if any clean-up is required in case of an error, it likely will need to be implemented manually. A good practice is to verify that the script is doing what it is supposed to do using indirect methods–for example, checking the database to verify that the proper information was added.

Scripts may include other logic specifying rules concerning when and how server requests will be made. One example is setting synchronization points, which is done by specifying that the script should wait for an event at that point before proceeding. The synchronization points may be used to ensure that a specific action is invoked concurrently or to coordinate work between several scripts.

Performance testing scripts are software, so creating a performance testing script is a software development activity. It should include quality assurance and tests to verify that the script works as expected with the whole range of input data.

—ISTQB_CTFL_PT

Much can be written regarding error handling. One of the main issues (and this is specific to HTTP return codes) is the redirect. Tools are preprogrammed to know that the HTTP return codes in the 200s are OK; 400s and 500s are error states. It's those in the 300s range that cause issues (more on this shortly). Redirects are used across the Internet to improve usability – an example being if a user visits `www.ba.com`, they are redirected to `www.britishairways.com`. Unfortunately, sometimes the redirect is because of an error state and sends the user to an internal error page within the site. But tools may interpret the 300 return code as a legitimate redirect (which it is), which could then be interpreted as everything is working (which it may not be).

Synchronization points are a useful technique, especially where the possibility of a race condition (or similar) could exist. It must be understood that the use of synchronization points can affect performance results. For example, if a virtual user is locked within a synchronization point waiting for a condition that cannot be met, it may never exit this condition.

The final point is once again a deficiency with many performance test scripts. A performance engineer must always remember once they start creating test scripts, they are writing code. And, it also must be acknowledged that just like any other developers, performance engineers can also make mistakes.

The moral of the story is – test your scripts!

Summary   Performance scripts must verify expected results to confirm correct behavior. Error handling should be used to recover from error conditions and clean up after the error. Synchronization points are useful to avoid race conditions. As the performance scripts are code, they must be tested after every change to confirm correct execution.

4.2.7 Implementing Performance Test Scripts

PTFL-4.2.7 (K3) Implement performance test scripts consistent with the plan and load profiles

> *Performance test scripts are implemented based on the PTP and the load profiles. While technical details of implementation will differ depending on the approach and tool(s) used, the overall process remains the same. A performance script is created using an Integrated Development Environment (IDE) or script editor, to simulate a user or component behavior. Usually the script is created to simulate a specific operational profile (although it is often possible to combine several operational profiles in one script with conditional statements).*

> —ISTQB_CTFL_PT

As mentioned earlier, the virtual user script steps must replicate the steps real users or components perform, including the negative (incorrect) steps!

Summary   Performance scripts follow the performance test plan, load profile, and operational profile(s) defined.

> *As the sequence of requests is determined, the script may be recorded or programmed depending on the approach. Recording usually ensures that it exactly simulates the real system, while programming relies on knowledge of the proper request sequence.*

> —ISTQB_CTFL_PT

Writing the script without recording is very rare. Many performance engineers will go throughout their career never needing to write an entire script from scratch. But it can be guaranteed that many hours will be spent ensuring changes to the recorded script execute correctly. Any time a change is made to a script, it must be tested!

Summary   Although rare, performance scripts can be programmed. More common is recording user input actions to record the script.

If recording on the protocol level is used, an essential step after recording in most cases is replacing all recorded internal identifiers that define context. These identifiers must be made into variables that can be changed between runs with appropriate values that are extracted from the request responses (e.g., a user identifier that is acquired at login and must be supplied for all subsequent transactions). This is a part of script parameterization, sometimes referred to as 'correlation.' In that context the word correlation has a different meaning than when used in statistics (where it means relationship between two or more things). Advanced load testing tools may do some correlation automatically, so it may be transparent in some cases—but in more complex cases, manual correlation or adding new correlation rules may be required. Incorrect correlation or lack of correlation is the main reason why recorded scripts fail to playback.

—ISTQB_CTFL_PT

Correlation is needed when dynamic server values are hard-coded into the script. For example, a music website lists a range of different albums for sale. As humans, we might refer to one of these albums as The Proclaimers *Sunshine On Leith*. The system refers to this as SKU[7] 1049296. If we record a script that selects this album, it's recorded as information within the protocol call to the server (within the web_submit_form function):

---

[7]SKU – stock keeping unit – a number used as a unique primary key identifier to track inventory items in a stock management database.

```
1  □ SelectItem()
2     {
3
4         lr_think_time(12);
5
6         // DRAG ITEM INTO BASKET
7
8         lr_start_transaction("Item_In_Basket");
9
10        web_submit_form("put_in_basket",
11                        "Snapshot=t12.inf",
12                        ITEMDATA,
13                        "name=itempick","value=\"Sunshine On Leith\"", ENDITEM,
14                        "name=itemsku","value=1049296", ENDITEM,
15                        LAST);
16
17        lr_end_transaction("Item_In_Basket", LR_AUTO);
18
19        return 0;
20    └─}
```

Parameterization is where hard-coded values are replaced with parameters to allow the script to draw different data each time the script iterates (loops). If the album title was parameterized (as the script will need to choose at random from a list of albums), the SKU would remain the same without the performance engineer parameterizing this too. If the performance engineer were to rerun the script after parameterizing the name, the first iteration would pass. Any subsequent iterations though would fail, as there would be an incorrect SKU for the next album. It would be easy to parameterize the SKU along with the album name, as it could be extracted along with the album name from the stock database.

Dynamic server–created values, on the other hand, are unknown before execution. A session ID is a good example – no way to predict this before execution. Session IDs can be annoying, as once the script is recorded, the session ID may be kept active by replaying the script (as the "user" is still active as far as the server knows). The absolute best thing to do in this case is have a long lunch:

Seven course meal with three wines and brandy...[8]

Non-alcoholic options are also available.

---

[8] *Yes, Prime Minister* Episode 1 – "The Grand Design," lunch with the German Ambassador, just for Joe!

During this dining bonanza, the session ID will expire, and upon return replaying the script will pass an expired session ID and fail.

The steps to correlate these dynamic server values are shown in Figure 4-25.

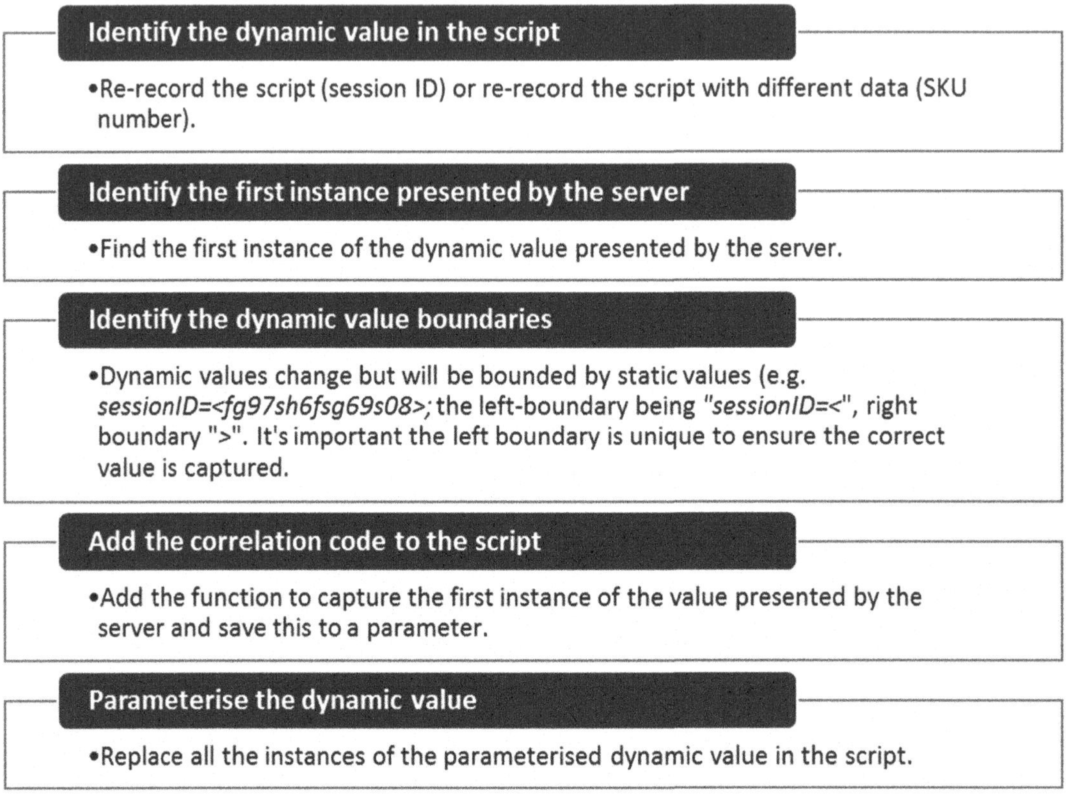

Identify the dynamic value in the script

- Re-record the script (session ID) or re-record the script with different data (SKU number).

Identify the first instance presented by the server

- Find the first instance of the dynamic value presented by the server.

Identify the dynamic value boundaries

- Dynamic values change but will be bounded by static values (e.g. *sessionID=<fg97sh6fsg69s08>;* the left-boundary being *"sessionID=<"*, right boundary *">"*. It's important the left boundary is unique to ensure the correct value is captured.

Add the correlation code to the script

- Add the function to capture the first instance of the value presented by the server and save this to a parameter.

Parameterise the dynamic value

- Replace all the instances of the parameterised dynamic value in the script.

Figure 4-25. *Steps to correlate*

And, of course, after the changes are made, test the script!

Summary   Internal identifiers (like session IDs) must be correlated to allow the script to run successfully. Correlation involves finding the first instance of the value sent from the server, capturing the value, and parameterizing all occurrences of the recorded value. Some tools automate correlation, or it can be done manually.

Running multiple virtual users with the same username and accessing the same set of data (as usually happens during playback of a recorded script without any further modification beyond necessary correlation) is an easy way to get misleading results. The data could be completely cached (copied from disk to memory for faster access) and results would be much better than in production (where such data may be read from a disk). Using the same users and/or data can also cause concurrency issues (e.g., if data is locked when a user is updating it) and results would be much worse than in production as the software would wait for the lock to free before the next user could lock the data for update.

—ISTQB_CTFL_PT

Data caching is a useful function in production systems but can also be the bane of many performance engineers. The cache is an area of memory reserved to temporarily store frequently accessed data. Computers, routers, and switches use caching to speed up memory access, browsers cache objects to stop retrieving the same object multiple times, client/server systems cache information at both the client and server, and databases cache frequently accessed records.

The problems with performance testing lie in the unintended use of the cache. If the cache is used in production, it should be used during the performance test. But there are several situations that could cause problems:

- If the browser cache is turned on, each virtual user might be using a cache when it may be the first time that "user" should have accessed the system (and hence download the objects). Performance engineers should check how web caching is set up on the client – many performance tools allow the cache to be cleared on each new user iteration.

- If the performance script has a limited set of user-defined data being used, it may be that records are cached, giving a false impression as to the speed at which the database responds. If the required data needs to be found on the disk, it will take much longer than accessing the data from the cache in RAM.

The steps to reduce the adverse effect of data caching are shown in Figure 4-26.

Consider the volume of user-defined data

- The volume of user-defined input data should be big enough to reduce the possibility of unintended data caching.

Consider the script data selection method

- Input data should be selected from the test data source to minimise the possibility of sequential selection (every virtual user using row 1 in the data source, then row 2, then row 3...) Random (pick any from a list) or unique (use this value once) data selection is the preferred data selection method.

Consider the volume of master data

- Ensure the test database is not too small. Small databases respond faster (as there are less rows to search) and increase the possibility of unintended caching (as there is less data to pick from).

Parameterise the input data

- Ensure the input values hard-coded in the script are replaced with dynamic parameters to allow a wide variety of values to be used as script input.

Figure 4-26. *Test data considerations*

Summary Reusing the same master or user-defined data can cause

- Data caching (reading from RAM rather than disk), meaning results are returned faster
- Concurrency issues due to record locking in the database, meaning results are returned slower

---

So scripts and test harnesses should be parameterized (i.e., fixed or recorded data should be replaced with values from a list of possible choices), so that each virtual user uses a proper set of data. The term "proper" here means different enough to avoid problems with caching and concurrency, which is specific for the system, data, and test requirements. This further parameter-

ization depends on the data in the system and the way the system works with this data, so it usually is done manually, although many tools provide assistance here.

—ISTQB_CTFL_PT

Although automated parameterization can be tempting, it's like doing a search and replace in a document. It can be that values that shouldn't be parameterized can unintentionally be replaced, or values that require parameterization are missed.

Summary   Script and test harness fixed values should be parameterized.

There are cases where some data must be parameterized for the test to work more than once-for example, when an order is created, and the order name must be unique. Unless the order's name is parameterized, the test will fail as soon as it tries to create an order with an existing (recorded) name.

—ISTQB_CTFL_PT

Unique transactional data often becomes a primary key in a database table and can be valuable to capture. This can be the advantage of capturing transactional data – as this output data can now be reused as input data for a later script. It can also be used as an expected result – this order number should be returned on a search for open orders for this customer.

Summary   Unique values must be parameterized for the script to work.

To match operational profiles, think times should be inserted and/or adjusted (if recorded) to generate a proper number of requests/throughput as discussed in Section 4.2.5.

—ISTQB_CTFL_PT

This is a good point. As an example, we can return to the code from earlier:

```
1  SelectItem()
2  {
3
4      lr_think_time(12);
5
6      // DRAG ITEM INTO BASKET
7
8      lr_start_transaction("Item_In_Basket");
9
10     web_submit_form("put_in_basket",
11                     "Snapshot=t12.inf",
12                     ITEMDATA,
13                     "name=itempick","value=\"Sunshine On Leith\"", ENDITEM,
14                     "name=itemsku","value=1049296", ENDITEM,
15                     LAST);
16
17     lr_end_transaction("Item_In_Basket", LR_AUTO);
18
19     return 0;
20  }
```

The *lr_think_time* represents some user action in the client – it took 12 seconds from getting the search results to placing the desired item in the basket. It might be the user who created this script is a new user, unfamiliar with the interface. An experienced user might only take 4 seconds. There are options here:

- The lr_think_time value could be parameterized, with the desired value being replaced by a variable being drawn from the user-defined dataset in the script.

- Some tools allow the think time to be handled according to a set of think time rules. When the performance engineer is testing the script, think time can be disabled (to speed up execution replay). It can be replayed as recorded or multiplied by a factor (e.g., 12 seconds x 1.5 = 18 seconds), with these values being hard-coded based on the recorded value. The third randomizes the think time based on the percentage multipliers (in the example, the time would be a random value between 6 and 18 seconds). The last option limits the think time to less than a value (e.g., if this was set to 10 seconds, the random value would be restricted between 6 and 10 seconds). See Figure 4-27.

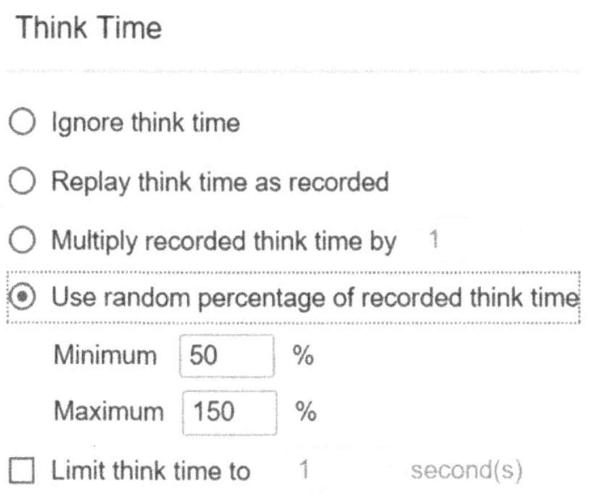

Think Time

○ Ignore think time

○ Replay think time as recorded

○ Multiply recorded think time by   1

◉ Use random percentage of recorded think time

    Minimum   50   %

    Maximum   150   %

☐ Limit think time to   1   second(s)

Figure 4-27. *Micro Focus LoadRunner think time runtime settings*

But this only affects the internal think time until the iteration is complete. Another setting that can be used is adding time onto the end of the iteration – known as pacing (Figure 4-28).

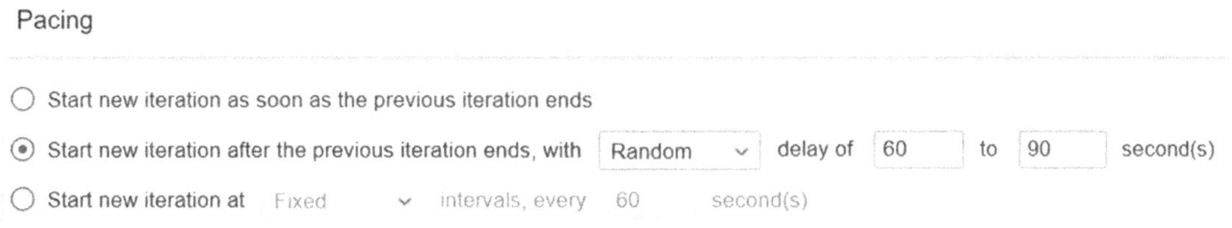

Pacing

○ Start new iteration as soon as the previous iteration ends

◉ Start new iteration after the previous iteration ends, with   Random   ∨   delay of   60   to   90   second(s)

○ Start new iteration at   Fixed   ∨   intervals, every   60   second(s)

Figure 4-28. *Micro Focus LoadRunner pacing runtime settings*

Pacing can be both fixed and random. An iteration can be delayed after the iteration is complete by a set time or can be started at a defined interval. The last could be problematic, as if the iteration takes longer than 60 seconds, and another iteration should start, it waits until the previous iteration ends and commences the next iteration immediately.

Summary   Think times can be adjusted to suit the operational profile.

When scripts for separate operational profiles are created, they are com-bined into a scenario implementing the whole load profile. The load profile controls how many virtual users are started using each script, when, and with what parameters. The exact implementation details depend on the specific load testing tool or harness.

—ISTQB_CTFL_PT

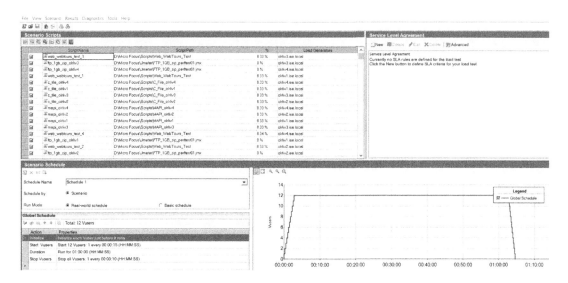

Figure 4-29. *LoadRunner – building a scenario*

Creating the full performance test scenario allows multiple user groups, each running a specified number of virtual users, with specific ramp-up, run duration, and ramp-down settings (Figure 4-29). Importantly, other variables, from the think time and pacing mentioned earlier, to the type of browser and bandwidth each user group uses, to individual environment variables to be set. The scenario then, during execution, allows the results and metrics to be captured, observed during runtime, and analyzed (Figure 4-30).

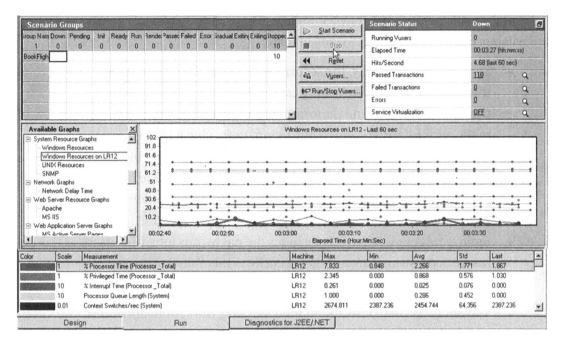

Figure 4-30. *LoadRunner – scenario execution*

Summary   A script is written to match the operational profile, which are combined into a scenario (the load profile).

4.2.8 Preparing for Performance Test Execution

PTFL-4.2.8 (K2) Understand the activities involved in preparing for performance test execution

> *The main activities for preparing to execute the performance tests include:*
>
> - *Setting up the system under test*
>
> - *Deploying the environment*
>
> - *Setting up the load generation and monitoring tools and making sure that all the necessary information will be collected*
>
> —ISTQB_CTFL_PT

Preparing the performance environment can cover a wide range of points beneath the syllabus points. Some things to consider are:

- Security – Occasionally, the security settings on the system under test are altered "to make testing easier." Although this may be true, it can alter the end-to-end performance. Any security added can add to the performance resource utilization. Removing it can remove this overhead. As well (and arguably more importantly), reducing the security on a test environment can create a vulnerability to become an attack vector for malicious users (both external and internal). Test environments must be secured as they would be in production to remove this possibility. This includes the passwords for virtual users (as weak passwords are another security vulnerability many test environments fall victim to).

- Test data – As previously mentioned, not only the system under test and performance test tool make up the performance environment. Master data is also included. Processes to manage the master data (source/ create/ refresh/ update) in the performance test master dataset are important. It also ties to security – sourcing or creating data that complies with the privacy regulations is required by law (as weakened security and production data in test is a recipe for disaster).

- Availability – A good performance environment makes the performance testing job much easier. But it also becomes useful for others to use as well – it can be typical that the environment is used for user training or some other form of testing. Proper scheduling of the environment for different user groups is a must. Change control/ configuration management are essential, as without these controls, time can be wasted chasing spurious performance results based on unauthorized changes.

Summary   The performance test execution tasks

- Set up the system under test

- Deploy the environment

- Set up load generators/monitoring tools and ensure necessary information is collected

It is important to ensure the test environment is as close to the production environment as possible. If this is not possible, then there must be a clear understanding of the differences and how the test results will be projected on the production environment. Ideally, the true production environment and data would be used, but testing in a scaled-down environment still may help mitigate a number of performance risks.

—ISTQB_CTFL_PT

Performing a gap analysis between the (planned) production environment and the planned and actual performance test environment can help cover any issues that could occur. This would include shortfalls in performance test results which could affect the achievement of the performance test objectives. Any shortfalls should be recorded as risks to the project and added to the risk register and evaluated. Any assumptions and constraints should also be captured to be dealt with.

Summary   The test environment should be as close to production-like as possible (both the hardware and test data), or there must be a documented understanding of the differences and how they will affect the results.

It is important to remember that performance is a non-linear function of the environment, so the further the environment is from production standard, the more difficult it becomes to make accurate projections for production performance. The lack of reliability of the projections and the increased risk level grow as the test system looks less like production.

—ISTQB_CTFL_PT

Remember extrapolation? This is the reason why it may not work. Extrapolation requires a prediction on the system under test's behavior beyond any gathered results data. It might work, but the risks of the extrapolation being wrong should always be acknowledged.

Summary   Performance is nonlinear. The bigger the difference between production and test environments, the less accurate the results.

The most important parts of the test environment are data, hardware and software configuration, and network configuration. The size and structure of the data could affect load test results dramatically. Using a small sample set of data or a sample set with a different data complexity for performance tests can give misleading results, particularly when the production system will use a large set of data. It is difficult to predict how much the data size affects performance before real testing is performed. The closer the test data is to the production data in size and structure, the more reliable the test results will be.

If data is generated or altered during the test, it may be necessary to restore the original data before the next test cycle to ensure that the system is in the proper state.

—ISTQB_CTFL_PT

A good tip is to set a database or virtual machine restore point. This simple step can speed up any environment refresh needed, but at the same time limit the performance testing being executed. Returning to a known starting point can ensure multiple runs are executed under the same conditions and return similar results – particularly useful when isolating an issue. It can however restrict the observation of database performance as the dataset expands. As well, it can take time to refresh a large dataset. A project once used a database that was very comprehensive but took 26 hours to restore to a known starting point after a performance test cycle was complete. That amount of time placed pressure on the schedule, so as strange as it might be, sometimes there can be too much data. The performance tests in this case would have been better to be written to use the test system database in whatever state it was in, to save on the refresh time.

Summary   The important parts of the test environment are data and hardware, software, and network configurations. The closer the data size is to production, the more realistic the results.

If some parts of the system or some of the data is unavailable for performance tests for whatever reason, a workaround should be implemented. For example, a stub may be implemented to replace and emulate a third-party component responsible for credit card processing. That process is often referred to as "service virtualization" and there are special tools available to assist with that process. The use of such tools is highly recommended to isolate the system under test.

—ISTQB_CTFL_PT

A range of service virtualization tools exist (including both commercial and open source). They allow the creation and deployment of virtual API sets to replicate the behavior of a system or externally sourced service. This is particularly useful for performance testing a single tier – the other tiers in the system might be replaced with service virtualization. Performance engineers should consider the nature of the API (languages/libraries/frameworks), along with the protocol used in communication between the service provider and the system under test.

Summary   Service virtualization can allow testing to continue if components or data are missing by replacing the missing components or data feeds.

There are many ways to deploy environments. For example, options may include using any of the following:

- *Traditional internal (and external) test labs*

- *Cloud as an environment using Infrastructure as a Service (IaaS), when some parts of the system or all of the system is deployed to the cloud*

- *Cloud as an environment using Software as a Service (SaaS), when vendors provide the load testing service*

—ISTQB_CTFL_PT

Performance engineers should consider the advantages and disadvantages of any deployment option, as has been mentioned earlier. It should be noted that, although not explicitly mentioned in the syllabus, these environments might also be virtualized, adding to the complexity. Things to note include:

- Production likeness – Like virtual environments, the two cloud options might be chosen for cost reasons rather than production likeness. When looking at virtual environments, the difference between the test and production environments were considered; the same should be done here.

- Monitoring – It can be difficult to get low-level monitoring information from the cloud provider. Arrangements should be made for the provision of such – either access via the performance engineer's monitoring tool(s) or the provision for the cloud provider to supply these results.

- Change control/configuration management – Performance engineers must abide by The Golden Rule of Test Environments During Performance Test Development and Execution:

We work as a team, and we do what the performance engineer says!

Unauthorized changes can have a major impact on the performance test results – best avoid these. As well, any authorized changes made to the environment (whether for defect repair or performance tuning the environment) must be recorded.

Summary   Test environments are deployed using the following:

- Traditional internal/external test labs
- Cloud environments using Infrastructure as a Service (IaaS)
- Cloud environments using Software as a Service (SaaS)

Depending on the specific goals and the systems to test, one test environment may be preferred over another. For example,

- *To test the effect of a performance improvement (performance optimization), using an isolated lab environment may be a better option to see even small variations introduced by the change.*

—ISTQB_CTFL_PT

An isolated environment allows The Golden Rule of Test Environments During Performance Test Development and Execution to reign supreme! It can remove extraneous factors that could affect the outcome of the performance test.

To load test the whole production environment end-to-end to make sure the system will handle the load without any major issues, testing from the cloud or a service may be more appropriate. (Note that this only works for SUTs that can be reached from a cloud).

To minimize costs when performance testing is limited in time, creating a test environment in the cloud may be a more economical solution.

—ISTQB_CTFL_PT

Cloud testing is becoming more popular for several reasons:

1. Scaling – Scaling the load can be easier due to the availability of resources.

2. External load – Because the load is coming from "outside the firewall," the full end-to-end infrastructure (firewall/proxy/ internal bandwidth) can be tested.

3. Available as a service – Vendors (such as IBM and Micro Focus) have cloud performance testing as a service. Performance engineers can create the tests and scenarios, then execute using the vendor's cloud servers.

4. Cost – Obtaining cloud resource can be a cost-effective option (when both licensing and maintenance are also considered) against internal servers. Much of the time, older hardware is used in test environments, which may be OK for functional testing,

even some limited testing of non-functional test types (security/usability/maintainability), although performance may have an impact on testing these.

Summary   Test environments can differ depending on the performance test type.

Whatever approach to deployment is used, both hardware and software should be configured to meet the test objective and plan. If the environment matches production, it should be configured in the same way. However, if there are differences, the configuration may have to be adjusted to accommodate these differences. For example, if test machines have less physical memory than the production machines, software memory parameters (such as Java heap size) may need to be adjusted to avoid memory paging.

—ISTQB_CTFL_PT

Compromises such as the memory mentioned earlier are always a possibility in any performance test project. If configuration changes (such as changing the Java heap size) are needed, these changes must be analyzed, and the results added as required to the project risk register. Any configuration changes could compromise the overall performance objectives and need to be treated as a risk. For example, if the project is testing a Citrix server farm with ten servers, might suggest taking a single server for performance testing and applying 10% of the load through that single server. The risks relate to the fact we are only testing 10% of the load and thus cannot check the rest of the infrastructure (specifically load balancing and network bandwidth). This type of test could also succumb to the Law of Diminishing Returns,[9] coupled with the danger of extrapolation also possibly affecting the performance test results.

Summary   The test environment should be configured to meet the performance test objectives. If the environment differs from production, the configuration can be adjusted to compensate for the difference.

---

[9]Although the Law of Diminishing Returns relates to economics, the applicability to performance means if one server gives 100% of the required performance, it isn't necessarily true that two servers will give 200%.

Proper configuration/emulation of the network is important for global and mobile systems. For global systems (i.e., one which has users or processing distributed worldwide) one of approaches may be to deploy load generators in places where users are located. For mobile systems network emulation remains the most viable option due to the variances in the network types that can be used. Some load testing tools have built-in network emulation tools and there are standalone tools for network emulation.

—ISTQB_CTFL_PT

As mentioned in Chapter 3.2, each option has good and bad points. Network emulation allows full control over the test infrastructure, with either software or hardware devices simulating the network conditions (bandwidth, latency, and packet loss). The good side of network virtualization is the performance engineer has full control over the infrastructure with no extraneous load on the network (unless the performance engineer puts it there). The downside of network virtualization is a virtual network may not match the real-world network, the performance engineer does NOT have full control, and extraneous load (which will affect the production load to varying degrees) is NOT present.

Summary   For global environment network configuration, load generators should be distributed to match the source of users. For mobile environments, network emulation should be used to simulate different network conditions.

The load generation tools should be properly deployed, and the monitoring tools should be configured to collect all necessary metrics for the test. The list of metrics depends on the test objectives, but it is recommended to collect at least basic metrics for all tests (see Section 2.1.2).

Depending on the load, specific tool/load generation approach, and machine configuration, more than one load generation machine may be needed. To verify the setup, machines involved in load generation should be monitored too. This will help avoid a situation where the load is not maintained properly because one of the load generators is running slowly.

Depending on the setup and tools used, load testing tools need to be configured to create the appropriate load. For example, specific browser emulation parameters may be set or IP spoofing (simulating that each virtual user has a different IP address) may be used.

—ISTQB_CTFL_PT

These items (having been covered earlier) are important, as the ability to generate the correct level and type of load in a production-like (and tested) environment cannot be undervalued.

Summary   For global environment network configuration, load generators should be distributed to match the source of users. For mobile environments, network emulation should be used to simulate different network conditions.

Before tests are executed, the environment and setup must be validated. This is usually done by conducting a controlled set of tests and verifying the outcome of the tests as well as checking that the monitoring tools are tracking the important information.

—ISTQB_CTFL_PT

Refer to the initial and final environment acceptance tests in Chapter 3.1. The test environment delivered should match that which was planned, should be enough to support the performance objectives, and, hopefully, should be production-like. Any monitoring should capture the required metrics, store them, and make the results available for analysis.

Summary   The performance test environment must be tested!

To verify that the test works as designed, a variety of techniques may be used, including log analysis and verifying database content. Preparing for the test includes checking that required information gets logged, the system is in the proper state, etc. For example, if the test changes the state of the system significantly (add/change information in database), it may be necessary to return the system to the original state before repeating the test.

—ISTQB_CTFL_PT

Testing the tests should become second nature to all performance engineers.

Summary   The performance test scripts and scenarios must be tested!

4.3 Execution

PTFL-4.3.1 (K2) Understand the principal activities in running performance test scripts

"It's quite exciting," said Sherlock Holmes, *with a yawn.*

—Conan Doyle, 1887

First – a warning. Performance test execution can be boring. It might involve sitting in a dark office after hours watching little graphs creep across the screen. Performance engineers sometimes execute tests after hours to minimize the impact of normal organization network traffic interfering with the executing performance test. As well, the performance test can interfere with organization traffic.

If after-hours execution is required, it's important for performance engineers to consider the following personal security points (along with the downside of not following them):

1. Notification – Inform site security you will be in the office late (the author was held at gunpoint while his ID was checked due to security being "unaware" of a late-night performance test running within a high security site!).

2. Access – Never, EVER, remove your security pass when running performance tests, especially if you need to open security doors (a colleague of the author was once found asleep in the toilets the next morning due to having left his security pass at his desk for a call of nature).

3. Transport – Ensure your chosen mode of transport is operating at the time you plan to finish work and leave (another colleague slept on the office floor one night, as the only available cab company in the area had closed for the night before he called. His other choice was a 10-mile walk back to the hotel). If you're driving – be careful driving tired!

4. Food – It's a good idea to have access to more than the contents of the office vending machines; you will get sick of eating Doritos and chocolate bars after a few days. And please be careful ordering pizza. Remember the security pass? You can probably

guess what happened – pizza on a bench outside the office, with everything (including the security pass) safely locked up inside the building...

5. Office ergonomics – If your office has motion-sensitive lights, you have a choice. You could either:

    a. Stand and wave your arms

    b. Stand and wave your arms to music, creating an impromptu aerobics session

    c. Bring a Frisbee – A short lob into the air and catch it yourself to reactivate the lights

    or

    d. (My favorite) Sit in darkness...

Performance test execution involves generation of a load against the SUT according to a load profile (usually implemented by performance testing scripts invoked according to a given scenario), monitoring all parts of the environment, and collecting and keeping all results and information related to the test. Usually advanced load testing tools/harnesses perform these tasks automatically (after, of course, proper configuration). They generally provide a console to enable performance data to be monitored during the test and permit necessary adjustments to be made (see Section 5.1). However, depending on the tool used, the SUT, and the specific tests being executed, some manual steps may be needed.

—ISTQB_CTFL_PT

Performance engineers should look to automate result collection as much as possible. If the tool can gather the results automatically, it can solve many problems. But there may be monitoring options that exist separately to the tool. Monitoring tools such as the Splunk set or more specific tools like AppDynamics (application monitoring) or Fiddler (network monitoring) could always augment any performance test monitoring.

Summary   The performance test generates the load as defined by the load profile, load against the system, allowing the system to be monitored to collect results and metrics. These can be monitored during the test through the tool, and adjustments to the execution can be made.

Performance tests are usually focused on a steady state of the system, i.e., when the system's behavior is stable. For example, when all simulated users/threads are initiated and are performing work as designed. When the load is changing (for example, when new users are added), the system's behavior is changing, and it becomes more difficult to monitor and analyse test results. The stage of getting to the steady state is often referred to as the ramp-up, and the stage of finishing the test is often referred to as the ramp-down.

—ISTQB_CTFL_PT

The concept of ramp-up/steady state/ramp-down looks at, in most cases, starting and stopping the virtual users as part of the planned load profile. This goes on to form the typical load test shape of the running virtual users (Figure 4-31).

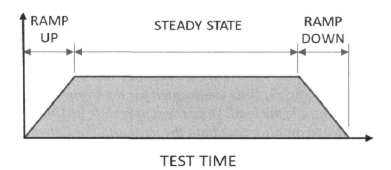

Figure 4-31. *Ramp-up, steady state, and ramp-down*

Summary   Performance tests focus on a steady system state under load to gather results. If the environment state is changing, results analysis becomes more difficult.

It is sometimes important to test transient states, when the system's behavior is changing. This may apply, for example, to the concurrent logging of a large number of users or spike tests. When testing transient states, it is important to understand the need for careful monitoring and analysis of the results, as some standard approaches—such as monitoring averages—may be very misleading.

—ISTQB_CTFL_PT

Testing in a constant state can make the job of analyzing performance tests much easier. Unfortunately, it's rare that a system exists for an extended period in a continual constant state. Small fluctuations in load will occur, and these are conditions tests should replicate. These fluctuations can be manipulated by varying the think time and pacing of the virtual user iterations. Initially, think time and pacing should be fixed to allow the test to run in a constant state. If issues are discovered, they can then be investigated with multiple runs of the performance test to diagnose the root cause. Once any initial defects have been identified and removed, think time and pacing randomization can be introduced. These small timing variations create a more realistic simulation of real load.

Summary   In some situations, the ramp-up/ramp-down form part of the performance test. Careful monitoring/analysis is required.

During the ramp-up it is advisable to implement incremental load states to monitor the impact of the steadily increasing load on the system's response. This ensures that sufficient time is allocated for the ramp-up and that the system is able to handle the load. Once the steady state has been reached, it is a good practice to monitor that both the load and the system's responses are stable and that random variations (which always exist) are not substantial.

—ISTQB_CTFL_PT

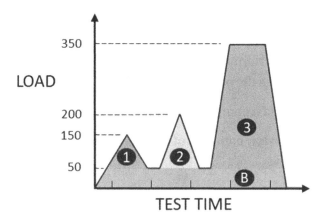

Figure 4-32. *Load profile diagram*

In every performance test project, the question always comes up around the rate at which the virtual users log in (Figure 4-32). How quickly can this be done?

If the login transaction does form an active part of the performance test, virtual user ramp-up is defined by the load profile. For example, the performance test could replicate users are arriving at work to log in to an organization-based client/server system. For this test, the ramp-up forms an active part of the load test and should match the rate at which staff members would log in (Figure 4-33).

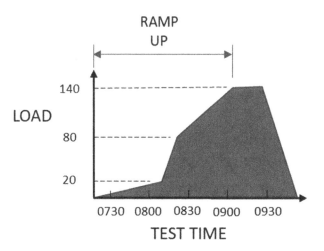

Figure 4-33. *Ramp-up*

In this case, the ramp-up rate changes, as many staff might arrive on the 08:00 train (a typical requirement in these situations).

If the objective of the performance test relates to the duration (i.e., the time after ramp-up is completed), then the objective would be twofold:

1. Log the users in fast enough to not waste time

2. Log the users in slow enough not to cause the system under test to fail

The performance test proper starts once the virtual users are logged in. But until then, performance engineers should always keep a watching eye on the system performance, just to be sure. For example, if Active Directory (AD) is involved in the test, it could be the performance AD is the production AD. Similar to the network that both production and performance testing are using, care must be taken before flooding both with performance traffic!

Summary   Ramp-up should be fast enough not to waste time and slow enough not to adversely affect the system under test.

It is important to specify how failures should be handled to make sure that no system issues are introduced. For example, it may be important for the user to logout when a failure occurs to ensure that all resources associated with that user are released.

—ISTQB_CTFL_PT

A fundamental issue every performance engineer will face is defining the term "failure." The ISTQB Foundation syllabus defines this in the following (Figure 4-34):

A person can make an error (mistake), which can lead to the introduction of a defect (fault or bug) in the software code or in some other related work product. An error that leads to the introduction of a defect in one work product can trigger an error that leads to the introduction of a defect in a related work product. For example, a requirements elicitation error can lead to a requirements defect, which then results in a programming error that leads to a defect in the code. If a defect in the code is executed, this may cause a failure, but not necessarily in all circumstances. For example, some defects require very specific inputs or preconditions to trigger a failure, which may occur rarely or never...

In addition to failures caused due to defects in the code, failures can also be caused by environmental conditions. For example, radiation, electromagnetic fields, and pollution can cause defects in firmware or influence the execution of software by changing hardware conditions.

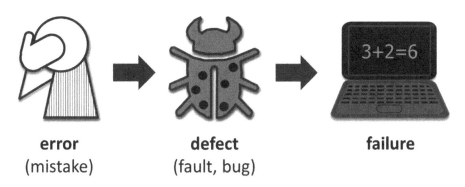

error	defect	failure
(mistake)	(fault, bug)	

Figure 4-34. *Error-defect-failure (from ISTQB CTFL)*

The difficulty for performance engineers is the definition of a performance defect can, by and large, fit this definition. But let's say a performance test has a goal of a two-second maximum response time under a defined load for a particular transaction. After running the test, the actual response time maximum was 2.1 seconds – a fail based on the requirement. Is the system "broken"? Or is it simply 5% slower than the desired and is not based on a defect caused by an error? Could it be a defect in the original specifications – why two seconds?

Another issue is the language we use. If a performance engineer calls this a failure (as in "The test failed..."), in almost every instance the stakeholders think "functional failure" – something is broken.

An important task for performance engineers in any performance project is to define the meaning of "a performance defect." Although the example did use transaction time, stakeholders should be encouraged to think beyond only transaction times as performance test goals. If a particular transaction time under load is desired, the nature of this time must be specified. If the objective is to achieve a two-second response time under load, it should be specified if that time is:

1. The maximum time – The maximum time a transaction can take during this performance test. If the requirements specified 2 seconds and out of 15,000 transactions, one was 2.1 seconds, the test would be defined as a failure.

2. The average time – The mean value of the transaction results. Unfortunately, some tools by default report average time in graphical form which can subsequently be misinterpreted by stakeholders. It should be acknowledged that an average will have a lot of data points above that line as well as below it. Performance engineers must ensure if the requirement states an average, stakeholders must understand there can be a significant deviation of values both above and below the mean. To sum up averages

Say you were standing with one foot in the oven and one foot in an ice bucket. According to the percentage people, you should be perfectly comfortable.

—Bobby Bragan

3. A percentile – A percentage of transactions completed within the specified requirement. For example, if the requirement states the 90th percentile as the goal, 90% of the transactions would need to complete within the stated two-second time.

A problem that exists within the performance space is the "black and white" nature of functional testing. Once again, most stakeholders think of the system as either working or not working. Tends to be different shades of gray. We can take this into account by using a measurement tolerance. For example, the two-second response time mentioned earlier, a RAG status could be implemented to build in an element of gray between the black and white. If a tolerance of 10% above goal were to be used:

Tolerance	Range
Red	2.2 seconds +
Amber	2.01–2.2 seconds
Green	Up to 2 seconds

To refer to the maximum time example mentioned earlier, the 2.1-second response time would show in the results as amber – signaling to the stakeholders the goal was exceeded by a small (and maybe acceptable) amount.

Another important consideration is the recording of performance defects. Countless times, the performance engineers discover an issue, investigate, and pass the information to administrators and/or developers. They fix the problem, the performance engineer retests, and the issue has been mitigated. And nothing was recorded. This creates a problem – no details of the issue, no cause-effect information, and no remediation steps captured. Later, when reporting is done on the overall project, the return on investment for performance testing is sometimes questioned, as in the words of project management, "No defects were discovered!"

Summary   Performance test failures should be defined, with error handling steps run as needed.

If monitoring is built into the load testing tool and it is properly configured, it usually starts at the same time as the test execution. However, if stand-alone monitoring tools are used, monitoring should be started separately, and the necessary information collected such that subsequent analysis can be carried out together with the test results. The same is true for log analysis. It is essential to time-synchronize all tools used, so that all information related to a specific test execution cycle can be located.

—ISTQB_CTFL_PT

The statement on time-synching different tools together is vital as it addresses one of the shortfalls of disparate monitoring. Analysis involves the merging of this results information to discover the effects and their causes to eventually determine the root cause of a performance issue. If there is no common reference point, it makes this comparison and merging of results much less certain.

Summary   Performance test monitoring should be properly configured, starting when the test begins (either automatically within the performance test tool or manually for external tools). All monitoring should be time synched.

Test execution is often monitored using the performance test tool's console and real-time log analysis to check for issues and errors in both the test and the SUT. This helps to avoid needlessly continuing with running large-scale tests, which might even impact other systems if things go wrong (e.g., if fail-

ure occur, components fail, or the generated loads are too low or high).
These tests can be expensive to run, and it may be necessary to stop the test
or make some on-the-fly adjustments to the performance test or the system
configuration if the test deviates from the expected behavior.

—ISTQB_CTFL_PT

Previously, in this chapter, some remarks were made about boredom regarding performance test execution. Occasionally, it can get a bit more exciting (but only a bit). Although a necessary evil, the need to "babysit" performance tests can pay off for the reason mentioned in the syllabus. Removing a single virtual user with troublesome data or a script-related error can save time in the long run.

Summary   Test execution is monitored to spot issues in the tests themselves and the test system. If an issue exists, it can be fixed while execution continues, or the test can be stopped.

One technique for verifying load tests which are communicating directly on the protocol level is to run several GUI-level (functional) scripts or even to execute similar operational profiles manually in parallel to the running load test. This checks that response times reported during the test only differ from the response times measured manually at the GUI level by the time spent on the client side.

—ISTQB_CTFL_PT

In Chapter 1.4, UI load generation was covered. This is similar – we can run background load on the system to create the correct load profile; the shortfall of this is any client-side processing being done can be excluded from the transaction times (Figure 4-35).

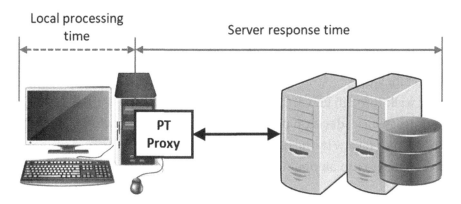

Local processing time

Server response time

Figure 4-35. *Protocol scripts missing client processing time*

If the requirement is for a 100-user load test, 98 could be protocol virtual users, with 2 GUI virtual users in addition. The protocol virtual users create the background load with the two GUI virtual users giving a realistic response time by including the client-side processing.

Summary   Protocol-level scripts can be run, but do not capture client-side processing. With a small number of GUI users, the performance test can measure the client-side performance time.

In some cases when running performance testing in an automated way (for example, as a part of Continuous Integration, as discussed in Section 3.4) checks must be done automatically, since manual monitoring and intervention may not be possible. In this case, the test set up should be able to recognize any deviations or problems and issue an alert (usually while properly completing the test). This approach is easier to implement for regression performance tests when the system's behavior is generally known but may be more difficult with exploratory performance tests or large-scale expensive performance tests that may need adjustments to be made dynamically during the test.

—ISTQB_CTFL_PT

The CI-based alert reporting works well with the RAG status mentioned earlier. In these cases, if alerts are flagged by the automated tests, they can be assessed by the performance engineer, and if needed further tests can be run. A good set of metrics is vital in the DevOps space to allow performance engineers, administrators, and developers to assess if the latest code drop achieves the minimum performance requirements. The process gives the stakeholders a decision point within the workflow to accept or reject the build.

A process walk-through for CI/CD automation is shown in Figure 4-36. At each automated process stage, decision points allow the process to continue, or deployment can be stopped after review by the development team. At both unit and system tests, the scripts are designed to run automatically without intervention (Figure 4-36).

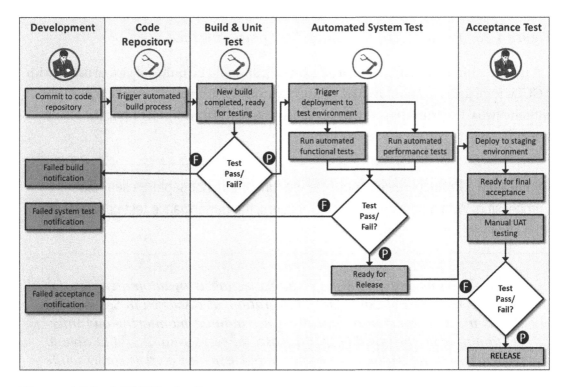

Figure 4-36. *A CI/CD pipeline*

The range of tools available in the CI/CD space grows larger by the day. A good source of information surrounding this space is `https://devops.com/` – with a wealth of information (including blogs on continuous testing). Tool information can be found at the following link:

`https://blog.xebialabs.com/2016/06/14/periodic-table-devops-tools-v-2/`

Summary   For continuous integration, both execution and checks are automated. Issues should be recognized, and alerts sent. This approach is good for regression but is more difficult for exploratory or tests requiring manual adjustment.

4.4 Analyzing Results and Reporting

PTFL-4.4.1 (K4) Analyze and report performance test results and implications

The world is full of obvious things which nobody by any chance ever observes.

—Conan Doyle, 1901

"They say that genius is an infinite capacity for taking pains," he remarked with a smile. "It's a very bad definition, but it does apply to detective work."

—Conan Doyle, 1887

You know my methods. Apply them.

—Conan Doyle, 1890

Section 4.1.2 discussed the various metrics in a performance test plan. Defining these up front determines what must be measured for each test run. After completion of a test cycle, data should be collected for the defined metrics.

—ISTQB_CTFL_PT

Additionally, in Chapters 1.1 and 2.1.2, a standard set of generic metrics were outlined. Ultimately, whatever set of metrics are captured, whether they be via the test tool or another source of monitoring, this is the point where performance engineers earn their money. A performance engineer can only become a good performance engineer by mastering results analysis.

When analyzing the data, it is first compared to the performance test objective. Once the behavior is understood, conclusions can be drawn which provide a meaningful summary report that includes recommended actions. These actions may include changing physical components (e.g., hardware, routers), changing software (e.g., optimizing applications and database calls), and altering the network (e.g., load balancing, routing).

—ISTQB_CTFL_PT

Having gathered these facts, Watson, I smoked several pipes over them, trying to separate those which were crucial from others which were merely incidental.

—Conan Doyle, 1894

Cause-effect (also known as causality or causation) states one event, process, or state (a cause) contributes to the production of another event, process, or state (an effect). This was considered in Chapter 1.5 – available memory is running low (a cause), leading to paging commencing (an effect).

It needs to be stated, however, that more often the initially identified effect is the end of a chain of causality. It usually manifests (at least initially) in a transaction time exceeding a stated goal. Performance engineers need to scroll through the chain to find the initial cause.

There can also be a danger, as specified by folks even older than Holmes:

Post hoc ergo propter hoc

(after it, therefore because of it)

The modern interpretation is correlation does not imply causation (although this is slightly different from that above, it's still relevant). Occasionally, the wrong conclusion can be drawn. For example, if the available memory drops low, simultaneously the CPU utilization spikes, are the two related? It may, or it could be a memory leak from one process and another separate process spiking the CPU.

Final point, don't stop too early. Once again, countless times performance engineers see the CPU utilization is running at 100%, and they identify that as the problem and stop investigating (Inspector Lestrade, anyone?). The next step is always worth considering – which process or processes are using the CPU? Does this CPU utilization correspond with a business process running?

Summary   Analysis begins with the test objectives. The results are then compared to obtain conclusions and from which subsequent recommendations can be drawn (changes to hardware, software, and/or infrastructure).

When analyzing the data, it is first compared to the performance test objective. Once the behavior is understood, conclusions can be drawn which provide a meaningful summary report that includes recommended actions. These actions may include changing physical components (e.g., hardware, routers), changing software (e.g., optimizing applications and database calls), and altering the network (e.g., load balancing, routing).

The following data is typically analyzed:

- **Status of simulated (e.g., virtual) users**. *This needs to be examined first. It is normally expected that all simulated users have been able to accomplish the tasks specified in the operational profile. Any interruption to this activity would mimic what an actual user may experience. This makes it very important to first see that all user activity is completed since any errors encountered may influence the other performance data.*

—ISTQB_CTFL_PT

In Chapter 1.2, the levels of concurrency were defined. The three levels are:

- Application concurrency (all virtual users on the system under test)

- Business process concurrency (virtual users all completing the same business process)

- Transaction concurrency (all virtual users performing the same step simultaneously)

Concurrency should form part of the load profile created as part of the performance test. Of course, the load profile should replicate the behavior of real users, including a small number of users using negative data to simulate real users making a mistake. At the end of the performance test, the status of the virtual users is usually shown as a virtual user passed/failed graph or table of results.

The virtual user status information gives limited data, but it can show individual virtual users or virtual user groups that may have problems relating to one or more of the following:

- Bad user-defined data

- A script error (especially if all virtual users running that script fail)

- A scenario issue (such as virtual users ramping up too quickly)

- A possible business process issue

- A possible database issue (connection pool/table locks)

This is not an exhaustive list, and anything at this stage should be investigated further.

Summary   Check the virtual user status, and look for issues/errors in completing the specified tasks.

- **Transaction response time**. *This can be measured in multiple ways, including minimum, maximum, average, and a percentile (e.g., 90th). The minimum and maximum readings show the extremes of the system performance. The average performance is not necessarily indicative of anything other than the mathematical average and can often be skewed by outliers. The 90th percentile is often used as a goal since it represents the majority of users attaining a specific performance threshold. It is not recommended to require 100% compliance with the performance objectives as the resources required may be too large and the net effect to the users will often be minor.*

—ISTQB_CTFL_PT

Much of the time, minimum times are ignored as they tend to be when a low number of virtual users are on the system at the beginning of a performance test. If the business stakeholders are setting response times as performance test requirements, these need to be defined as an average/maximum/percentile and need to be defined with a defined operational profile in mind.

Summary   Check the transaction response time:

- Minimum and maximum – Extremes of the system performance (outliers)

- Average – Can be skewed by the outliers

- Percentile – Usually 90th percentile, as it returns the time for most virtual users

100% compliance can be costly in resources.

- **Transactions per second**. *This provides information on how much work was done by the system (system throughput).*

—ISTQB_CTFL_PT

Some tools allow transactions to be grouped (e.g., database access, search, form submission, etc.) or separated into individual transactions per second. It should be stated in the graph in Figure 4-37 that each individual line represents a single transaction. Total transactions per second would be the sum of all individual graph lines at any time.

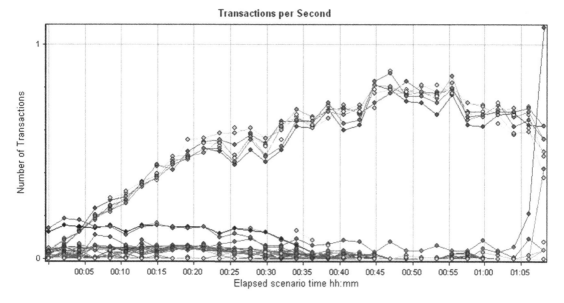

Figure 4-37. *Transaction count per second*

Summary   Check the transaction per second, as a measure of work performed by the system.

- **Transaction failures**. *This data is used when analyzing transactions per second. Failures indicate the expected event or process did not complete or did not execute. Any failures encountered are a cause for concern and the root cause must be investigated. Failed transactions may also result in invalid transactions per second data since a failed transaction will take far less time than a completed one.*

—ISTQB_CTFL_PT

As mentioned earlier in this chapter, for any failure to be a cause of concern the definition of performance "failure" must be defined. For example, it could be a bad set of input user-defined data for that iteration of that virtual user, and not a failure as far as the system under test is concerned. A failed transaction can take less time, but it will depend on the nature of the failure. For example, if the failure is caught by a client-side checkpoint, or a default error captured by the performance test tool, the failure might return quickly. Alternatively, if a search is done for an invalid record, it might take much longer to search or even time out.

Once again, the nature of the failure is important. It could be:

- A standard default failure the tool captures (such as those returned by HTTP return codes or similar)

- A failure relating to bad data

- A business process failure (such as selecting the wrong account for a business process)

- A custom checkpoint failure (a checkpoint created by the performance engineer to check some specific aspect of the system under test)

- A tool failure (such as a failure to access a data source)

Unless the source of the failure is obvious, it will require investigation.

Summary   Check the transaction failures, as a measure of work not completed successfully. Any failures must have the root cause of failure investigated. Failed transactions can affect the transactions per second.

- **Hits (or requests) per second**. *This provides a sense of the number of hits to a server by the simulated users during each second of the test.*

—ISTQB_CTFL_PT

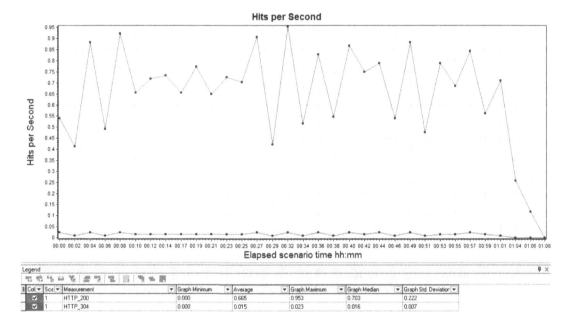

Figure 4-38. *Hits per second*

Hit per second records the number of hits made on the server by virtual users during each second of the performance test (Figure 4-38).

One problem easily seen with hits per second is the "plateau effect." The number of virtual users increases, but the number of hits per second reaches a point and then flatlines, possibly demonstrating a saturation point. More on the plateau effect will follow.

317

Summary   Check the hits (server requests) per second.

Network throughput. This is usually measured in bits by time interval, as in bits per second. This represents the amount of data the simulated users receive from the server every second. (see Section 4.2.5)

—ISTQB_CTFL_PT

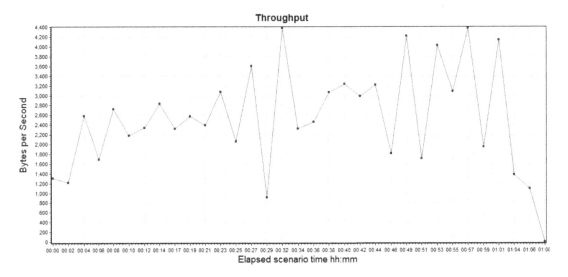

Figure 4-39. *Throughput (bytes per second)*

Throughput captures the amount of data in bytes the virtual users receive from the server at any given second during the performance test (Figure 4-39).

There is a somewhat misunderstood relationship between hits per second and throughput. A large vendor's performance tool training stated that hits per second and throughput should correspond. This was sometimes misinterpreted, as because the demo training website used for training had pages of the same size, both hits per second and throughput exactly mirrored each other. Consider the definitions of hits (a request to the server searching for an item) and throughput (information returned could result in zero to many items). One hit could result in throughput of 100kB, 100MB, or more.

A change in hits per second (an increase or decrease) should see a corresponding change in throughput (an increase or decrease in kind). But rarely do they exactly mirror each other.

Once again, the same plateau effect mentioned earlier can also be evident with network throughput.

Summary   Check the network throughput (bits per second), the amount of data received from the server.

- **HTTP responses**. *These are measured per second and include possible response codes such as: 200, 302, 304, 404, the latter indicating that a page is not found.*

                                                    —ISTQB_CTFL_PT

If any work is done in a web environment, the HTTP return codes become an extremely useful tool. A full list of return codes is available from W3C (`www.w3.org/Protocols/rfc2616/rfc2616-sec10.html`).

Any request made using the HTTP format will generate an HTTP response code in one of five classes. The first digit of the status code defines the class of response:

- 1xx Informational – The request was received, continuing process.

- 2xx Successful – The request was successfully received, understood, and accepted.

- 3xx Redirection – Further action needs to be taken in order to complete the request.

- 4xx Client Error – The request contains bad syntax or cannot be fulfilled.

- 5xx Server Error – The server failed to fulfill an apparently valid request.

The following requests/responses have been abbreviated:

Return Code	Client Request	Server Response
200 – OK, the resource was found.	`GET /index.html HTTP/1.1` `Host: www.example.com`	`HTTP/1.1 200 Found`

302 – Found, a redirection from the initial URL to a new URL.	`GET /index.html HTTP/1.1`
	`Host: www.example.com`
		`HTTP/1.1 302 Found`
		`Location: http://www.`
		`anotherexample .com/`
		`domains/example/`

304 – Not Modified, the resource has not been modified since the last download by the client; thus, a server retransmit isn't necessary, the client cached copy could be used.	`GET /index.html HTTP/1.1`
	`Host: www.example.com`
	`If-Modified-Since: Wed,`
	`05 Aug 2020 14:22:56 GMT`
	`If-None-Match:`
	`"c794ab9415dbcc1:0"`
		`HTTP/1.1 304 Not`
		`Modified`

404 – Page Not Found, the client could communicate with the server, but it was unable to find the requested resource. In the example, a simple typo becomes the problem.	`GET /index.html HTTP/1.1` `Host: www.examlpe.com`	`HTTP/1.1 404 Not Found`

Of note, a class not referred to earlier is the 5xx class denoting a server error. This typically will occur when the web server fails under load. Return codes in this class that appear frequently are the following:

500 – Internal Server Error, a generic error message sent when an unexpected condition was encountered on the server (in effect, it's broken, and we don't know why…).

502 – Bad Gateway, a gateway/proxy server received an invalid response from an upstream server, possibly as a result of excessive load.

503 – Service Unavailable, the server cannot handle the request (most often because it is overloaded). It's the best case for the server not supporting this load profile.

504 – Gateway Timeout, the gateway/proxy server did not receive a response from the upstream server within the timeout period.

Another class that can cause problems is the 3xx class. Many performance tools today will automatically fail a script if the tool receives a 4xx or 5xx class response. But class 3xx are different in that they could be part of a legitimate redirect (e.g., ba.com redirects to britishairways.com). The problem is when an internal error within the website occurs and the user is redirected to an internal site error page. This could be mistakenly interpreted by the tool as a legitimate redirect, and the script continues without raising an error. A useful backup to this problem occurring is to add an additional checkpoint into each page to confirm that the requested URL is the actual page the virtual user reaches during the performance test.

Summary   Check the HTTP responses per second (200, 302, 304, 404, and 500–504).

Although much of this information can be presented in tables, graphical representations make it easier to view the data and identify trends.

Techniques used in analyzing data can include:

- *Comparing results to stated requirements*

- *Observing trends in results*

- *Statistical quality control techniques*

- *Identifying errors*

- *Comparing expected and actual results*

- *Comparing the results to prior test results*

- *Verifying proper functioning of components (e.g., servers, networks)*

                                            —ISTQB_CTFL_PT

The table vs. graph question is interesting. The answer to which is better depends on the following:

1.   Personal preference – The graph and table in Figure 4-40 display the same information, and yet stakeholders will prefer one or the other. Occasionally, stakeholders cannot understand the information being displayed in the graph, whereas the numbers make more sense for them.

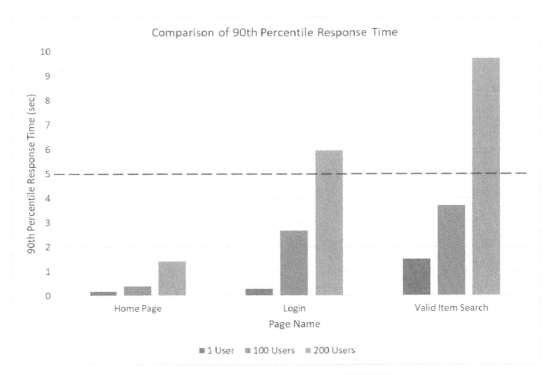

Figure 4-40. *Graph vs. table preference*

2. The nature of the information – The preceding information shows
    an absolute in the measurements (in this case, 90th percentile)
    or a "point in time." This is known as summary information. The
    alternative is progress information representing a change over
    a defined period. For summary information, either a table or a
    graph (such as the histogram shown above) can represent this
    data. But for progress information, the change over time is better
    represented by a line graph or similar (Figure 4-41).

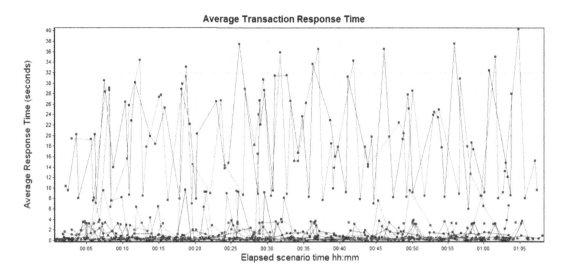

Figure 4-41. *Transaction response time*

In this instance, the change over time can be displayed much clearer than it could in tabulated data.

3. The relevance of the information – There can be a temptation to display large amounts of information. It is important to remember the KISS principle when analyzing and reporting – Keep It Simply Simple (a slightly more polite variation on the original that most ex-military personnel would remember). Sometimes, there can be a temptation to display EVERYTHING, even though a small number of metrics might show the relevant information. A good example is the graph in Figure 4-42.

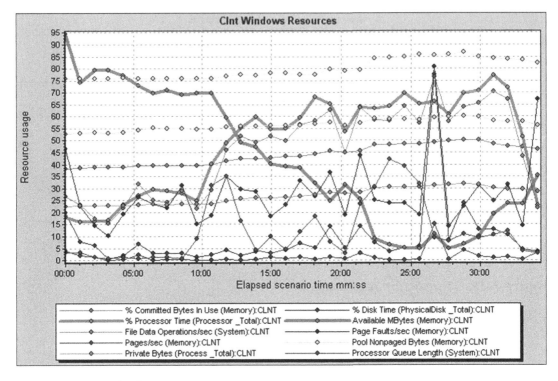

Figure 4-42. *Windows server resources*

There is a lot of unnecessary information within this graph – the relevant metrics will be looked at in more detail shortly.

Analysis Techniques

It is my business to know what other people don't know.

—Conan Doyle, 1892bc

In the syllabus bullet point reference earlier, several techniques are considered for analysis. Ultimately, it's the performance engineer's job to investigate and filter the performance test results data to either:

- Develop the cause-effect relationship chains to uncover the root cause of performance issues

- Prove the system under test has achieved the stated performance requirements

The first step is to consider the basic statistical information captured from the performance test. The initial basic statistics include:

- The **maximum**, **average**, and **minimum** transaction times (although the minimum isn't the most useful measure, it does come into play for the following percentile and standard deviation)

- The **percentile**, either a nominated percentile (90th/95th/98th) or a percentile graph to show the percentage measure progression

- The **standard deviation**, useful in two ways, to understand if the data is normally distributed and how disbursed the collected data is

These five measures can start to give some information regarding the performance from an overall point of view of the system under test. It might highlight a certain transaction or group of transactions that are performing poorly, allowing a starting point for analysis. From these measures, we can continue the statistical journey, considering the following.

The sample size of measures: How many data points for that transaction were collected? The sample size goal is to gather enough measurements to allow a conclusion to be made based on the gathered data. A minimum sample number should be established for each measure to allow those data points to be considered in terms of the initial measures listed earlier. For example, it would be foolish to predict the outcome of a federal election based on asking five random people at a bus stop who will win. The smaller the sample, the wider the confidence intervals and higher the probability of error. As a rule of thumb, the performance test should collect at least 20 data points for a measurement. But beware, as this is a number purely based on experience. A more calculated method can be the use of Creative Research Systems' sample size calculator.[10]

Outliers: Outliers tie in with the maximum/minimum/percentile measurements earlier. Much work has been done around statistical significance relating to the outliers – a result is statistically significant if it's within roughly 48% either side of the mean. This would mean that we reject measures from 0–2% and 98–100% of a measurement. This can be dangerous for performance engineers, as we can use the maximum measure as a performance goal. Earlier, it was mentioned that we reject the minimum measurements, due to them being gathered when the load level is very low. Accordingly, it may make more sense to reject 0–5% of measurements and keep the rest.

---

[10]www.surveysystem.com/sscalc.htm

Correlation and trends: This goes on to become the primary focus of analysis beyond the initial sample and high-level statistical analysis. Results from all previous relevant performance tests can be considered, as individually a pattern may not be discerned, but together they might show relevant cause-effect relationships.

Before proceeding further with analysis, a clarification is required. We must return to an earlier quote from Holmes:

I have no data yet. ***It is a capital mistake to theorize before one has data****. Insensibly one begins to twist facts to suit theories instead of theories to suit facts...*

—Conan Doyle, 1892

Often, performance engineers are too quick to jump to a conclusion as to what the root cause may be. Certainly, it can be a temptation, especially if we have a basis for that conclusion. But unless there is definitive proof, it is only a theory. A good performance engineer must always separate two things:

what we know; *and*

what we think.

Any one piece of information we can identify is what we know. What could have caused that is what we think. Unfortunately, unless you can find something that proves what you think is correct (and more than one thing is always preferred), what you think is wrong!

This point cannot be stressed highly enough. It often pays to write two lists – the first of what you know. Consider the graph from earlier (Figure 4-43).

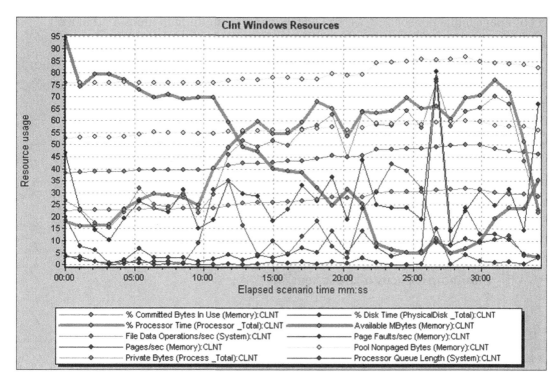

Figure 4-43. *Windows server resources*

Stop for a minute, study the graph and write **what you know** from this.

We know this graph shows the resources of a Windows machine. It also shows numerous measurements collected on that machine.

We know the bright pink line (available memory in MB) shows that the available memory reduces until, at about 22 minutes, there is less than 10% available memory. After 22 minutes, available memory continues to decrease. At 26 minutes, there was a brief positive spike which then dropped back to 5% at 28 minutes. Beyond that, available memory began to trend upward.

We know the gray line (% processor time – the percentage of elapsed time the process spends executing non-idle threads) begins at around 20%, increases until it hits 60% at 14 minutes, and peaks at just above 75% at 31 minutes. We also know that between 26 and 28 minutes, there were positive (upward) spikes in several measurements. There are many other things we know from that graph, but let's pause.

Now for a new list – **what you think**. From this, we can now surmise that based on the available memory, and knowing that as memory runs low, page faults start to occur as information is moved from RAM to the hard disk. Based on this, we should see a spike in both page faults per second, as the CPU looks for something in memory that isn't there, and % disk time as the thing the CPU is looking for is now on the disk.

To now consider causality, we could surmise that the cause of low available memory led to the effect of paging and disk activity. What's the next step we could take? Any of the following could be the next step:

- Match transaction times to the time paging occurred – Did the transaction times increase?

- Investigate the server – Which processes were running to cause the available memory to reduce?

- Investigate the load level – Did the paging occurrence match a peak in the level of virtual users (as in a stress test to determine the maximum capacity of the system)?

- Investigate the test environment – Could dynamic resource allocation be affecting the performance of a virtual machine on which the system is running?

Identifying correlation between metrics can help us understand at what point system performance begins to degrade. For example, what number of transactions per second were processed when the CPU reached 90% capacity and the system slowed?

—ISTQB_CTFL_PT

The easiest way to correlate performance test metrics (and could be argued by some the best and only way) is to work from a common starting point. In most cases, this relates to the X-axis on many of the metric graphs captured. This axis should be the execution time. There are two to choose from:

- The relative time (starting at 00:00:00 and proceeding)

- The absolute time (the actual clock time)

Problems exist with both. For example, if the performance test draws metrics from a tool external to the performance test tool, relative time will be problematic as the external tool may be using absolute time. If absolute time is used during the performance test, will that time match all the server times in the system under test (considering some servers may be based in a different time zone)?

Once a common frame of reference has been established, server logs and other monitoring tools can be compared to the execution results.

In looking at the results graphs (and to an extent seen previously), two shapes are significant. These are referred to as the exponential and the plateau (Figure 4-44).

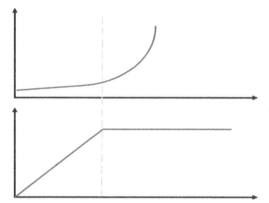

The exponential is where a point is reached where a significant change occurs at the "knee" of the graph. This change could be an exponential or linear increase, and be positive (upward), or negative (downward).

The plateau occurs when some limit is reached (usually corresponding to 0% or 100% in some metric).

Figure 4-44. *The exponential and plateau*

Based on this, a cause-effect relationship could then be derived based on the shared X-axis. For example, returning to what we know, the preceding graphs could show a cause-effect relationship. During the test, an exponential started at time X (the top graph), which also has a corresponding plateau in the bottom graph.

What we think would relate to the possible cause of this. Did the exponential cause the plateau or the plateau cause the exponential? Could another cause occurring at time X be the actual cause and what is seen in the graphs are a combination of effects?

Other considerations would be:

1. If the cause of the effect is discovered, is this the root cause? In most cases, the answer is no, so the search continues.

2. Why is your conclusion wrong? It always pays to ask yourself this question as it can save a lot of time to stop investigating down the wrong path.

3. If in doubt, ask! In almost every performance test, there could be someone who knows more about the system/infrastructure/ network/database than you.

There is nothing more deceptive than an obvious fact.

—Conan Doyle, 1892bv

It should be noted that cause-effect correlation can be a statistical exercise as well as a skilled performance engineer visual inspection exercise. Remembering back to the qualitative vs. quantitative analysis, the statistical (quantitative) method can be better. However, it's accepted it might be easier to find the cause-effect correlation visually and then measure afterward. The Excel function STANDARDIZE[11] is an underused function, and performance engineers should be using it much, much more.

Summary   Identifying correlation between metrics can help understand at what point system performance begins degrading.

Analysis can help identify the root cause of the performance degradation or failure, which in turn will facilitate correction. Confirmation testing will help determine if the corrective action addressed the root cause.

—ISTQB_CTFL_PT

The root cause can be an elusive adversary. It's always worth thinking back to the first principle – the nature of load being code executing in an environment. Can the executing code be identified that relates to the discovered issue?

Any performance engineer who states, "The problem is the CPU as it's running at 100% on server X," has not finished the job of analysis. Ultimately, whatever the root cause of any issue might be, proof is required.

Without proof, all that remains are theories.

Summary   Analysis identifes the root cause of identified issues. Confirmation testing determines if the fix corrects the issue.

---

[11] STANDARDIZE returns a normalized value (the number of standard deviations a given data point is from the mean) from a distribution based on the mean and the standard deviation of the dataset.

Reporting

Analysis results are consolidated and compared against the objectives stated in the performance test plan. These may be reported in the overall test status report together with other test results or included in a dedicated report for performance testing. The level of detail reported should match the needs of the stakeholders. The recommendations based on these results typically address software release criteria (including target environment) or required performance improvements.

—ISTQB_CTFL_PT

Reporting can be done after:

- Each performance test execution

- Each performance test cycle

- The completed performance test project

The reporting aim is twofold:

1. To report against the requirements, risks, and goals of the performance test

2. To prove the performance engineer's conclusions are correct based on the reported facts

A major consideration is the stakeholders to whom the report will be presented. Each stakeholder group may require different information.

Business stakeholders may be interested in the achievement of requirements and goals but will not delve into the technical detail. Technical stakeholders, on the other hand, probably will appreciate technical details relating to why the goal was achieved or not achieved. It may even be the case that separate reports are created for the different stakeholder groups.

The KISS principle should always be at the forefront of reporting. Performance engineers can fall into the trap of using the report to show how clever they are. In many cases, it may even be true. But it should be remembered that cleverness merely helps solve problems, whereas wisdom avoids problems. The best reports will always be understood by their audience, however technical the details they are reporting.

Reporting may also be based on a defined format coming directly from a performance test tool or be a custom-created format incorporating multiple feeds of information from a range of tools. Or, it may be a simple Excel spreadsheet. Whatever the format, the properties to consider are:

- KISS – Keep it simple; the least experienced stakeholder should understand its contents.

- Standard information sets – Provide a standard set of understood metrics (with descriptions if necessary).

- Automation – As much as possible, automate the collection of results and the creation of standard reports.

There is a word of warning on the last point. Tools such as LoadRunner can automate the creation of reports based on created report templates. There are however sections within these reports that state

Insert text here...

Unfortunately, it's surprising how often new performance engineers miss this bit.

Summary   Analysis results are consolidated and compared against the performance test objectives, reporting the overall test status and details in the performance test report. The report details should match the needs of the stakeholders, with recommendations.

A typical performance testing report may include:

Executive Summary

This section is completed once all performance testing has been done and all results have been analyzed and understood. The goal is to present concise and understandable conclusions, findings, and recommendations for management with the goal of an actionable outcome.

—ISTQB_CTFL_PT

It's not surprising that many people looking at a performance test report may not get past the executive summary. Care should be taken with this section to include:

1. A unique report identifier – Allowing the reader to quickly see the report type (execution, cycle, or completion report), along with a means of uniquely identifying this document.

2. The reporting period – When was the execution/cycle/ performance test project covered by this report?

3. The key conclusions, findings, and recommendations.

Test Results

Test results may include some or all of the following information:

- *A summary providing an explanation and elaboration of the results.*

- *Results of a baseline test that serves as "snapshot" of system performance at a given time and forms the basis of comparison with subsequent tests. The results should include the date/ time the test started, the concurrent user goal, the throughput measured, and key findings. Key findings may include overall error rate measured, response time and average throughput.*

- *A high-level diagram showing any architectural components that could (or did) impact test objectives.*

- *A detailed analysis (tables and charts) of the test results showing response times, transaction rates, error rates and performance analysis. The analysis also includes a description of what was observed, such as at what point a stable application became unstable and the source of failures (e.g., web server, database server).*

—ISTQB_CTFL_PT

Additionally, the following factors could also be added:

1. Progress against the performance test plan

2. New performance test quality risks and/or performance project risks identified in the reporting time period

Test Logs/Information Recorded

A log of each test run should be recorded. The log typically includes the following:

- *Date/time of test start*

- *Test duration*

- *Scripts used for test (including script mix if multiple scripts are used) and relevant script configuration data*

- *Test data file(s) used by the test*

- *Name and location of data/log files created during test*

- *HW/SW configuration tested (especially any changes between runs)*

- *Average and peak CPU and RAM utilization on web and database servers*

- *Notes on achieved performance*

- *Defects identified*

—ISTQB_CTFL_PT

This list is self-explanatory. A few points:

1. Average and peak CPU and RAM utilization (or any other metric) can be included if they are useful in proving your conclusions, findings, and recommendations are correct.

2. Hardware and software configuration changes during the reporting period should be recorded, with the total changes consolidated and included within the final performance test completion report.

3. Defects identified – It's helpful to include further information on changes to existing performance defects (such as the retesting of repaired performance defects).

Recommendations

Recommendations resulting from the tests may include the following:

- *Technical changes recommended, such as reconfiguring hardware or software or network infrastructure*

- *Areas identified for further analysis (e.g., analysis of web server logs to help identify root causes of issues and/or errors)*

- *Additional monitoring required of gateways, servers, and networks so that more detailed data can be obtained for measuring performance characteristics and trends (e.g., degradation)*

—ISTQB_CTFL_PT

Added to this:

- Any further performance testing required based on newly discovered defects and/or performance quality risks

- Any lessons learned discovered as part of the performance testing conducted in the reporting period

Finally, we return to what we know and what we think. Any recommendations should lead with "What we know." A summary of facts should be provided to back up any recommendations.

It's always a good tip to start "What we think" with the phrase, "In my opinion…." This provides a clear marker between the facts gathered and proved with any supposition performance engineers make regarding the performance testing conducted. Anything included in the "What we think" section should as much as possible be reflected in the performance test data gathered, pointing the direction any further investigation will continue.

Summary   A typical performance test report contains

- Executive summary – Presents concise conclusions, findings, and recommendations understandable by all stakeholders

- Test results – A summary of the results, comparisons between baselines and subsequent tests, architectural components that impacted test objectives, and a detailed analysis

- Test logs/information recorded – Including date/time, test duration, scripts used, test data used, results data, CPU/RAM notes, and defects

- Recommendations – Including technical changes recommended, areas identified for further analysis, and additional monitoring required for further tests

Chapter 4 Questions

Note: This section is the largest in the syllabus, with 50% of the exam questions coming from this section alone.

1. Which of the following is NOT a key objective of performance testing?

   A. The identification of necessary changes

   B. The identification of performance-related risks

   C. The identification of opportunities for improvements

   D. The identification of trends predicting lower-level performance

2. A company is reengineering an in-house system to move into a cloud environment. A product risk was identified relating to systems running in a cloud environment not performing to the expected level. The system will receive transaction inputs from multiple large manufacturing plants around the globe to be scheduled for shipping to customer sites. Two objectives exist for this project:

   i. The transaction submit response time between the plant and the cloud instance must be within two seconds to all plants from the time the transaction submit is sent when ten concurrent manufacturing flows are submitting data.

ii. The system must handle 400 transaction submits per minute with no degradation failures in resource utilization.

Which of the following combination is correct?

A. (i) and (ii) are both technical objectives.

B. (i) and (ii) are both user-based objectives.

C. (i) is a user-based objective; (ii) is a technical objective.

D. (i) is a technical objective; (ii) is a user-based objective.

3. You are working for an international shipping company. The number of shipments handled by the shipping system each day averages 120,000 packages, evenly spread across 24 hours. Shipments contain everything from birthday gifts to high-value retail goods to special shipments (dangerous goods and medical supplies). SLAs exist for special shipments:

- As a customer, I must be able to access the open shipping records any time to check on their status and expected arrival time.

- As a customer, I want available delivery time slots presented within three seconds when booking a shipment.

- As a customer, I want to secure my transactions to avoid theft of deliveries.

This project will be using DevOps as the development methodology. Which of the following statements is true?

A. DevOps projects do not require a performance test plan.

B. A key performance objective is the three-second response time under a 5000 shipment/hr load.

C. A key performance objective is the authentication and authorization of user logins responding within three seconds.

D. A key performance objective is the three-second response time.

4. You are working for a large legal firm running as a partnership. The firm has had problems in the past with overbilling staff time. In a business goal update by the senior partners, a new microservice system is being implemented to track correct billing of the firm lawyers. These microservices will be deployed as a customized SaaS solution running in the cloud to allow the firm's staff to work from home. Each of the 1200 lawyers must track each six-minute block of time throughout the eight-hour standard workday. This can be done in the following ways:

- Automatically by assigning a case file number to the billing system – as the lawyer's machine is active in the case files, time is booked to the server.

- Manually by bulk booking six-minute time blocks several times a day to case file numbers.

Which of the following performance test objectives would be suitable for this project?

A. A key performance indicator is testing the SaaS system with a load of 1200 users submitting time every six minutes.

B. A key performance indicator is testing the SaaS system with a mixed load of 1200 manual and automated users submitting time.

C. A key performance indicator is testing the SaaS system with a mixed load of 1200 manual and automated users submitting manual time every six minutes.

D. A key performance indicator is testing the SaaS system with a load submitting 7200 transactions/hour.

5. You are working for a large legal firm run as a partnership. The firm has had problems in the past with overbilling staff time. In a business goal update by the senior partners, a new microservice system is being implemented to track correct billing of the firm lawyers. These microservices will be deployed as a customized SaaS solution running in the cloud to allow the firm's staff to work from home. Each of the 1200 lawyers must track each six-minute

block of time throughout the eight-hour standard workday. You have been asked to prepare a presentation for the firm partners regarding your plan for performance testing. Which of the following is the best example of information that should be shared with these stakeholders?

A. The repeatability of planned performance tests must be communicated, with the time booking performance tests repeated with minimum effort.

B. The technical stakeholders must be clear about their tasks and when they are scheduled.

C. The planned approach to generating required load profiles must be explained and the expected involvement of the cloud services team made clear.

D. The steps required to make performance tests repeatable must be communicated, including the participation of key staff and technical issues.

6. You are working for a large legal firm run as a partnership. The firm has had problems in the past with overbilling staff time. In a business goal update by the senior partners, a new microservice system is being implemented to track correct billing of the firm lawyers. These microservices will be deployed as a customized SaaS solution running in the cloud to allow the firm's staff to work from home. Each of the 1200 lawyers must track each six-minute block of time throughout the eight-hour standard workday. Two stakeholder considerations exist for this project:

   i.   Where test environments are to be shared with other ongoing projects, the scheduling of performance tests must be communicated with other project teams to ensure the test results will not be adversely impacted.

   ii. Project risks must be communicated. These include constraints and dependencies concerning the setup of the tests and infrastructure requirements.

Which of the following combination is correct?

A. (i) and (ii) are both for business-focused stakeholders.

B. (i) and (ii) are both for technical-focused stakeholders.

C. (i) is for business-focused stakeholders; (ii) is for technical-focused stakeholders.

D. (i) is for technical-focused stakeholders; (ii) is for business-focused stakeholders.

7. You are working for a large legal firm run as a partnership. The firm has had problems in the past with overbilling staff time. In a business goal update by the senior partners, a new microservice system is being implemented to track correct billing of the firm lawyers. These microservices will be deployed as a customized SaaS solution running in the cloud to allow the firm's staff to work from home. Each of the 1200 lawyers must track each six-minute block of time throughout the eight-hour standard workday. You have been asked to prepare a presentation for the IT team regarding your plan for performance testing. Which of the following is the best example of information that should be shared with these stakeholders?

A. Mitigation for the potential impact on real users if performance testing needs to be executed in the production environment must be communicated and accepted.

B. Awareness of the balance between the cost of planned performance tests and how representative the performance testing results should be covered, compared to production conditions.

C. The connection between performance quality risks and performance test objectives must be clearly stated.

D. The plan containing the high-level activities, costs, time schedule, and milestones.

8. You are working for a large legal firm run as a partnership. The firm has an old web application publishing staff biographies and case information internally. The application is a two-tier application, with a web front end using HTTPS to communicate with the web servers and database back end using the open source GNU Data Access (GDA) APIs, as shown in the following:

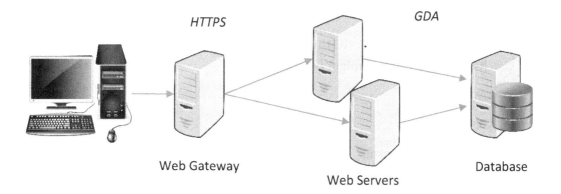

You are asked to performance test this application. Due to cost, the test environment only has one web server available, with a full-sized production-like database back end and no gateway. The business stakeholders would like a full load pushed through the system. Which of the following options would you recommend for creating a load test?

A. As each web server can support 50% full load, a full 100% load test cannot be run. A 50% load test would be the best option.

B. A full 100% load test could be run by pushing 50% load through the web server and 50% load applied directly to the database.

C. A full 100% load test could be run, with careful note taken of the failure point to show the maximum capacity of the web server.

D. A full 100% load test could be run directly against the database, as many performance issues are found in the database.

9. If a performance test is testing a web service, which protocol listed in the syllabus might be used?

    A. HTTPS

    B. RTE

    C. SOAP

    D. JSON

10. If a performance test is testing a remote desktop, which protocol listed in the syllabus might be used?

    A. TruClient

    B. MQSeries

    C. Windows Sockets

    D. Citrix ICA

11. If a performance test is testing network access, which protocol listed in the syllabus might be used?

    A. LDAP

    B. SMP

    C. JDBC

    D. HTML

12. A performance test has been written to create a directory on a target server and copy a 1GB file across the network to the target server to test the network. A code section is as follows:

```
char sourcefile[] = "D:\\Data\\1GB.zip";
char new_dir[] = "\\\\server1.ise.local\\PerfTestTarget";

lr_start_transaction("DataTransfer_MakeDir");

/* Create a directory '\\server1.ise.local\PerfTestTarget' and
make it the current directory */
if (mkdir(new_dir)) {
```

```
    // If test directory exists, output message
    lr_output_message ("Create directory %s exists", new_dir);
    }
else {
    // If test directory is created, output message
    lr_output_message ("Created new directory %s", new_dir);
    lr_think_time(10);
    }
lr_start_transaction("DataTransfer_1GB");

lr_end_transaction("DataTransfer_MakeDir", LR_AUTO);

// Copies the xcopy command to the variable 'command'
sprintf(command, "xcopy %s %s /y", sourcefile, new_dir);

// runs the xcopy command to copy the file to the test dir
system(command);

lr_end_transaction("DataTransfer_1GB", LR_AUTO);
lr_think_time(10);
```

It is suspected a problem exists with the script, with some transaction response times takes much longer than they should. Which of the following is the reason for the suspected delay?

A. The **DataTransfer_1GB** transaction begins before the **DataTransfer_MakeDir** transaction ends, causing a delay.

B. The problem could exist with intermittent latency problems caused by variable traffic on the network while the test is running.

C. The DataTransfer_MakeDir transaction is not in the right place and should be moved after the if (mkdir(new_dir)) statement.

D. The lr_think_time statement is within the **DataTransfer_MakeDir** transaction and is only executed when a new directory is created.

13. Which of the following statements about transactions are NOT true?

    A. Transactions can be nested so that individual and aggregate activities can be measured.

    B. By increasing load and measuring transaction times, it is possible to determine the cause of degradation with the response times alone.

    C. The transaction response times collected during the performance test show how this measurement changes under different loads imposed on the system.

    D. The transaction response time plus the think time equals the elapsed time for that transaction.

14. You are working for a large legal firm run as a partnership. The firm has had problems in the past with overbilling staff time. In a business goal update by the senior partners, a new microservice system is being implemented to track correct billing of the firm lawyers. These microservices will be deployed as a customized SaaS solution running in the cloud to allow the firm's staff to work from home. Each of the 1200 lawyers must track each six-minute block of time throughout the eight-hour standard workday either automatically or manually via the case file.

    An identified operational profile is a lawyer entering manual time. You have determined that lawyers entering manual time will access the system on average once every 60–90 minutes to enter time for that period against the case files worked on. What further information would be required to complete the load profile?

    A. The ratio between the users updating times manually and automatically.

    B. The size of the case files being downloaded each time the lawyer changes cases.

C. The hours of overtime the users work to accurately model the transaction numbers.

D. The size of the time entries being sent to model the volume of traffic.

15. What is the difference between an operational profile and a load profile?

A. There is no practical difference between load and operational profiles.

B. A load profile describes the business process; the operational profile describes the predicted behavior of the business processes.

C. The operational profile describes the business process; the load profile describes the number and way the virtual users will run the business processes.

D. Performance tests can be built with a large number of operational profiles, but can only contain one load profile.

16. Identifying data for an operational profile considers the users interacting with the system. Which of the following four steps are undertaken during identification?

i.   Use a top-down approach to create simple broad operational profiles and possibly broken down further if needed to achieve performance test objectives.

ii.   Gather different types of user personas and their roles (e.g., standard user, registered member, administrator, user groups with specific privileges).

iii. Estimate numbers of users for each role/task per unit of time over a given time period.

iv.   Document different generic tasks performed by those users/roles (e.g., browsing a website for information, searching a website for a particular product, performing role-specific activities).

    A. ii, iii, iv

    B. i, iii, iv

    C. i, ii, iv

    D. i, ii, iii

17. You are working for a large legal firm run as a partnership. You have been asked to performance test an existing network link between the firm's main office and the firm's data center. It simulates a Saturday, where a case deadline is forcing 150 staff to work on the weekend. The total load varies throughout the day based on a combination of FTP transfers, web traffic, and email as shown in the following:

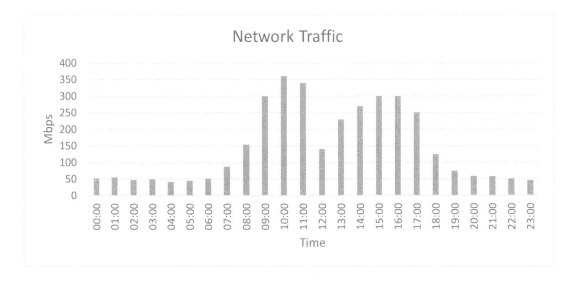

The peak load at 10:00 is made up of 50% FTP traffic, 20% web traffic, and 30% email.

Each planned FTP operational profile user consumes 10Mbps.

Each planned web operational profile user consumes 3Mbps.

Each planned email operational profile user consumes 1Mbps.

The peak load to be replicated is 360Mbps, and 150 virtual user licenses for your tool are available. How would a load test be designed to test the network to meet the desired load?

A. A test scenario would consist of 30 web virtual users, 45 email virtual users, and 75 FTP virtual users.

B. A test scenario would consist of 24 web virtual users, 108 email virtual users, and 18 FTP virtual users.

C. A test scenario would consist of 36 web virtual users, 72 email virtual users, and 18 FTP virtual users.

D. A test scenario would consist of 60 web virtual users, 30 email virtual users, and 15 FTP virtual users.

18. You are working for a large legal firm run as a partnership. You have been asked to performance test an existing network link between the firm's main office and the firm's data center. It simulates a normal weekday traffic. The total load varies throughout the day based on a combination of FTP transfers, web traffic, and email as shown in the following:

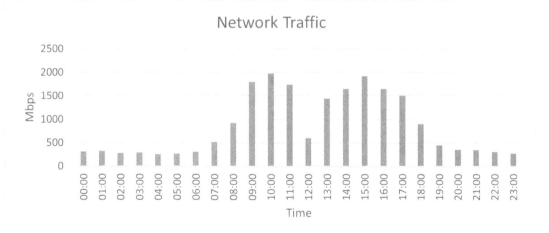

The peak load at 15:00 is due to a court filing deadline where documents for cases must be submitted via STARTTLS secure email/SFTP transfer. These transfers must have a success rate of

100%. The weekday load at 15:00 is made up of 50% SFTP traffic, 20% web traffic, and 30% email.Each planned email operational profile user consumes 1Mbps.

Each planned web operational profile user consumes 3Mbps.

Each planned SFTP operational profile user consumes 10Mbps.

The 15:00 load peak to be replicated is 1920Mbps. What are the differences between this scenario and the previous scenario in Q17?

i.   The load has increased between weekdays and the weekend.

ii.   The overall traffic percentages are different between the weekend and weekdays.

iii.   Traffic peaks have changed between weekdays and the weekend.

iv.   There are no court submissions on the weekend, as the courts do not hear cases.

v.   The protocols have changed between the weekend and the weekday traffic.

vi.   A new 100% success rate for email/FTP transfers to the courts.

   A.   i, iii, v, vi

   B.   i, ii, iv, vi

   C.   ii, iii, iv, v

   D.   i, ii, iii, iv, v, vi

19.   The focus of batch processing lies principally on the throughput of the batch processing system and its ability to complete within a given time period. A batch payment system is being performance tested for different payment types (bank transfer, Stripe, Worldpay, ACI Worldwide, PayPal, Amazon Pay, Apple Pay, and AmEx/Visa/Mastercard credit cards). There is a concern in the business that payments be as fast as possible, as there are SLAs

with each payment provider that must be met. Working with the stakeholders to create an operational profile for this batch process, which would be the best option?

A. A single operational profile could be used to save time and scripting, as these are all payment options that would pass the same data.

B. The payments could be separated into different operational profile groups of the same payment type (bank transfer; Stripe/Worldpay/ACI; PayPal, Amazon Pay, Apple Pay/AmEx, Visa, Mastercard) as each payment type is different.

C. A separate end-to-end payment option would be created for every payment provider, as every different payment to each provider could take different times to process.

D. Single payment types would be tested based on the percentage of payments processed of that type, and payment types that have been identified as slow.

20. What is an advantage to conducting performance testing at the user interface level?

A. It's the easiest method for manual scripting.

B. It's scalable because the client is included.

C. It's an effective way to assess the user experience.

D. It's the best way to handle data correlation.

21. What is one disadvantage to conducting performance testing at the protocol level?

A. It might affect the scalability of the performance test due to the test execution resource overhead running longer scripts.

B. It might not capture the time required for the client to render the server response in the user interface.

    C. It might make data correlation more difficult due to session information changing each time the test is executed.

    D. It might make the script more difficult to analyze as more code will need to be written to help execution.

22. You have a requirement to create two scripts for a system within a logistics organization. The first script is to test a client-server version of a shipping business process where an internal staff member logs in to the shipping system in the morning, creates shipments for different customers phoning to transport goods, and logs out in the evening. The second script tests the web version, where customers can create their own shipments. Which of the following combinations would represent the best way to develop these performance test scripts?

    A. The client-server script would log in once, perform many iterations of adding shipments, and log out once; the web script would log in once, perform many iterations of adding shipments, and log out once.

    B. The client-server script would log in, perform an add shipment, and log out each iteration; the web script would log in, perform an add shipment, and log out each iteration.

    C. The client-server script would log in, perform an add shipment, and log out each iteration; the web script would log in once, perform many iterations of adding shipments, and log out once.

    D. The client-server script would log in once, perform many iterations of adding shipments, and log out once; the web script would log in, perform an add shipment, and log out each iteration.

23. The way to create a performance script depends on the nature of the tool, the system under test, and the script being created. Which of the following is NOT an option to create a script?

    A. The script can be created by recording communication between the client and the system or component at the protocol level.

B. The script can be created by recording at the GUI level by capturing GUI actions of a single client.

C. The script can be created by converting available system source code into an executable client.

D. The script can be created by programming protocol requests, GUI actions, or API calls.

24. What is correlation in terms of performance testing?

A. Correlation is capturing a server-presented value to replace input data at replay.

B. Correlation is a statistical relationship between two or more performance test results.

C. Correlation is an automated parameterization of performance test input data.

D. Correlation is capturing a server-presented value.

25. You are working for a logistics organization, shipping goods around the world. A customer can log in to the website and create shipments. Each shipment's details contain shipping information input by the customers (address information from the sender and shipment receiver) and system-supplied information hidden from the end user (customer ID/shipment ID/etc.). You have recorded the script, and initially it replayed fine. After you replaced the hard-coded input data, it replays the first iteration, but every subsequent iteration fails. Which of the following is the most likely cause of this issue?

A. A server-supplied session ID has not yet been correlated.

B. The first input data record is correct; the subsequent parameterized data is wrong.

C. A system-supplied value has not been parameterized.

D. The system cannot handle the applied load.

26. You are working for a logistics organization, shipping goods around the world. The organization is moving internal systems across to cloud-based virtual machines running Software as a Service systems. During test execution, you notice a wide variation in response time while running the same load test with the same data at different times of the day. Which of the following are NOT possible reasons for this variation in response time?

    A. The variations in the load generators for each run could be affecting the response time.

    B. The changing volume of network traffic affecting available bandwidth could be affecting the response time.

    C. The caching of the load test data on the database could be affecting the response time.

    D. More concurrent processes running in the cloud virtual machines could be affecting the response time.

27. You are working for a large legal firm run as a partnership. A system tracking lawyer's time spent on a case is being load tested, with the execution schedule requiring the 90-minute load test to be executed four times each day, with a 15-minute gap between each run. You find, however, the system login behaves differently each time the test is rerun. In the first run of the day, the individual login transactions complete in less than two seconds, with the following runs taking up to eight seconds on average. Other transactions behaved the same across each run, with little variation. What could be the possible issue with this load testing?

    A. A problem with the user login information not being cached on the client machine, leading to user details being resent by the load test

    B. A problem logging the virtual users out at the end of the test, leading to old session still running from previous tests causing queueing

    C. A problem with congestion on the network due to increased production casework being conducted at the same time during the execution time

    D. A problem with server RAM running low causing the system to page to hard disk, leading to a delay in processing time for the login process

28. You are working on a national integrated database project that allows citizens to register to vote, with voter numbers in the millions. Voters can register to vote online, change their address, or remove themselves from the voter register if they move. The government has two SLAs:

Section 1 Personal data

1 a) Safeguards must be applied with reference to two criteria: **the need to know** (only those officials to whom the information be permitted shall view records); **and the right to know** (voters are permitted to view their own data).

Section 2 Voter usability

2 a) When checking their voter registration, the voter information should be returned within five seconds of the request under peak pre-election load.

You have conducted your tests and have determined the following percentile metrics:

<3-second response time: 85% of the time <6-second response time: 95% of the time

<5-second response time: 90% of the time <10-second response time: 100% of the time

---

Which of the following statements would be the best response to the project stakeholders (the minister and senior civil servant) on the test results?

A. The test failed as the system is deemed too slow. The requirements should be reviewed to ensure that the response time of less than five seconds is required 100% of the time, or if this time could be increased.

B. The test has provisionally passed, as 95% of the voter requests responded within six seconds, which is within the 20% tolerance for time measurements and could be tuned to reduce the time further.

C. There is insufficient information to report the results back to the stakeholders at this point, as the performance testing is only reporting response times, and no further information on resource utilization is available.

D. Clarify SLA 2 a) with the stakeholders in reporting the full results to check if the response time target is the maximum, the average, or a percentile time, allowing the stakeholders to then make a pass/fail decision.

CHAPTER 5

Tools

ISTQB Keywords

load generator

A tool that generates a load for a system under test.

load management

The control and execution of load generation, and performance monitoring and reporting of the component or system.

monitoring tool

A software tool or hardware device that runs concurrently with the component or system under test and supervises, records, and/or analyzes the behavior of the component or system.

performance testing tool

A test tool that generates load for a designated test item and that measures and records its performance during test execution.

5.1 Tool Support

PTFL-5.1.1 (K2) Understand how tools support performance testing

—ISTQB_CTFL_PT

"... Bring with you a jemmy, a dark lantern, a chisel, and a revolver. S.H."

It was nice equipment for a respectable citizen to carry through the dim, fog-draped streets.

—Conan Doyle, 1908

© Keith Yorkston 2021
K. Yorkston, *Performance Testing*, https://doi.org/10.1007/978-1-4842-7255-8_5

As previously stated, manual performance testing is fraught with problems. By far the largest are controlling the users while the test is running and gathering disparate data for the results. Manual performance testing tends to give load that is not reproducible and results that are almost impossible to correlate back to user actions. Surprisingly, it also adds to the cost of any project using manual performance testing, as the cost of both the users involved in the test and the hardware they use must be a consideration. In effect, manual performance testing gives poor results, takes additional time to organize, and any issues found very rarely can be investigated.

If project stakeholders suggest manual performance testing, performance engineers tend to start looking for easily accessible fire escapes.

Performance engineers will get to know certain tools well. These tools could be commercial (Micro Focus LoadRunner or Performance Center; IBM Rational Performance Tester) or open source (JMeter; Gatling). They may work in a single environment or with a single protocol or may operate across a wide range of environments and protocol types.

Many today share a common architecture. The diagram used earlier in the book relates to the following syllabus points (Figure 5-1).

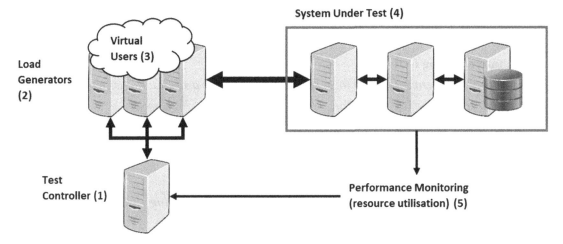

Figure 5-1. *View of the tool components of a performance test*

Performance testing tools include the following types of tool to support performance testing.

Load Generators (2)

The generator, through an IDE, script editor or tool suite, is able to create and execute multiple client instances that simulate user behavior according to a defined operational profile. Creating multiple instances in short periods of time will cause load on a system under test. The generator creates the load and also collects metrics for later reporting.

—ISTQB_CTFL_PT

The load management console or test controller (1) passes the executable scripts to the load generator. It's the load generator's responsibility to execute the scripts and capture the performance script–related test results (such as the executing virtual user status, any checkpoints internal to the script, and other basic default result sets specified by the tool in use). Of note, the load generator will not capture specific monitoring information from the system under test (such as CPU/memory/etc.). It can in fact be the subject of monitoring, as while performance tests are executing, it can be helpful for the performance engineer to know the state of health of the load generators.

Summary   Load generators create load by executing multiple client instances (virtual users) simulating user behavior.

When executing performance tests, the objective of the load generator is to mimic the real world as much as is practical. This often means that user requests coming from various locations are needed, not just from the testing location. Environments that are set up with multiple points of presence will distribute where the load is originating from so that it is not all coming from a single network. This provides realism to the test, though it can sometimes skew results if intermediate network hops create delays.

—ISTQB_CTFL_PT

This all forms part of the individual operational profiles and the overall load profile for the performance test. It also touches on the performance test environment, all of which were covered earlier in the book.

Summary   Load generators mimic real user behavior, including setting up multiple load generators to simulate distributed load, but can skew results if additional network hops are needed.

Load Management Console (1)

The load management console provides the control to start and stop the load generator(s). The console also aggregates metrics from the various transactions that are defined within the load instances used by the generator. The console enables reports and graphs from the test executions to be viewed and supports results analysis.

—ISTQB_CTFL_PT

The load management console (or controller) lives up to its name – it controls the performance test. In this tool, the load profile is converted into a performance test scenario with the appropriate numbers and types of virtual users, scripts, and runtime settings to match the real-world behavior of users on the system under test. The performance test is subsequently executed from the load management console, also gathering the results from both the load generators and the performance monitors. These results are consolidated into a single result set upon completion of the performance test. Many performance tools also allow real-time monitoring during the performance test, available through the load management console.

Summary   The load management console controls the performance test. It starts and stops the test, controls the load generators, and collects metrics during the test, which can be viewed during the test and generate test reports after completion.

Monitoring Tool (5)

Monitoring tools run concurrently with the component or system under test and supervise, record and/or analyses the behavior of the component or system. Typical components which are monitored include web server queues, system memory and disk space. Monitoring tools can effectively support the root cause analysis of performance degradation in a system under test and may also be used to monitor a production environment when the product is released. During performance test execution monitors may also be used on the load generator itself.

—ISTQB_CTFL_PT

Much has already been said on monitoring. But the last consideration is the amount of resources the monitoring tool itself uses. Monitoring should be performed selectively as the greater the amount of metrics captured, and the rate at which each measurement is sampled can influence the performance test. Much of the time, this resource drain is negligible, but depending on the testing performed, it could be an issue.

Summary   Monitoring collects metric information (both direct test results like transaction times and indirect results like CPU, memory, disk IO, and queueing). This can support root cause analysis and aid reporting. It can also monitor production environments and load generators.

License models for performance test tools include the traditional seat/site-based license with full ownership, a cloud-based pay-as-you-go license model, and open source licenses which are free to use in a defined environment or through cloud-based offerings. Each model implies a different cost structure and may include ongoing maintenance. What is clear is that for any tool selected, understanding how that tool works (through training and/or self-study) will require time and budget.

—ISTQB_CTFL_PT

The licensing model for the selected tool would of course depend on the tool itself, its developers, and the licensing arrangement an organization has with the vendor. Open source tools also have licensing, although it may be somewhat different from the commercial. Performance engineers must be familiar with the licensing model used by all tools involved in the performance test. Beware of tools sourced through Google – always make a point of reading any licensing agreement. It could be that a tool is free to use for personal or educational use but may require a licensing fee if used commercially.

Whichever tool is selected, the performance engineer must get the most from it. It can be a benefit to practice using the tool against a wide range of environments and systems. A wide range of resources exist online for both commercial and open source tools.

It can even be useful to use the tool of choice to record accessing sites like Facebook, Amazon, or YouTube. It can be an interesting exercise to see the amount of data being passed from the client back to the server...

Summary   Licensing models include traditional seat/site-based licenses, cloud-based pay-as-you-go licenses, and open source licenses. Training on the tool requires budget and time.

5.2 Tool Suitability

PTFL-5.2.1 (K4) Evaluate the suitability of performance testing tools in a given project scenario

Before moving on, it is worth considering the limitations surrounding open source tools. Yes, they don't cost much to obtain. But there can be hidden costs to an open source tool – it might take longer to create tests, or support and training for the tool might be lacking. Many commercial tools are sold with support packages and training bundled into the purchase price. If an organization works in a high-risk environment, the tool may require certification (and each time it's upgraded, it might need to be recertified). Many commercial tools are sold on the premise that the tool vendor has achieved this required certification as it becomes a selling point for the commercial tool. The issue of warranty and associated liability is also a factor – some organizations will reject the use of open source tools purely because there is no legal warranty relationship between the open source tool supplier and user under the GNU license. Security too can be a blocker – some online tools can be downloaded from a number of different sites, and if you pick the wrong site, you might get some unofficial "add-ins" included. Finally, finding a skilled user for the tool can be daunting, especially if the tool in question is less common. Commercial tools usually have consultants either working for the vendor or certified by the vendor who will have the required knowledge.

This shouldn't be taken as an indictment of open source tools, merely a reminder of the potential challenges in using open source tools.

Commercial tools can have their own problems – the first of which is cost. Tool licensing and maintenance costs can run to a tidy sum, and this might be prohibitively expensive for some organizations. Some tools charge by the protocol needed and the number of virtual users required, so the bigger the test, the higher the cost. Support, even though it's paid for, might not be adequate. Or the commercial tool might use a proprietary scripting language to build performance test scripts rather than a standard, well-known language.

The following factors should be considered when selecting a performance testing tool.

Compatibility

In general, a tool is selected for the organization and not only for a project. This means considering the following factors in the organization:

- **Protocols**: *As described in Section 4.2.1, protocols are a very important aspect to performance tool selection. Understanding which protocols a system uses and which of these will be tested will provide necessary information in order to evaluate the appropriate test tool.*

- **Interfaces to external components**: *Interfaces to software components or other tools may need to be considered as part of the complete integration requirements to meet process or other inter-operability requirements (e.g., integration in the CI process).*

- **Platforms**: *Compatibility with the platforms (and their versions) within an organization is essential. This applies to the platforms used to host the tools and the platforms with which the tools interact for monitoring and/or load generation.*

—ISTQB_CTFL_PT

The one constant in information technology is change. New languages, upgrades of operating system and tools, new protocols, new software development methodologies, all are in a continuous cycle. Coupled to that are the older legacy systems that continue to fulfill an organization business need.

It can pay to perform a periodic proof of concept against various systems within the organization with the tool of choice. Occasionally, a tool that previously worked against an older system won't work against a later version. A good example was LoadRunner, where the latest version of the tool was designed to work against the latest version of Oracle/SAP/etc. If the tool was upgrading to a later version, it was sometimes necessary to patch the tool backward to enable it to continue operating against earlier versions of systems.

Although the need for a specific project needing a specific tool always exists, in general the organization should always be looking for the maximum return on investment on the time, effort, and money used to obtain and use a performance tool.

Summary   A tool is selected for an organization, not a project, considering the required protocols, interfaces to external components, and platforms.

Scalability

Another factor *to consider is the total number of concurrent user simulations the tool can handle. This will include several factors:*

- *Maximum number of licenses required*

- *Load generation workstation/server configuration requirements*

- *Ability to generate load from multiple points of presence (e.g., distributed servers)*

—ISTQB_CTFL_PT

As more organizations move toward the goal of digital transformation, flexible workforces, remote working, and cloud-based computing, the nature of the way systems are accessed and used is also changing. Organizations are growing, shrinking, merging, and acquiring others or being acquired. Acquiring licenses for more users or different protocols should always be a consideration when sourcing a performance tool. Understanding the licensing model can help with future proofing the tool.

Summary   User simulations supported by the tool are a consideration, including the maximum number, load generator requirements, and multiple load generation points.

Understandability

Another factor to consider is the level of technical knowledge *needed to use the tool. This is often overlooked and can lead to unskilled testers incorrectly configuring tests, which in turn provide inaccurate results. For testing requiring complex scenarios and a high level of programmability and customization, teams should ensure that the tester has the necessary skills, background, and training.*

—ISTQB_CTFL_PT

A basic set of questions to ask of any potential performance tool is:

- Is the tool easy to use (how long to create a virtual user script or performance test)?

- Is the tool easy to understand (including the tool itself, the virtual user scripts, the configuration of the performance test, etc.)?

- Is the tool easy to learn (for performance engineers to develop expertise in the tool) and the language the tool uses (is it an old language like ANSI C or a not-well-known language like Scala vs. Java or Python)?

- Is the tool attractive (regarding results and reporting)?

A historic issue with open source tools is this usability aspect. These tools are developed by groups of highly technical developers and performance engineers. It has only been in recent times that usability has been thought important. Commercial tools have had an advantage in the usability stakes – part of the selling of these tools is to make the process of performance testing "look easy."

Summary   Performance engineers need the necessary technical knowledge, skills, background, and training to use the tool.

Monitoring

Is the monitoring provided by the tool sufficient? Are there other monitoring tools available in the environment that can be used to supplement the monitoring by the tool? Can the monitoring be correlated to the defined transactions? All of these questions must be answered to determine if the tool will provide the monitoring required by the project.

When monitoring is a separate program/tools/whole stack then it can be used to monitor production environment when the product is released.

—ISTQB_CTFL_PT

In all that has been spoken on monitoring, the basic question remains. Can the performance tool capture what is needed, and can it report on the results once the data is gathered?

Summary   Tool monitoring should provide enough coverage, correlate against defined transactions, and (if the tools alone do not have sufficient coverage) integrate with other monitoring tools. Monitoring can also be continued within the production environment.

Chapter 5 Questions

1. What is the purpose of a load management console?

    A. It creates the load on the network to allow performance testing by executing the performance scripts.

    B. It aggregates the performance test results to allow analysis after the performance test.

    C. It executes the load profile designed into the performance test and aggregates the results of the test.

    D. It simulates user behavior according to the operational profiles built into the performance test.

2. Which of the following factors are relevant for selecting a performance tool?

i. Monitoring	ii. Scalability	iii. Maintainability
iv. Understandability	v. Performance	vi. Compatibility

   A. i, iii, v, vi

   B. i, ii, iv, vi

   C. ii, iii, iv, v

   D. i, ii, iii, iv, v, vi

3. According to the syllabus, which of the statements regarding tool licensing is NOT true?

   A. A freeware license model which is free to use, but could incur costs associated with the purchase of load generators and performance scripts.

   B. A cloud-based pay-as-you-go license model allows flexibility to buy virtual users, but could be an issue as load is generated outside the organization domain.

   C. A seat/site-based license model allows full ownership, but could include extra maintenance cost annually to the vendor for support and upgrades.

   D. An open source license model which is free to use, but could incur extra costs in building and maintaining assets as training and support are limited.

CHAPTER 6

Final Thoughts

The only easy day was yesterday…

—US Navy SEALs

Being a performance engineer isn't easy. The more technology changes, the more a good performance engineer is needed. A good performance engineer:

- Learns continuously – As each new bit of technology needs to be understood, as well as understanding how it will communicate and integrate with older technology.

- Communicates well – In both spoken and written forms. Performance engineers will need to communicate with and potentially present to both business and technical stakeholders in language they understand.

- Understands the psychology of the users – Looking at a system under test and understanding the motivation and thought processes of users will help write better performance scripts and scenarios.

- Understands risk – In defining the scope of performance risk, identifying risk, assessing this risk quantitatively, and effectively mitigating performance quality risk with performance testing and performance project risk with better processes to save time and money.

- Experiments to get answers – Scientific method, like performance testing, involves creating hypotheses (the performance requirements), deriving predictions on performance from them (what we think), and then carrying out performance tests to confirm these (what we know).

© Keith Yorkston 2021
K. Yorkston, *Performance Testing*, https://doi.org/10.1007/978-1-4842-7255-8_6

- Writes things down(!) – A historic failure of many performance engineers, now corrected in the performance test plans, environment specifications and acceptance tests, the scripts and scenarios, results and reports the performance tests generate.

Finally, continue being curious. How does this system/application/API/protocol work? How could it integrate/communicate/adversely affect existing systems or components? How would the users access and use this system?

Education never ends, Watson. It is a series of lessons, with the greatest for the last.

—Conan Doyle, 1917

Performance testing is the ultimate mix of business and technology, wrapped in quality. It's the testing type that includes elements of functionality and reliability on top of performance. The type that when it's done well, users never notice. But when it's bad, they all know. It's sometimes very challenging, but always fulfilling to those conducting it.

Need an Exam?

To take the exam, make contact with an authorized exam provider. iSQI is a global exam provider for the ISTQB Certified Tester Foundation Level – Performance Tester. For more information, go to `www.isqi.org`.

APPENDIX A

References

Standards

[ISO9126] ISO/IEC 9126-1:2001, Software engineering – Product quality – Part 1: Quality model

[ISO25000] ISO/IEC 25000:2005, Software Engineering – Software Product Quality Requirements and Evaluation (SQuaRE)

[ISO25010] ISO/IEC 25010:2011, Systems and software engineering – Systems and software Quality Requirements and Evaluation (SQuaRE) – System and software quality models

[ISO29119] ISO/IEC/IEEE 29119-3:2013, Software and systems engineering – Software testing – Part 3: Test documentation

[ISO Guide 73] ISO GUIDE 73:2009, Risk management – Vocabulary

[NIST 800-30] NIST SpPub 800-30, Rev 1, Guide for Conducting Risk Assessments (2012) – `http://nvlpubs.nist.gov/nistpubs/Legacy/SP/nistspecialpublication800-30r1.pdf`

ISTQB Documents

All syllabi and the glossary used remain the Copyright of the International Software Testing Qualifications Board (ISTQB).

[ISTQB_UT_SYL] ISTQB Foundation Level Usability Testing Syllabus, Version 2018

[ISTQB_ALTA_SYL] ISTQB Advanced Level Test Analyst Syllabus, Version 2012

[ISTQB_ALTTA_SYL] ISTQB Advanced Level Technical Test Analyst Syllabus, Version 2012

[ISTQB_ALTM_SYL] ISTQB Advanced Level Test Manager Syllabus, Version 2012

[ISTQB_FL_SYL] ISTQB Foundation Level (Core) Syllabus, Version 2018

© Keith Yorkston 2021
K. Yorkston, *Performance Testing*, https://doi.org/10.1007/978-1-4842-7255-8

[ISTQB_FL_AT] ISTQB Foundation Level Agile Tester Syllabus, Version 2014

[ISTQB_GLOSSARY] ISTQB Glossary of Terms used in Software Testing, `http://glossary.istqb.org`

[ISTQB_CTFL_PT] ISTQB Certified Tester Advanced Level Syllabus Security Tester Version 2016

Books

[Anderson04] G. W. Anderson, "mySAP Tool Bag for Performance Tuning and Stress Testing," Prentice-Hall, 2004, ISBN: 0131448528

[Anderson01] Lorin W. Anderson, David R. Krathwohl (eds.) "A Taxonomy for Learning, Teaching and Assessing: A Revision of Bloom's Taxonomy of Educational Objectives," Allyn & Bacon, 2001, ISBN 978-0801319037

[Bath & McKay 2014] Graham Bath, Judy McKay, "The Software Test Engineer's Handbook," Rocky Nook, 2014, ISBN 978-1-933952-24-6

[Bondi 2014] A.B. Bondi, "Foundations of Software and System Performance Engineering: Process, Performance Modeling, Requirements, Testing, Scalability, and Practice," Addison-Wesley Professional, 2014, ISBN: 9780133038149

[Conan Doyle 1887] *A Study in Scarlet* (1887)

[Conan Doyle 1890] *The Sign of the Four* (1890)

[Conan Doyle 1892bc] *The Adventures of Sherlock Holmes* (1892) "The Adventure of the Blue Carbuncle"

[Conan Doyle 1892bv] *The Adventures of Sherlock Holmes* (1892) "The Boscombe Valley Mystery"

[Conan Doyle 1892cb] *The Adventures of Sherlock Holmes* (1892) "The Adventure of the Copper Breeches"

[Conan Doyle 1892ci] *The Adventures of Sherlock Holmes* (1892) "A Case of Identity"

[Conan Doyle 1893] *The Strand Magazine* (December 1893) "The Adventure of the Final Problem"

[Conan Doyle 1894] *The Memoirs of Sherlock Holmes (1894)* "The Adventure of the Final Problem"

[Conan Doyle 1908] His Last Bow (1908) "The Adventures of the Bruce-Partington Plans"

[Conan Doyle 1901] *The Strand Magazine* (August 1901–April 1902) "The Hound of the Baskervilles"

[Molyneaux09] Ian Molyneaux, "The Art of Application Performance Testing: From Strategy to Tools," O'Reilly, 2009, ISBN: 9780596520663

[Microsoft07] Microsoft Corporation, "Performance Testing Guidance for Web Applications," Microsoft, 2007, ISBN: 9780735625709

[M_o_R] AXELOS, "Management of Risk Guidance for Practitioners," The Stationery Office, 2010, ISBN: 9780113312740

[Stamatis03] D.H. Stamatis, "Failure Mode and Effect Analysis: FMEA from Theory to Execution" (Rev 2), American Society for Quality Press, 2003, ISBN: 9780873895989

[van Veenendaal12] E. van Veenendaal, "Practical Risk-Based Testing: The PRISMA Approach," UTN Publishers, 2012, ISBN: 9789490986070

Papers and Articles

[Arif et al] M.M. Arif, W. Shang & E. Shihab, "Empirical Study on the Discrepancy Between Performance Testing Results from Virtual and Physical Environments," Empirical Software Engineering, June 2018, Volume 23, Issue 3, pp1490–1518

[Stecklein et al] Stecklein, J. Dabney, J. Dick, B. Haskins, B. Lovell, R. Moroney, G., "Error Cost Escalation Through the Project Life Cycle," Report JSC-CN-8435, June 2004, https://ntrs.nasa.gov/citations/20100036670

[Schneier 2008] The Security Mindset – www.schneier.com/blog/archives/2008/03/the_security_mi_1.html

APPENDIX B

Question Answers

Chapter 1

Question	Correct	Notes
1	B	Scalability is a type of performance testing.
2	C	Usability and functional stability are the options from the syllabus. Component and integration are test levels, not quality characteristics. Capacity and resource utilization are subcharacteristics beneath performance efficiency. Usability and efficiency include one correct characteristic (usability) and efficiency being the characteristic tested with performance testing.
3	D	Tests must align to the defined expectations, not build the defined expectations. Performance user stories are written before test results are obtained. Performance tests should be affordable, as per the syllabus.
4	A	Availability Testing (1) and Efficiency Testing (5) are not performance test types.
5	A	Endurance Testing is testing to determine the stability of a system under a significant load over a significant time period within the system's operational context.
6	C	Integration testing tests the interfaces between components and systems – including dataflows and workflows.
7	B	Issues with crowd-based load generation are controlling the users – making it hard to reproduce the load in subsequent tests and organize the testers.

(continued)

© Keith Yorkston 2021
K. Yorkston, *Performance Testing*, https://doi.org/10.1007/978-1-4842-7255-8

Question	Correct	Notes
8*	D	Saturation of one or more resources is listed in the syllabus as a cause of slow response under moderate to heavy load. Resource limits can create bottlenecks in the system, slowing the entire system.
9*	B	Disk fragmentation can increase the time it takes to find and retrieve data from disks (note this becomes less of a problem with SSD disks). The syllabus suggests this as a cause of degradation over time.

*NOTE: Both questions 8 and 9 relate directly to the syllabus. It could be that an inefficient database design or implementation could cause the system to slow under load. The database could be the bottleneck under load. It's important to distinguish the syllabus points, as the exam questions will always refer to the syllabus.

Chapter 2

Question	Correct	Notes
1	A	Alerts and warnings are an operational environment metric.
2	D	D – A long-running issue with performance requirements/user stories created by business stakeholders is the lack of measurable metrics. A isn't correct, as times are easily understood. For B, test execution MAY take longer, but it's not guaranteed. For C, transaction times are the end effect of a performance test. It might be true that lower levels of performance cannot be determined, but the leader in this question was the reference to requirements earlier in the question.
3	C	As per the bullet point list in Section 2.2.
4	A	As per the bullet point list in Section 2.3.
5	C	Probe effect is the unintended change in behavior of a component or system caused by measuring it. A – Performance testing WILL have an impact on performance but is not the answer matching the definition. B and D are incorrect.

(continued)

Question	Correct	Notes
6	B	A is the performance test tool. C is the log analysis tool. D is the performance monitoring tool.
7	A	A associates with a loss of resource over time leading to less resource to service system transactions, which can be typical for endurance testing. B is typical for stress testing. C is typical for spike testing. D is typical for scalability testing.

Chapter 3

Question	Correct	Notes
1	A	A is correct according to the syllabus. Defining the performance test scope early in the project is vital, as it informs performance engineers of the project "field of play." Planning can then proceed based on this scope.
2	C	C is correct according to the syllabus. Performance test procedures outline the steps the performance test will take. Defining the procedure occurs after the performance test conditions and cases are created.
3	B	B is correct according to the syllabus. Analysis of the performance test basis allows performance test conditions to be created.
4	A	A is correct according to the syllabus. Contingent action plans form part of the control measures taken if the performance project plan begins to slip.
5	D	D is correct according to the syllabus. Aggregating results needs results firstly to be generated and analyzed. Aggregation then allows a simpler view of the results and analysis than the raw results data.
6	B	B is correct according to the syllabus. Performance test cases are created after the test conditions and before the test procedures.
7	D	D is correct. Resource utilization could be an issue in any environment, as any executing code requires resources to run.

(continued)

Question	Correct	Notes
8	A	Memory leaks can be caused by C-based languages which allow direct heap management – in effect, a developer could make a mistake with memory management allowing a memory leak to occur. Languages like Java allow garbage collection, which can "tidy up" memory and reduce (but not eliminate) the probability of memory leaks.
9	C	C (performance risk impact) is determined during risk assessment. The question referred to the characteristics for risk identification. Time behavior, capacity, and resource utilization are covered in the syllabus.
10	B	A is incorrect – it would create a baseline for the existing product in its current environment, but it wouldn't address the product risk. C could remove the GUI, allowing more virtual users to be executed on the load generator(s). But, once again, it doesn't address the product risk. D is a good idea – database tuning can often improve performance. But, as this is the first iteration, it would be difficult to performance test through the UI with a full dataset. B is the best response, as it addresses the product risk directly.
11	C	C is correct – the SDLC steps are from the syllabus. Test-driven development (B) isn't a development methodology but may be used within an iterative/incremental project. COTS and sequential are incorrect.
12	B	B is the correct combination of each sentence taken from the syllabus.

Chapter 4

Question	Correct	Notes
1	D	D is the correct answer – the identification of trends predicting lower-level performance is not a key objective, but a function of performance test results analysis.

(continued)

Question	Correct	Notes
2	C	C is correct – option (i) focuses on the response time (a user-based metric) vs. option (ii) based on resource utilization (a technical metric looking at the ability to provide an adequate service with those resources).
3	B	B is correct – the objective quantifies the load (120,000/24hrs=5000 shipments) with the response time (3 sec). A – DevOps can (and should) use performance test plans; C has the response time reference, but incorrectly references only authentication/authorization; D only refers to the response time.
4	B	B is correct – it includes both user types submitting time (not specifically manual bulk upload or automatic). A includes users submitting time only every six minutes (no bulk upload) and no breakdown of the users. C has a mixed load, but automated time submission. D – The transaction number is incorrect (1200 users x 10 time submissions per hour=12,000 times submitted).
5	A	From syllabus Section 4.1.3 – A is a business-focused factor; the other answers are technical focused.
6	D	From syllabus Section 4.1.3 – (i) is a technical factor; (ii) is a business factor.
7	A	From syllabus Section 4.1.3 – D is a technical-focused factor; the other answers are business focused.
8	B	B is correct – 50% of load could be pushed via HTTPS and 50% via GDA to apply 100% load to the server. A only pushes 50% HTTPS as total load. C pushes 100% load through the web server causing 200% load through this server. D only pushes GDA against the DB, and not through the web server.
9	C	A – web; B – remote access; C – web service; D – database.
10	D	A – TruClient; B – SOA; C – network; D – remote access.
11	A	A – network; B – mobile; C – database; D – web.

(continued)

Question	Correct	Notes
12	D	D is correct – the lr_think_time is inside the DataTransfer_MakeDir transaction, meaning this transaction would have an extra ten seconds added to it. A – Although not the neatest code, the DataTransfer_1GB starting won't affect the DataTransfer_MakeDir timing, as transactions can be nested. B – Latency could exist, but is irrelevant to the question. C – The DataTransfer_MakeDir start transaction needs to begin to time making the directory, thus is in the right place.
13	B	Section 4.2.2 contains A, C, and D. B is not in this section – response time is the end result of any performance issue; the first sign a problem might exist is a transaction slowing, but further investigation using resource utilization would be needed.
14	A	A gives the number of users running the transaction to give the load profile. The operational profile describes a single user journey. B – File size is not relevant as it would relate to input data. C – Overtime is not relevant, as the operational profile specified a standard day. D – Transaction size is not relevant, as per B.
15	C	As per the ISTQB definitions for load profile and operational profile.
16	A	A is in the syllabus as part of constructing operational profiles.
17	B	24 web x 3Mbps = 72Mbps; 72 + 108 + 180 = 360Mbps 108 email x 1Mbps = 108Mbps; 24 + 108 + 18 = 150 users 18 ftp x 10Mbps = 180Mbps.
18	A	i) TRUE – Traffic has changed between the weekend and weekdays. ii) FALSE – Both have 50% (S)FTP/20% web/30% email traffic. iii) TRUE – The 1500 peak weekdays is relatively higher than the weekend. iv) FALSE – Nothing says they do or don't in the question. v) TRUE – FTP (weekend) vs. SFTP (weekday). vi) TRUE – 100% successful court submissions not in the weekend specification.

(continued)

Question	Correct	Notes
19	D	A – As different payments follow different business processes, A is incorrect.
		B – Within each group are differences; PayPal and Apple Pay have different networks/etc.
		C – Every payment provider could be looked at as being exhaustive; do we need to test separate Barclays Visa from Bank of America Visa?
		D is the best answer – each different payment type could be done based on the % of total use and associated risk.
20	C	C is correct – it measures the total transaction time, including client-side processing. Protocol-based scripts may not capture this.
		A is subjective – it may be easy or may not.
		B – Scalability is reduced with UI scripting; often, only a single UI script can run on a load generator.
		D – Data correlation can be difficult, as UI scripts often don't capture hidden information like session IDs/etc.
21	B	B is correct, as protocol scripts don't include client-side processing in times they capture.
		A – Protocol scripts can be more efficient, running many Vusers from a single load generator.
		C – Data correlation is easier, as hidden values can be captured.
		D – Difficult or easy is subjective.
22	D	D is correct – the internal user logs in once, performs many transactions, and logs out at the end of the day. Web users typically log in, do their transaction, then log out. There will be many more single customers booking shipments than individual internal users booking many transactions.
23	C	C is not an option in the syllabus (Section 4.2.6). Converting source code could create much more code to maintain in a test and most often isn't written as a performance test. Specifically, creating code with performance testing as the goal is more efficient.
24	A	Correlation is capturing a server-presented value and reusing that value as an input parameter in the script.

(continued)

Question	Correct	Notes
25	C	C is correct – the first iteration ran with the data that was hard-coded in the script as the first row of parameterized data. A – A server-side session ID would fail on the first iteration because an expired session ID would be passed. B – Could be true, but unlikely that the only valid data was the first set. D – A shipping organization would need to book more than one shipment to remain profitable.
26	A	A – If the same test is running on the same load generators, the probability the load generators are causing the time variation is very low. B – Changing network conditions could affect the response time. C – Database caching could cause the DB to respond faster (which may or may not be an intended effect). D – Processes running within the same environment could consume resources needed by the system under tests.
27	B	B is correct – cleaning up old user sessions at the end of a test run can ensure then environment is the same for the next test execution. A – User session caching locally on a client would not cause this effect. C – Congestion would slow all transactions, not just the login. D – Paging would, once again, slow down all transactions.
28	D	D is the best option – report the results and let the stakeholders decide if the system is acceptable. A – It's not known if the <5 sec response time is a maximum time goal. B – No tolerance is mentioned in the scenario. C – The stakeholders are not technical, so more technical information would be irrelevant.

Chapter 5

Question	Correct	Notes
1	C	A – Load generator. B – Part of load management console. C – Load management console. D – A performance test script.
2	B	Maintainability (iii) and performance (v) are test types.
3	A	A is incorrect, as the freeware model doesn't exist in the syllabus (Section 4.2.6), but hey, it's a tool question, after all!

Index

Printed in the United States
by Baker & Taylor Publisher Services